BLACK CAT

I'LL TAKE MANHATTAN

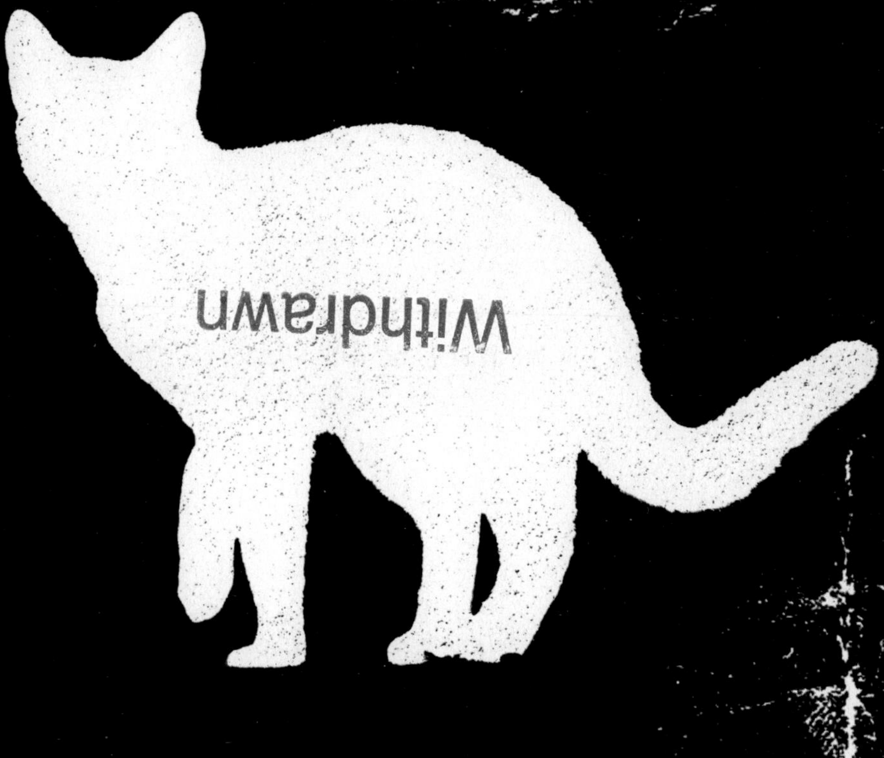

Felicia Hardy is a world-renowned thief known as the **Black Cat**. At the behest of her former mentor and current patron, the **Black Fox**, Felicia and her crew--**Bruno and Doctor Korpse**--pulled off a series of heists, stealing from the **Frick Collection**, the **Fantastic Four**, **Dr. Strange**, **Wolverine**, **Iron Fist**, and **Iron Man**. Their haul? A painting, the original deed to Manhattan, and an old book, as well as the schematics for the dimension-hopping Randall Gate and a key for said gate. It's all been in service of the ultimate heist: breaking into the extradimensional vault of the **New York Thieves Guild**, currently run by the deadly **Odessa Drake**.

Now, with all the pieces in place, Felicia and the Fox are finally ready to put their plan into action...

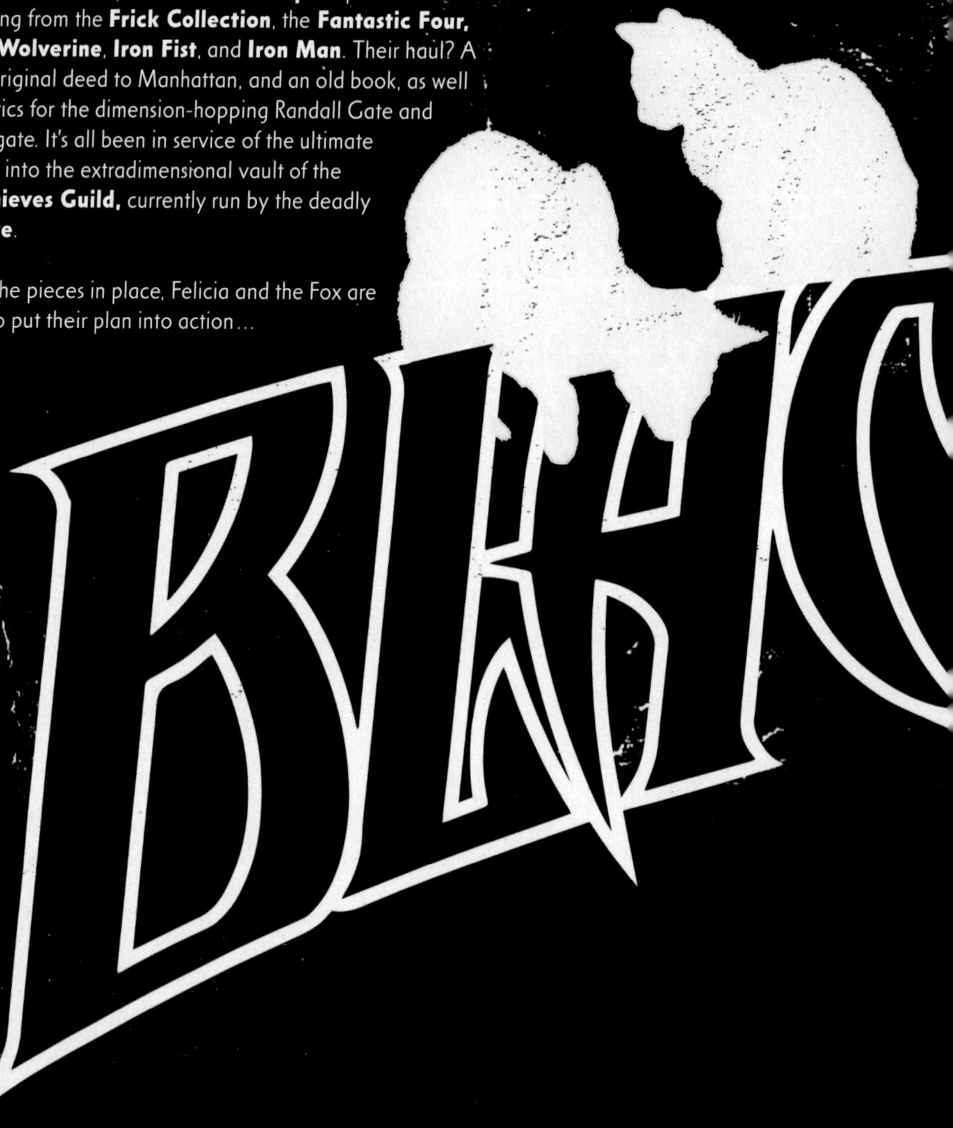

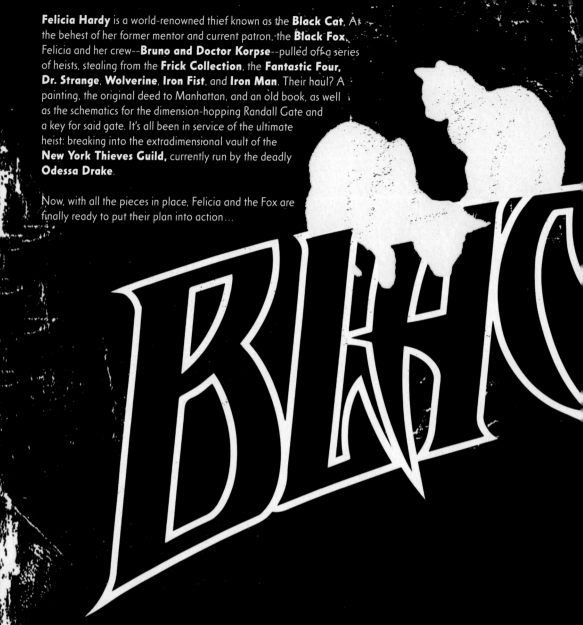

collection editor **JENNIFER GRÜNWALD** ♦ assistant editor **DANIEL KIRCHHOFFER**
assistant managing editor **MAIA LOY** ♦ assistant managing editor **LISA MONTALBANO**
vp production & special projects **JEFF YOUNGQUIST** ♦ book designer **SARAH SPADACCINI** with **JAY BOWEN**
svp print, sales & marketing **DAVID GABRIEL** ♦ editor in chief **C.B. CEBULSKI**

BLACK CAT VOL. 5: I'LL TAKE MANHATTAN. Contains material originally published in magazine form as BLACK CAT (2020) #5-7 and BLACK CAT ANNUAL (2021) #1. First printing 2021. ISBN 978-1-302-92789-9. Published by MARVEL WORLDWIDE, INC., a subsidiary of MARVEL ENTERTAINMENT, LLC. OFFICE OF PUBLICATION: 1290 Avenue of the Americas, New York, NY 10104. **Printed in Canada.** KEVIN FEIGE, Chief Creative Officer; DAN BUCKLEY, President, Marvel Entertainment; JOE QUESADA, EVP & Creative Director; DAVID BOGART, Associate Publisher & SVP of Talent Affairs; TOM BREVOORT, VP, Executive Editor; NICK LOWE, Executive Editor, VP of Content, Digital Publishing; DAVID GABRIEL, VP of Print & Digital Publishing; JEFF YOUNGQUIST, VP of Production & Special Projects; ALEX MORALES, Director of Publishing Operations; DAN EDINGTON, Managing Editor; RICKEY PURDIN, Director of Talent Relations; JENNIFER GRÜNWALD, Senior Editor, Special Projects; SUSAN CRESPI, Production Manager; STAN LEE, Chairman Emeritus. For information regarding advertising in Marvel Comics or on Marvel.com, please contact Vit DeBellis, Custom Solutions & Integrated Advertising Manager, at vdebellis@marvel.com. For Marvel subscription inquiries, please call 888-511-5480. **Manufactured between 7/9/2021 and 8/10/2021 by SOLISCO PRINTERS, SCOTT, QC, CANADA.**

10 9 8 7 6 5 4 3 2 1

KCAT

I'LL TAKE MANHATTAN

writer   **JED MacKAY**

BLACK CAT #5-7

artists   **MICHAEL DOWLING**
color artist   **BRIAN REBER**
letterer   **FERRAN DELGADO**
cover art   **PEPE LARRAZ** & **MARTE GRACIA**
assistant editor   **LINDSEY COHICK** & **DANNY KHAZEM**
editor   **NICK LOWE**

BLACK CAT ANNUAL #1

artist   **JOEY VAZQUEZ**
color artist   **BRIAN REBER**
letterer   **FERRAN DELGADO**
cover art   **C.F. VILLA** & **BRIAN REBER**
assistant editor   **LINDSEY COHICK** & **DANNY KHAZEM**
editor   **NICK LOWE**

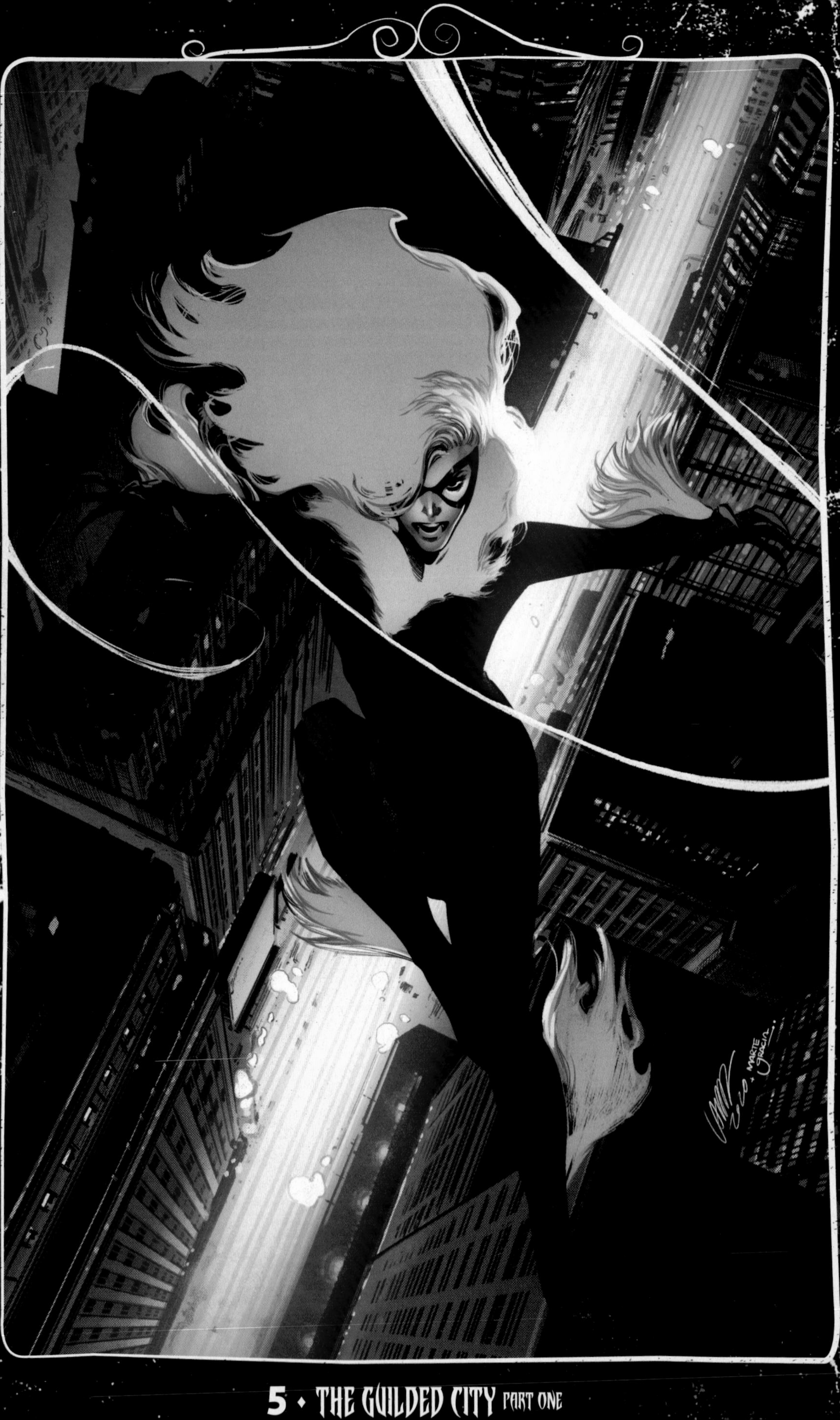

5 • THE GUILDED CITY PART ONE

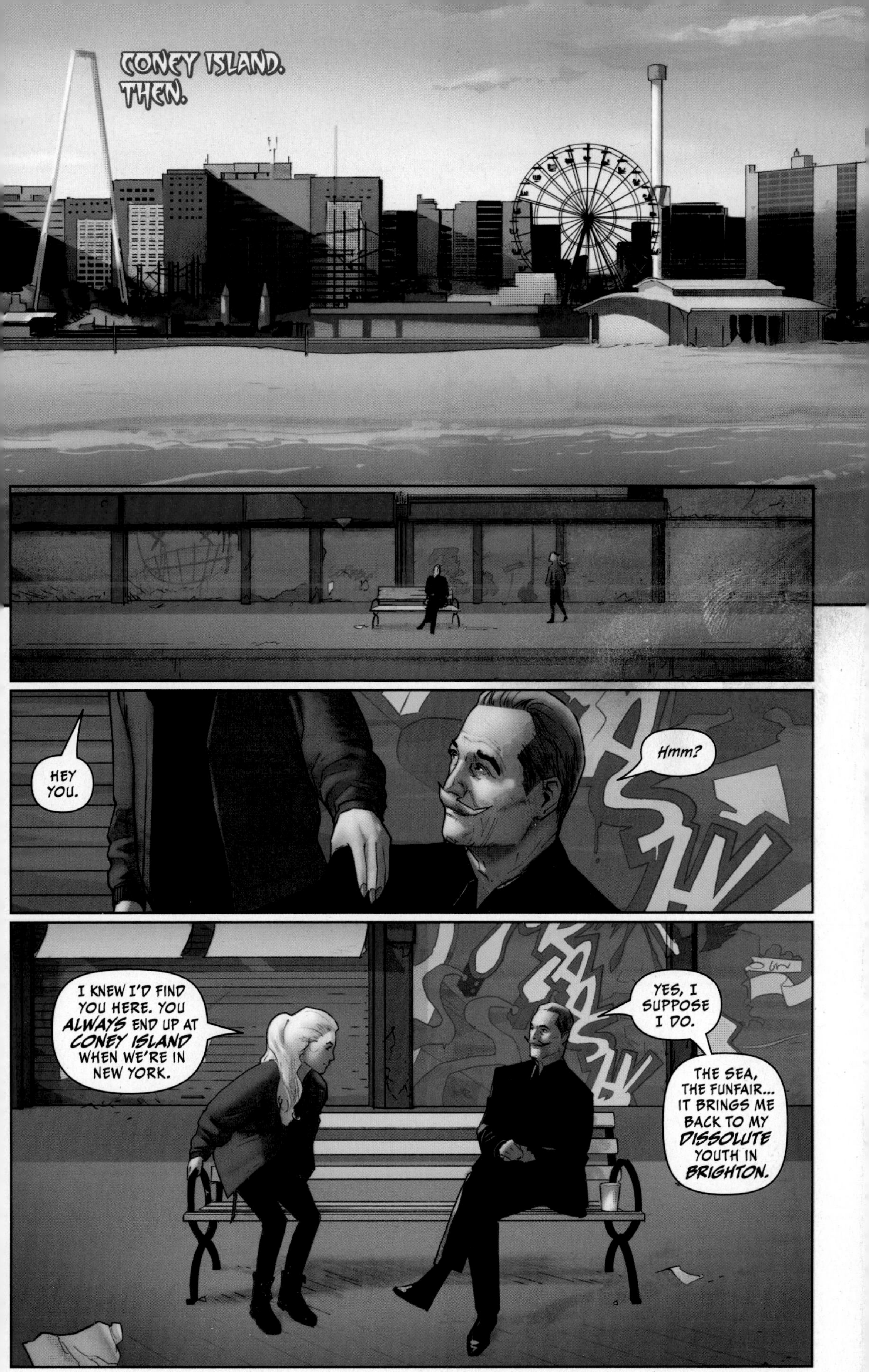
CONEY ISLAND.
THEN.
HEY YOU.
Hmm?
I KNEW I'D FIND YOU HERE. YOU ALWAYS END UP AT CONEY ISLAND WHEN WE'RE IN NEW YORK.
YES, I SUPPOSE I DO.
THE SEA, THE FUNFAIR... IT BRINGS ME BACK TO MY DISSOLUTE YOUTH IN BRIGHTON.

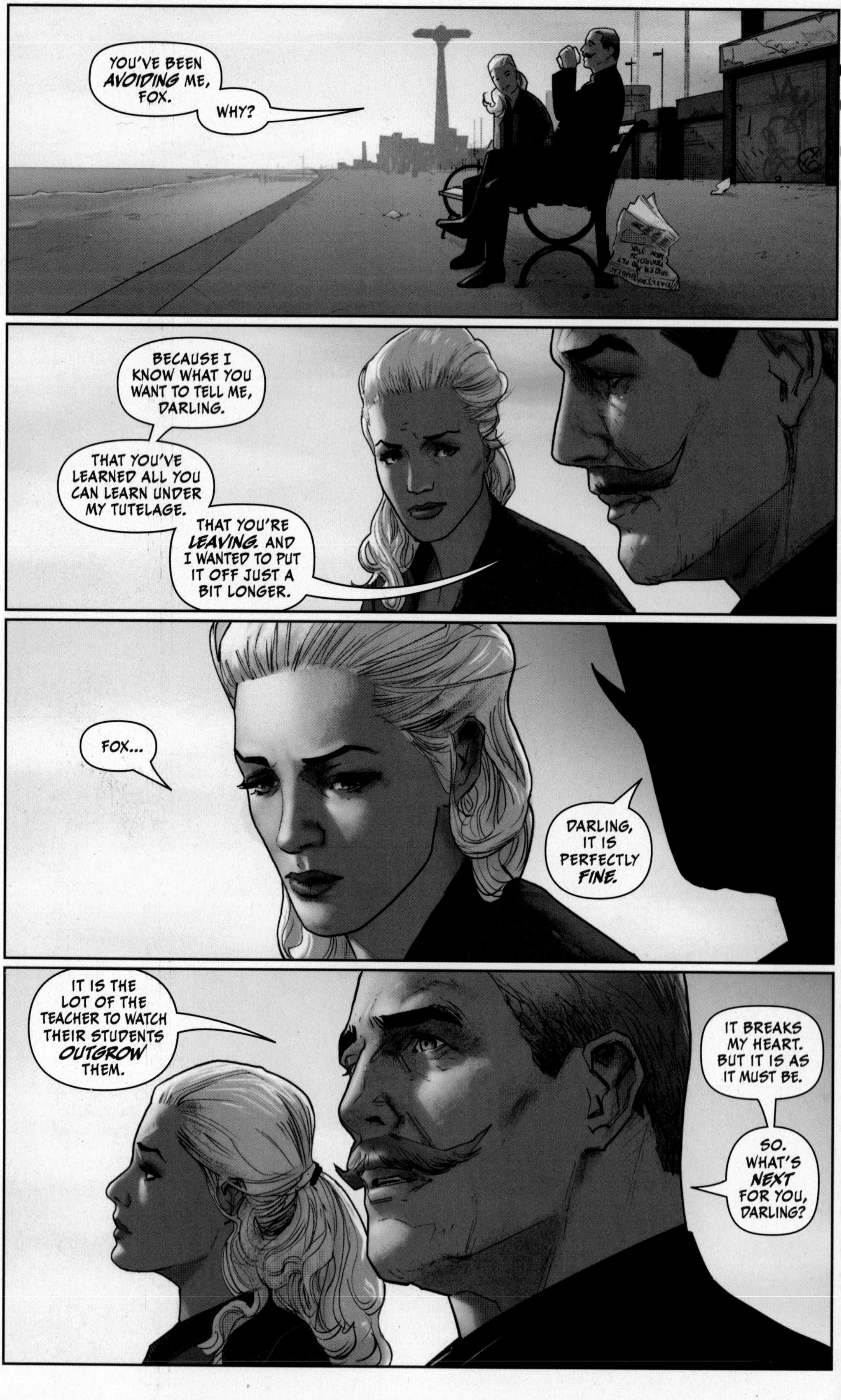
YOU'VE BEEN AVOIDING ME, FOX.
WHY?
BECAUSE I KNOW WHAT YOU WANT TO TELL ME, DARLING.
THAT YOU'VE LEARNED ALL YOU CAN LEARN UNDER MY TUTELAGE.
THAT YOU'RE LEAVING. AND I WANTED TO PUT IT OFF JUST A BIT LONGER.
FOX...
DARLING, IT IS PERFECTLY FINE.
IT IS THE LOT OF THE TEACHER TO WATCH THEIR STUDENTS OUTGROW THEM.
IT BREAKS MY HEART. BUT IT IS AS IT MUST BE.
SO. WHAT'S NEXT FOR YOU, DARLING?

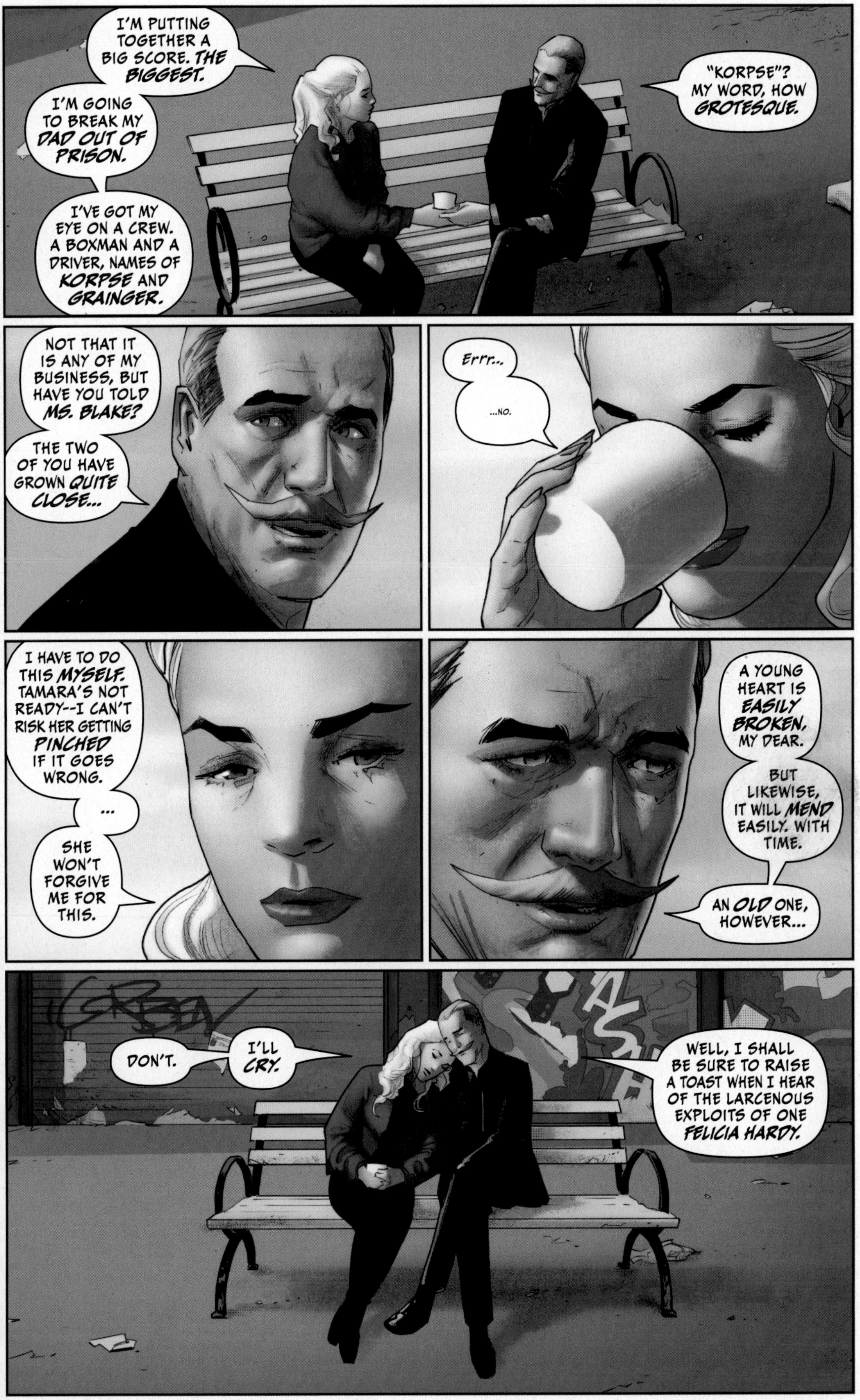
I'M PUTTING TOGETHER A BIG SCORE. THE BIGGEST.
I'M GOING TO BREAK MY DAD OUT OF PRISON.
I'VE GOT MY EYE ON A CREW. A BOXMAN AND A DRIVER, NAMES OF KORPSE AND GRAINGER.
"KORPSE"? MY WORD, HOW GROTESQUE.
NOT THAT IT IS ANY OF MY BUSINESS, BUT HAVE YOU TOLD MS. BLAKE?
THE TWO OF YOU HAVE GROWN QUITE CLOSE...
Errr..
...NO.
I HAVE TO DO THIS MYSELF. TAMARA'S NOT READY--I CAN'T RISK HER GETTING PINCHED IF IT GOES WRONG.
...
SHE WON'T FORGIVE ME FOR THIS.
A YOUNG HEART IS EASILY BROKEN, MY DEAR.
BUT LIKEWISE, IT WILL MEND EASILY. WITH TIME.
AN OLD ONE, HOWEVER...
DON'T.
I'LL CRY.
WELL, I SHALL BE SURE TO RAISE A TOAST WHEN I HEAR OF THE LARCENOUS EXPLOITS OF ONE FELICIA HARDY.

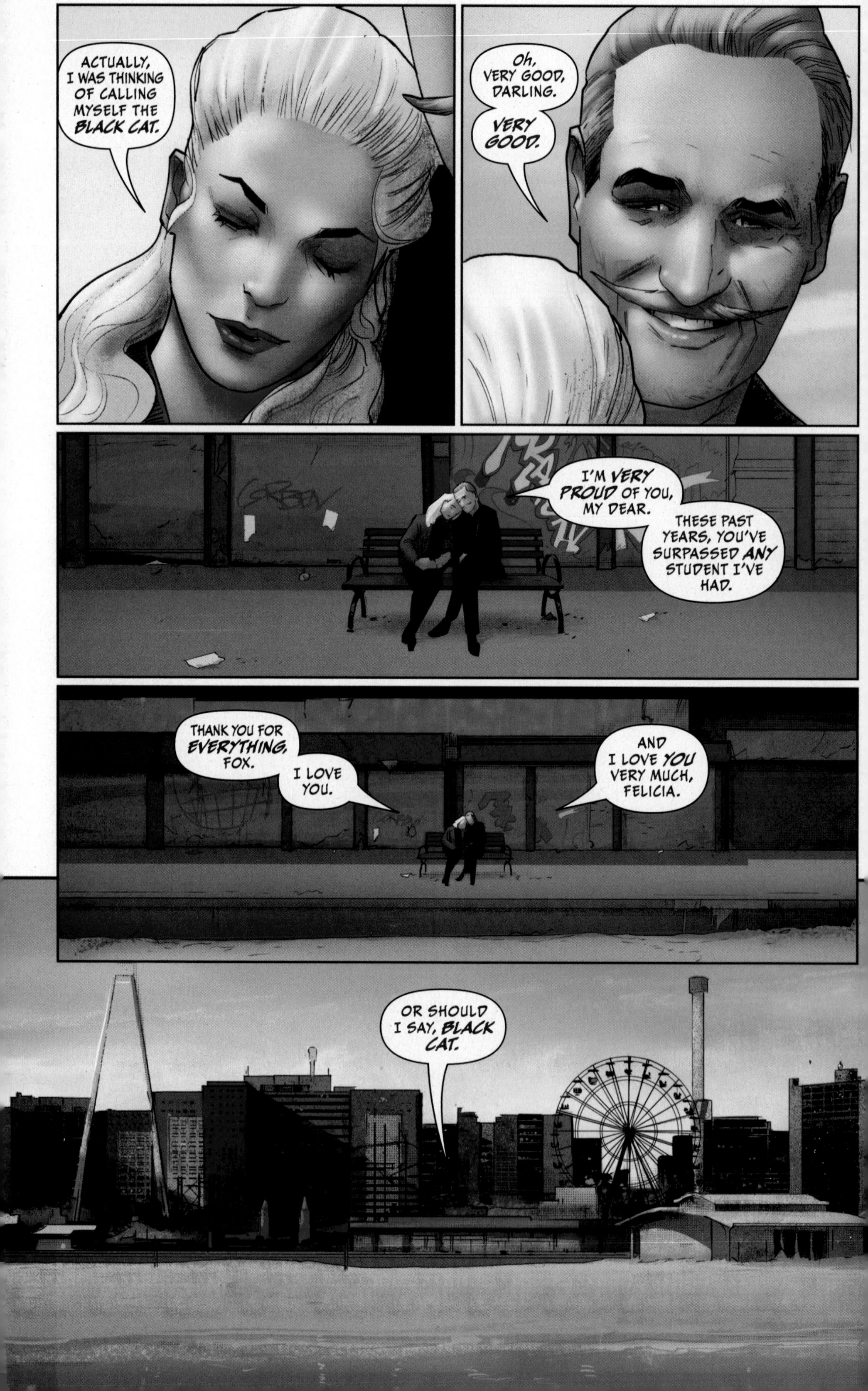
ACTUALLY, I WAS THINKING OF CALLING MYSELF THE BLACK CAT.
Oh, VERY GOOD, DARLING.
VERY GOOD.
I'M VERY PROUD OF YOU, MY DEAR.
THESE PAST YEARS, YOU'VE SURPASSED ANY STUDENT I'VE HAD.
THANK YOU FOR EVERYTHING, FOX.
I LOVE YOU.
AND I LOVE YOU VERY MUCH, FELICIA.
OR SHOULD I SAY, BLACK CAT.

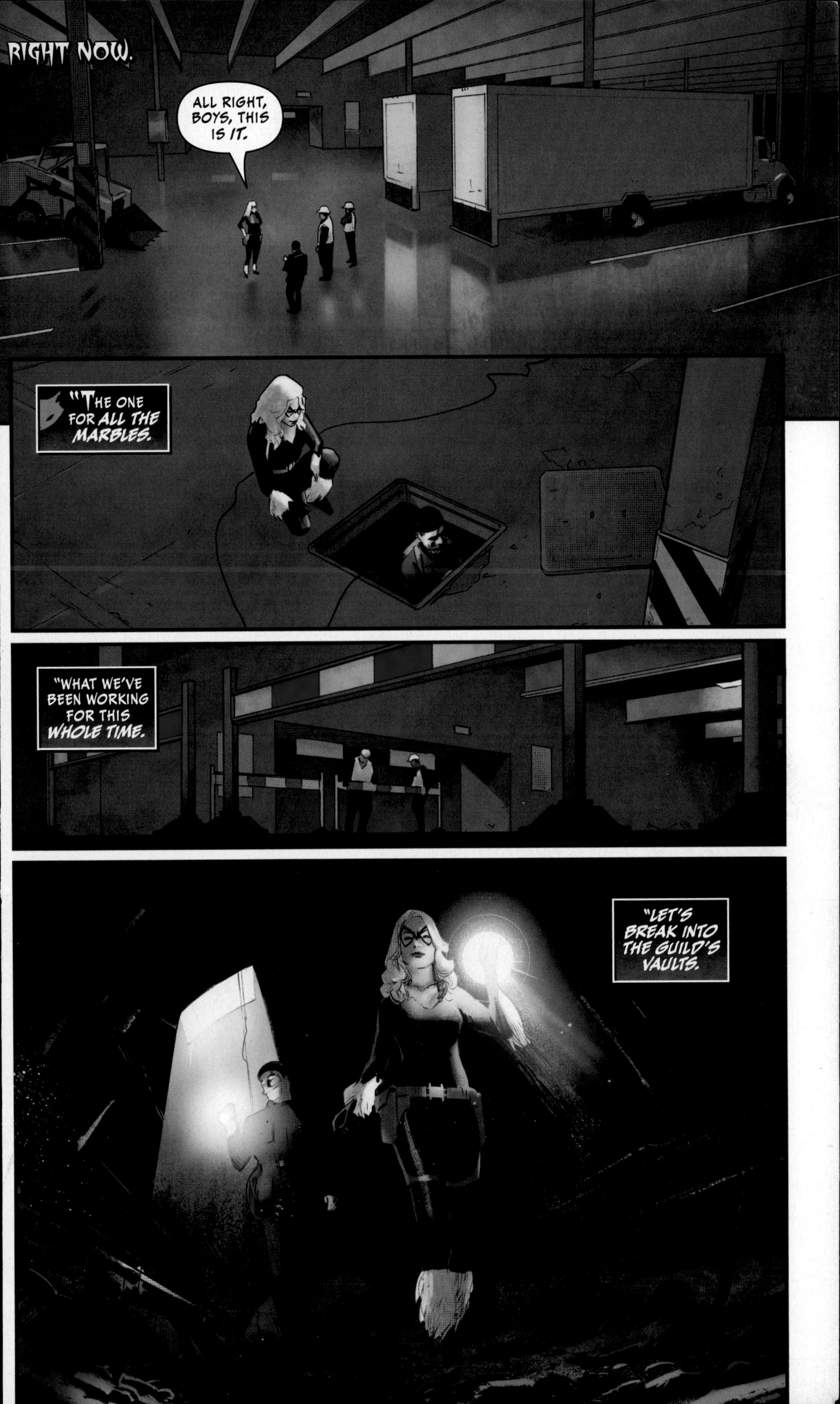
RIGHT NOW.
ALL RIGHT, BOYS, THIS IS IT.
"THE ONE FOR ALL THE MARBLES.
"WHAT WE'VE BEEN WORKING FOR THIS WHOLE TIME.
"LET'S BREAK INTO THE GUILD'S VAULTS.

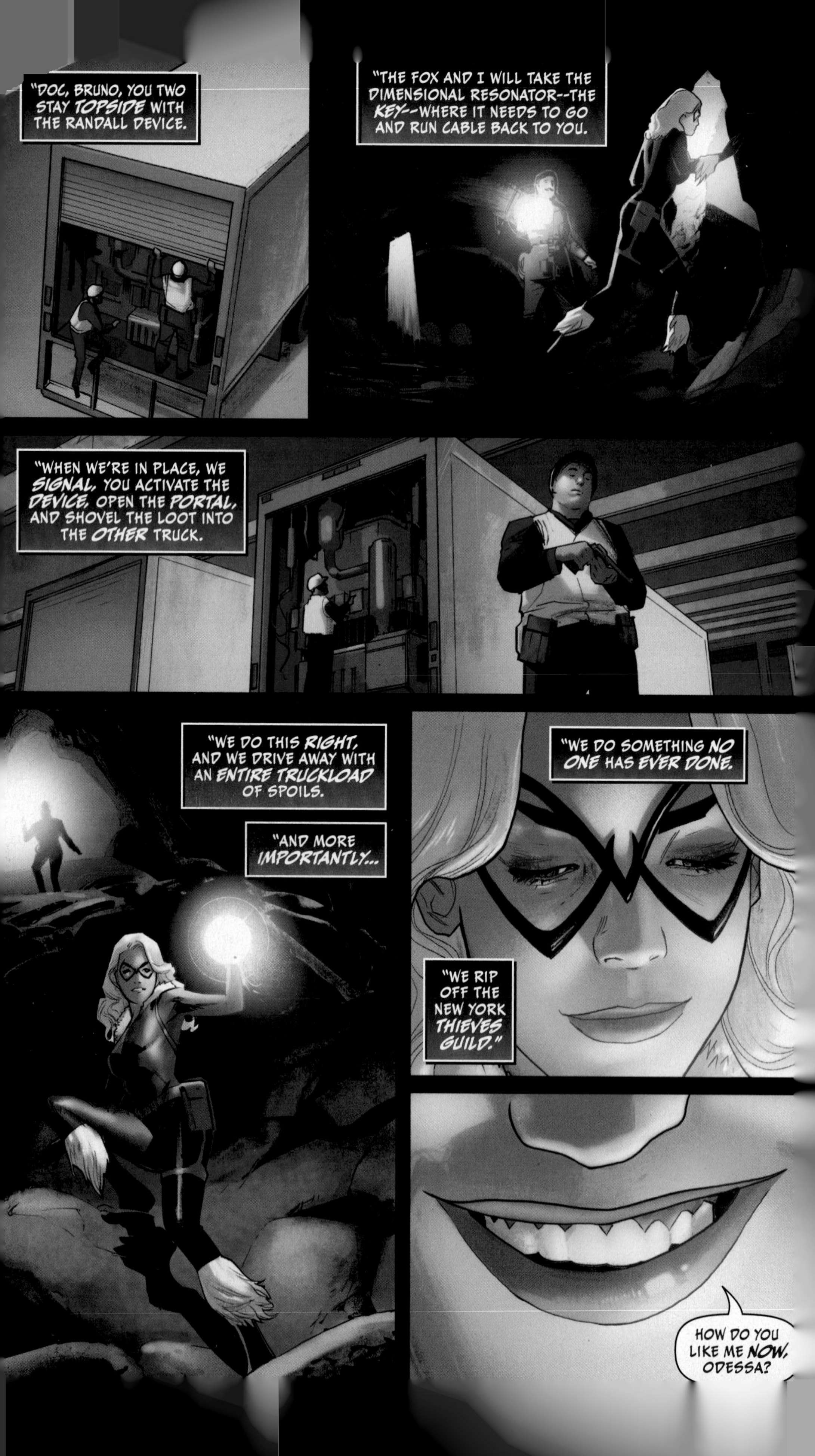
"DOC, BRUNO, YOU TWO STAY TOPSIDE WITH THE RANDALL DEVICE.
"THE FOX AND I WILL TAKE THE DIMENSIONAL RESONATOR--THE KEY--WHERE IT NEEDS TO GO AND RUN CABLE BACK TO YOU.
"WHEN WE'RE IN PLACE, WE SIGNAL, YOU ACTIVATE THE DEVICE, OPEN THE PORTAL, AND SHOVEL THE LOOT INTO THE OTHER TRUCK.
"WE DO THIS RIGHT, AND WE DRIVE AWAY WITH AN ENTIRE TRUCKLOAD OF SPOILS.
"AND MORE IMPORTANTLY...
"WE DO SOMETHING NO ONE HAS EVER DONE.
"WE RIP OFF THE NEW YORK THIEVES GUILD."
HOW DO YOU LIKE ME NOW, ODESSA?

I STILL DON'T UNDERSTAND WHY WE HAVE TO GO DOWN *THERE.*

DARLING, I FEAR THAT FOR THE SAKE OF *EXPEDIENCE,* THERE ARE SOME THINGS I DID NOT SHARE WITH YOU.

WELL, I DON'T LOVE *THAT.*

THE GUILD'S VAULTS AREN'T EXACTLY *VAULTS.*

THAT IS TO SAY, THEY DO POSSESS EXTREME AMOUNTS OF *WEALTH.*

BUT WHEN *ODESSA DRAKE* FIRST DECODED THE PAINTINGS OF ORLANDO, IT WAS NOT MERELY TO FIND A PLACE TO *HIDE* HER LOOT.

YOU SEE, WHEN THE NEW YORK GUILD WAS *EXCOMMUNICATED* FROM THE LARGER GUILDS, THEY ALSO LOST THE PATRONAGE OF *CANDRA,* THE IMMORTAL BEING WHO FOUNDED THEM.

WITH THAT PATRONAGE REVOKED, SO TOO WAS THE *ULTIMATE REWARD* WITH WHICH CANDRA KEPT THEIR LOYALTY: *ETERNAL LIFE.*

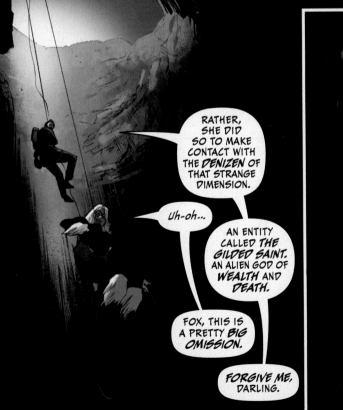

RATHER, SHE DID SO TO MAKE CONTACT WITH THE *DENIZEN* OF THAT STRANGE DIMENSION.

Uh-oh...

AN ENTITY CALLED *THE GILDED SAINT.* AN ALIEN GOD OF *WEALTH* AND *DEATH.*

FOX, THIS IS A PRETTY *BIG* OMISSION.

FORGIVE ME, DARLING.

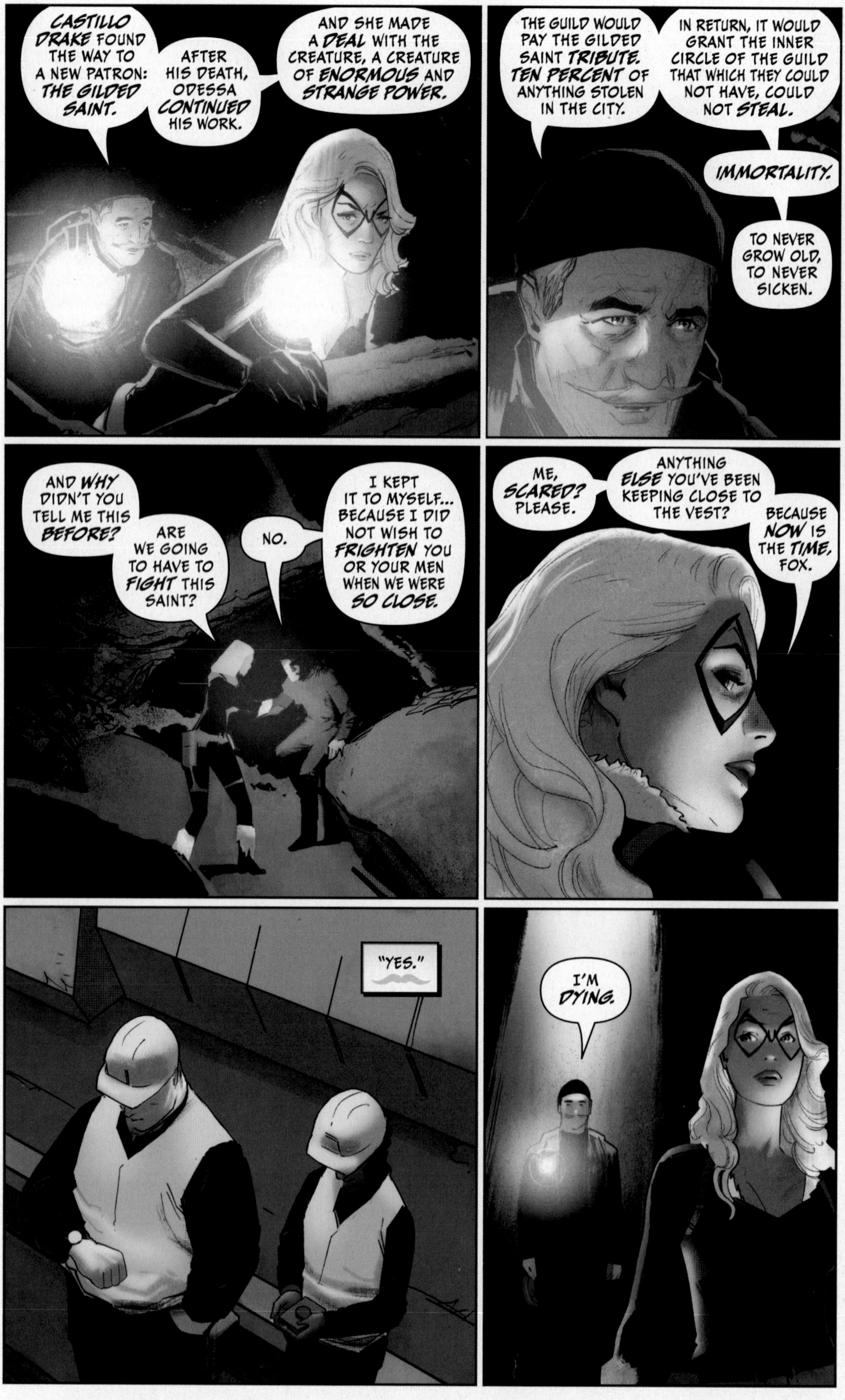
CASTILLO DRAKE FOUND THE WAY TO A NEW PATRON: THE GILDED SAINT.
AFTER HIS DEATH, ODESSA CONTINUED HIS WORK.
AND SHE MADE A DEAL WITH THE CREATURE, A CREATURE OF ENORMOUS AND STRANGE POWER.
THE GUILD WOULD PAY THE GILDED SAINT TRIBUTE. TEN PERCENT OF ANYTHING STOLEN IN THE CITY.
IN RETURN, IT WOULD GRANT THE INNER CIRCLE OF THE GUILD THAT WHICH THEY COULD NOT HAVE, COULD NOT STEAL.
IMMORTALITY.
TO NEVER GROW OLD, TO NEVER SICKEN.
AND WHY DIDN'T YOU TELL ME THIS BEFORE?
ARE WE GOING TO HAVE TO FIGHT THIS SAINT?
NO.
I KEPT IT TO MYSELF... BECAUSE I DID NOT WISH TO FRIGHTEN YOU OR YOUR MEN WHEN WE WERE SO CLOSE.
ME, SCARED? PLEASE.
ANYTHING ELSE YOU'VE BEEN KEEPING CLOSE TO THE VEST?
BECAUSE NOW IS THE TIME, FOX.
"YES."
I'M DYING.

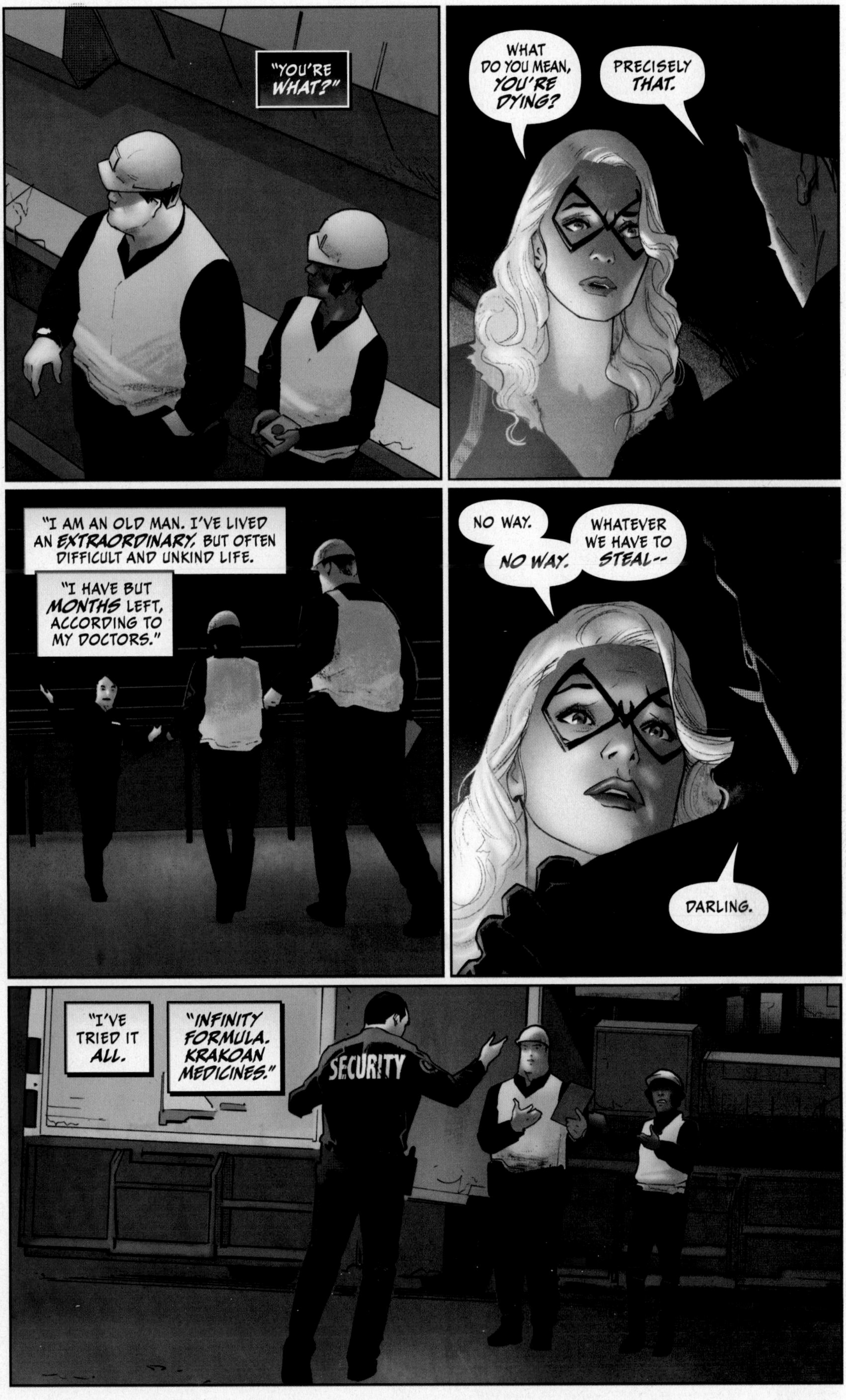
"YOU'RE WHAT?"
WHAT DO YOU MEAN, YOU'RE DYING?
PRECISELY THAT.
"I AM AN OLD MAN. I'VE LIVED AN EXTRAORDINARY, BUT OFTEN DIFFICULT AND UNKIND LIFE.
"I HAVE BUT MONTHS LEFT, ACCORDING TO MY DOCTORS."
NO WAY.
NO WAY.
WHATEVER WE HAVE TO STEAL--
DARLING.
"I'VE TRIED IT ALL.
"INFINITY FORMULA. KRAKOAN MEDICINES."
SECURITY

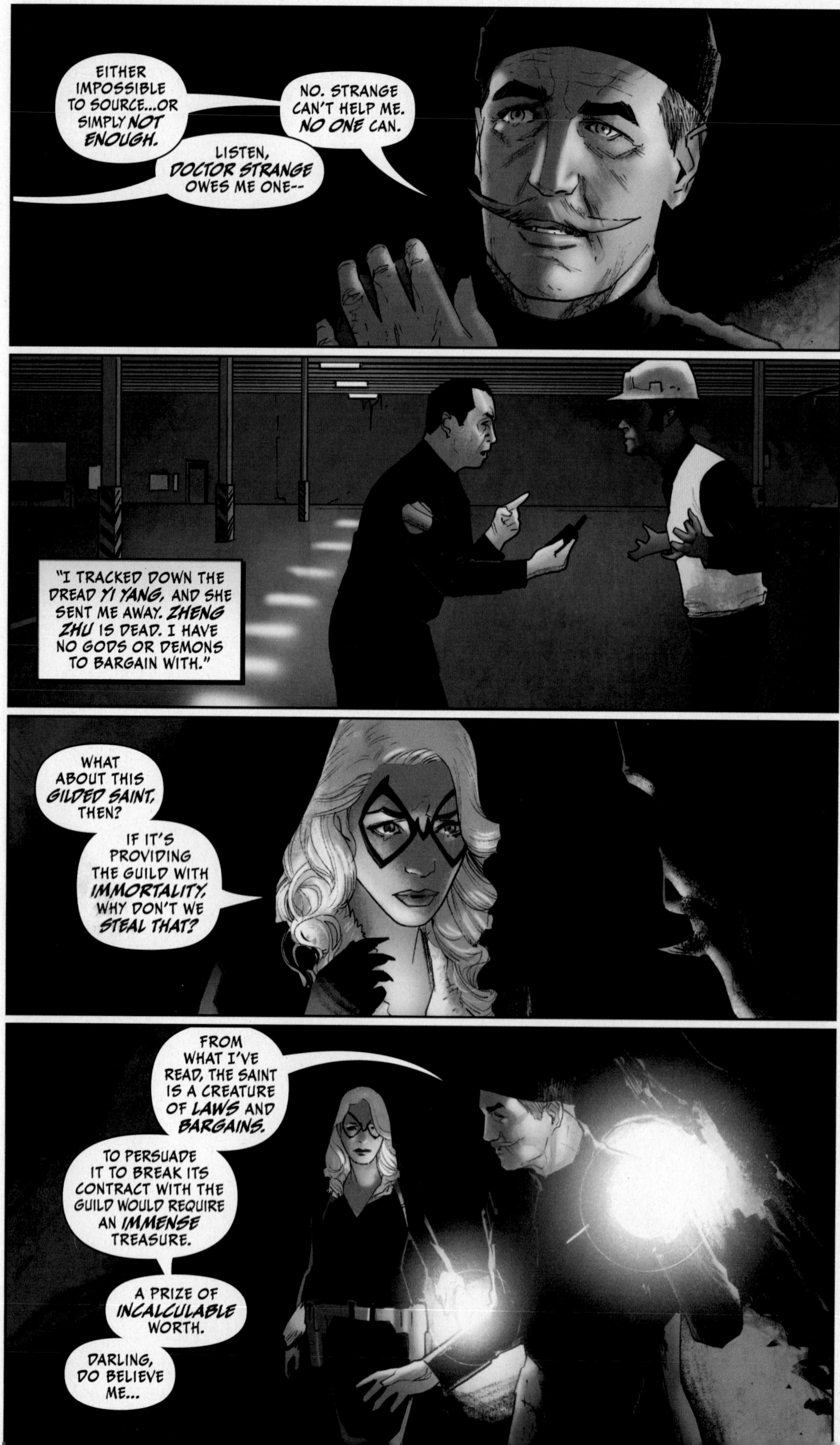
EITHER IMPOSSIBLE TO SOURCE...OR SIMPLY NOT ENOUGH.
LISTEN, DOCTOR STRANGE OWES ME ONE--
NO. STRANGE CAN'T HELP ME. NO ONE CAN.
"I TRACKED DOWN THE DREAD YI YANG, AND SHE SENT ME AWAY. ZHENG ZHU IS DEAD. I HAVE NO GODS OR DEMONS TO BARGAIN WITH."
WHAT ABOUT THIS GILDED SAINT, THEN?
IF IT'S PROVIDING THE GUILD WITH IMMORTALITY, WHY DON'T WE STEAL THAT?
FROM WHAT I'VE READ, THE SAINT IS A CREATURE OF LAWS AND BARGAINS.
TO PERSUADE IT TO BREAK ITS CONTRACT WITH THE GUILD WOULD REQUIRE AN IMMENSE TREASURE.
A PRIZE OF INCALCULABLE WORTH.
DARLING, DO BELIEVE ME...

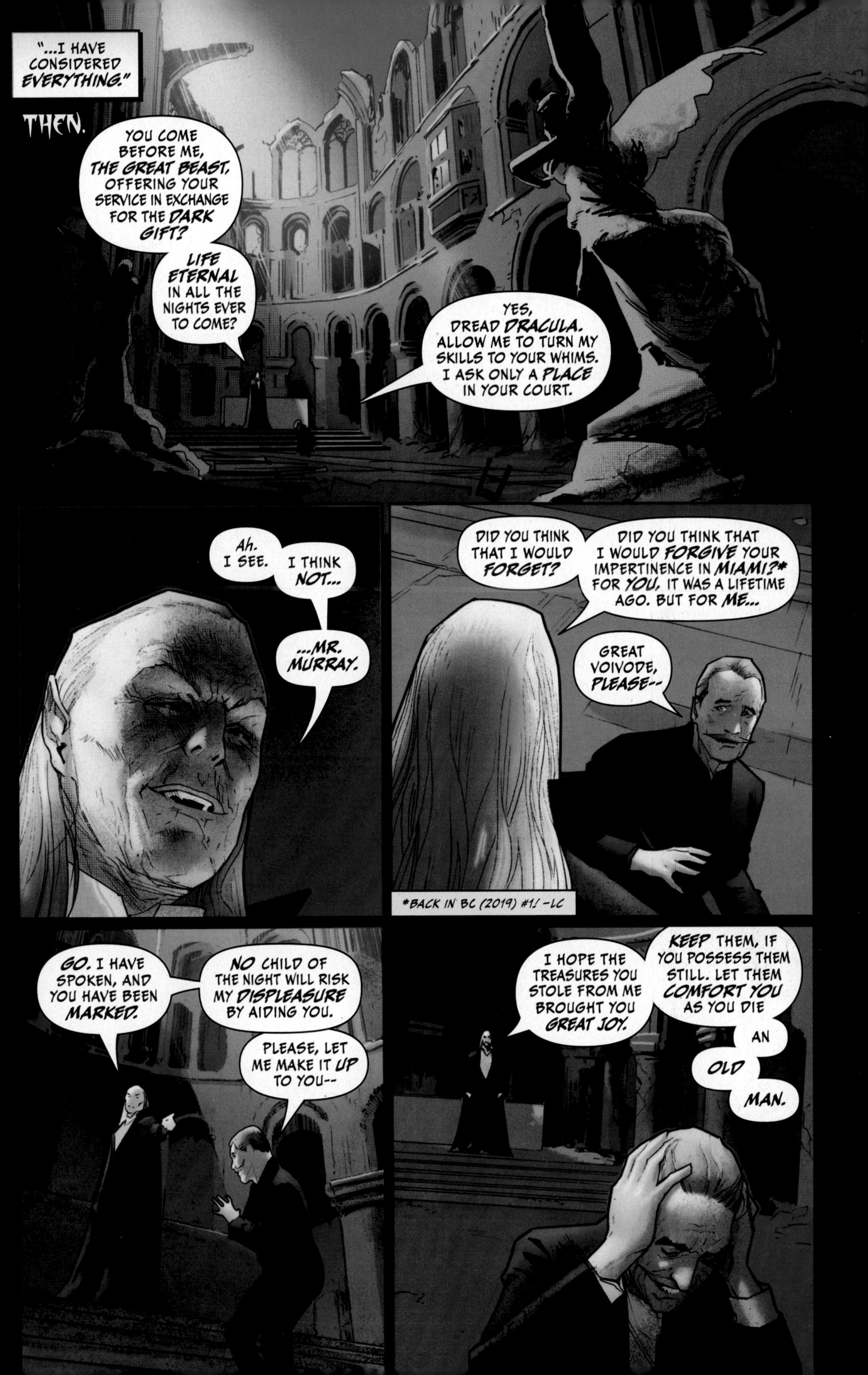
"...I HAVE CONSIDERED EVERYTHING."
THEN.
YOU COME BEFORE ME, THE GREAT BEAST, OFFERING YOUR SERVICE IN EXCHANGE FOR THE DARK GIFT?
LIFE ETERNAL IN ALL THE NIGHTS EVER TO COME?
YES, DREAD DRACULA. ALLOW ME TO TURN MY SKILLS TO YOUR WHIMS. I ASK ONLY A PLACE IN YOUR COURT.
AH. I SEE.
I THINK NOT...
...MR. MURRAY.
DID YOU THINK THAT I WOULD FORGET?
DID YOU THINK THAT I WOULD FORGIVE YOUR IMPERTINENCE IN MIAMI?* FOR YOU, IT WAS A LIFETIME AGO. BUT FOR ME...
GREAT VOIVODE, PLEASE--
*BACK IN BC (2019) #1! -LC
GO. I HAVE SPOKEN, AND YOU HAVE BEEN MARKED.
NO CHILD OF THE NIGHT WILL RISK MY DISPLEASURE BY AIDING YOU.
PLEASE, LET ME MAKE IT UP TO YOU--
I HOPE THE TREASURES YOU STOLE FROM ME BROUGHT YOU GREAT JOY.
KEEP THEM, IF YOU POSSESS THEM STILL. LET THEM COMFORT YOU AS YOU DIE
AN
OLD
MAN.

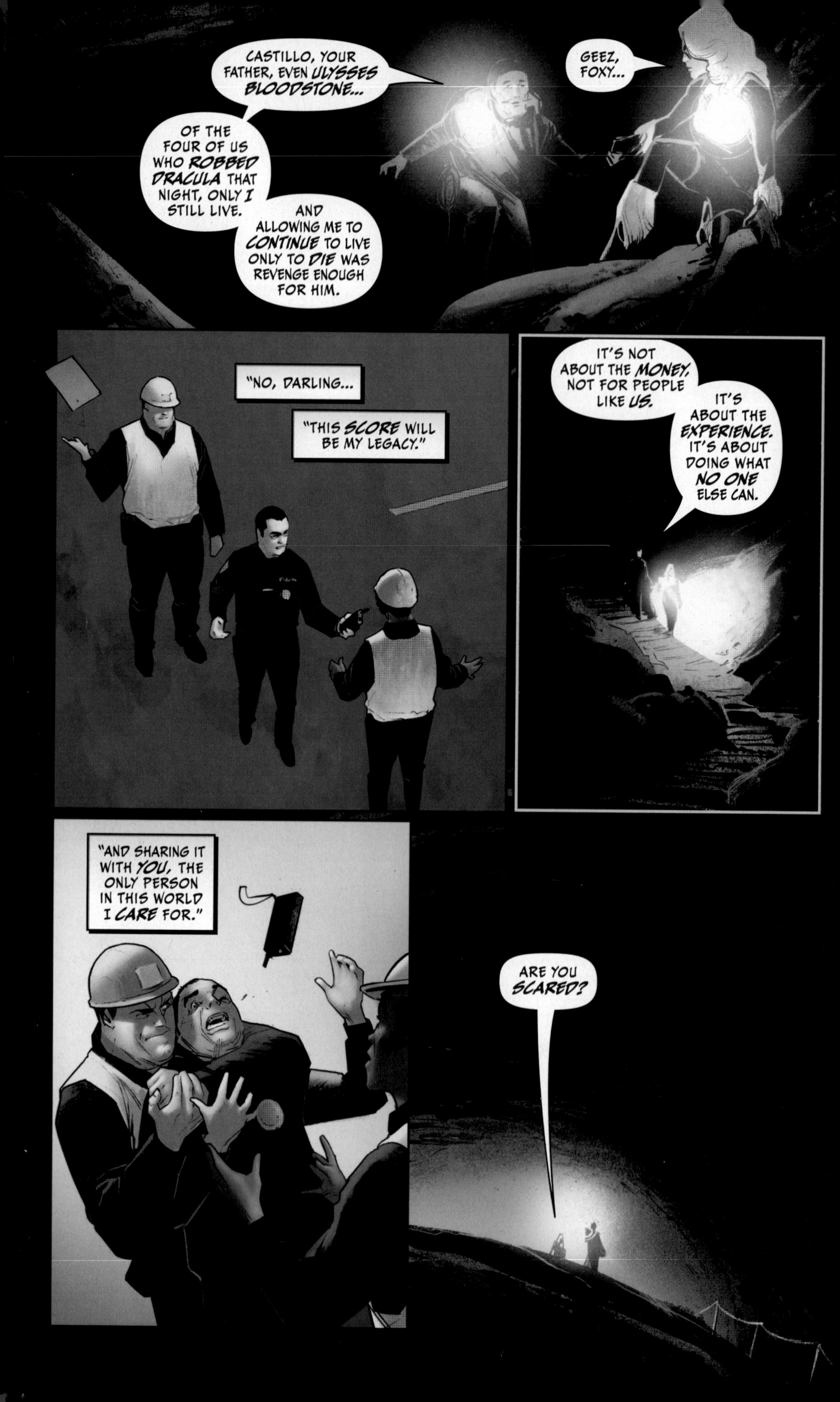
CASTILLO, YOUR FATHER, EVEN ULYSSES BLOODSTONE...
GEEZ, FOXY...
OF THE FOUR OF US WHO ROBBED DRACULA THAT NIGHT, ONLY I STILL LIVE.
AND ALLOWING ME TO CONTINUE TO LIVE ONLY TO DIE WAS REVENGE ENOUGH FOR HIM.
"NO, DARLING...
"THIS SCORE WILL BE MY LEGACY."
IT'S NOT ABOUT THE MONEY, NOT FOR PEOPLE LIKE US.
IT'S ABOUT THE EXPERIENCE. IT'S ABOUT DOING WHAT NO ONE ELSE CAN.
"AND SHARING IT WITH YOU, THE ONLY PERSON IN THIS WORLD I CARE FOR."
ARE YOU SCARED?

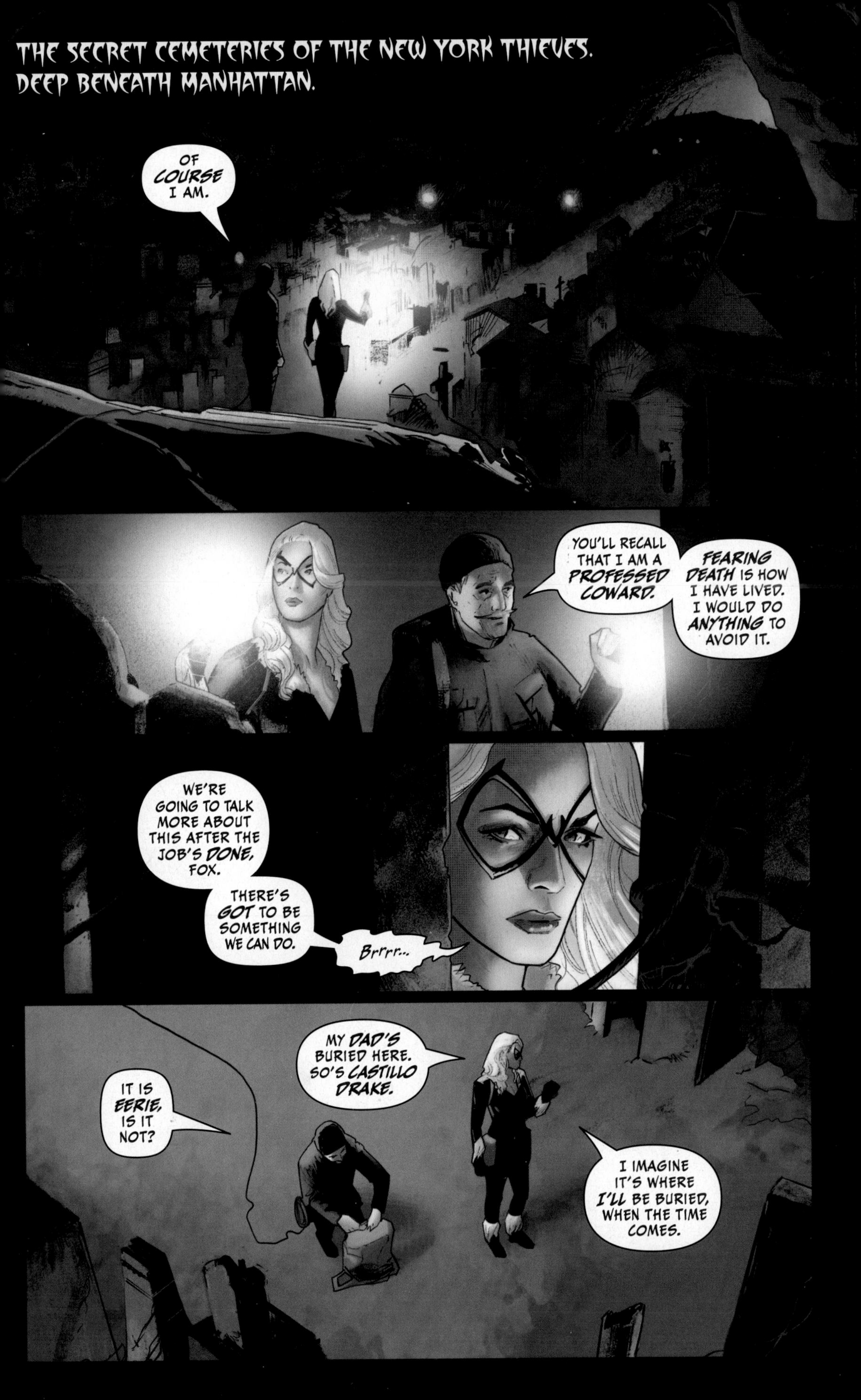
THE SECRET CEMETERIES OF THE NEW YORK THIEVES.
DEEP BENEATH MANHATTAN.
OF COURSE I AM.
YOU'LL RECALL THAT I AM A PROFESSED COWARD.
FEARING DEATH IS HOW I HAVE LIVED. I WOULD DO ANYTHING TO AVOID IT.
WE'RE GOING TO TALK MORE ABOUT THIS AFTER THE JOB'S DONE, FOX.
THERE'S GOT TO BE SOMETHING WE CAN DO.
Brrrr...
IT IS EERIE, IS IT NOT?
MY DAD'S BURIED HERE. SO'S CASTILLO DRAKE.
I IMAGINE IT'S WHERE I'LL BE BURIED, WHEN THE TIME COMES.

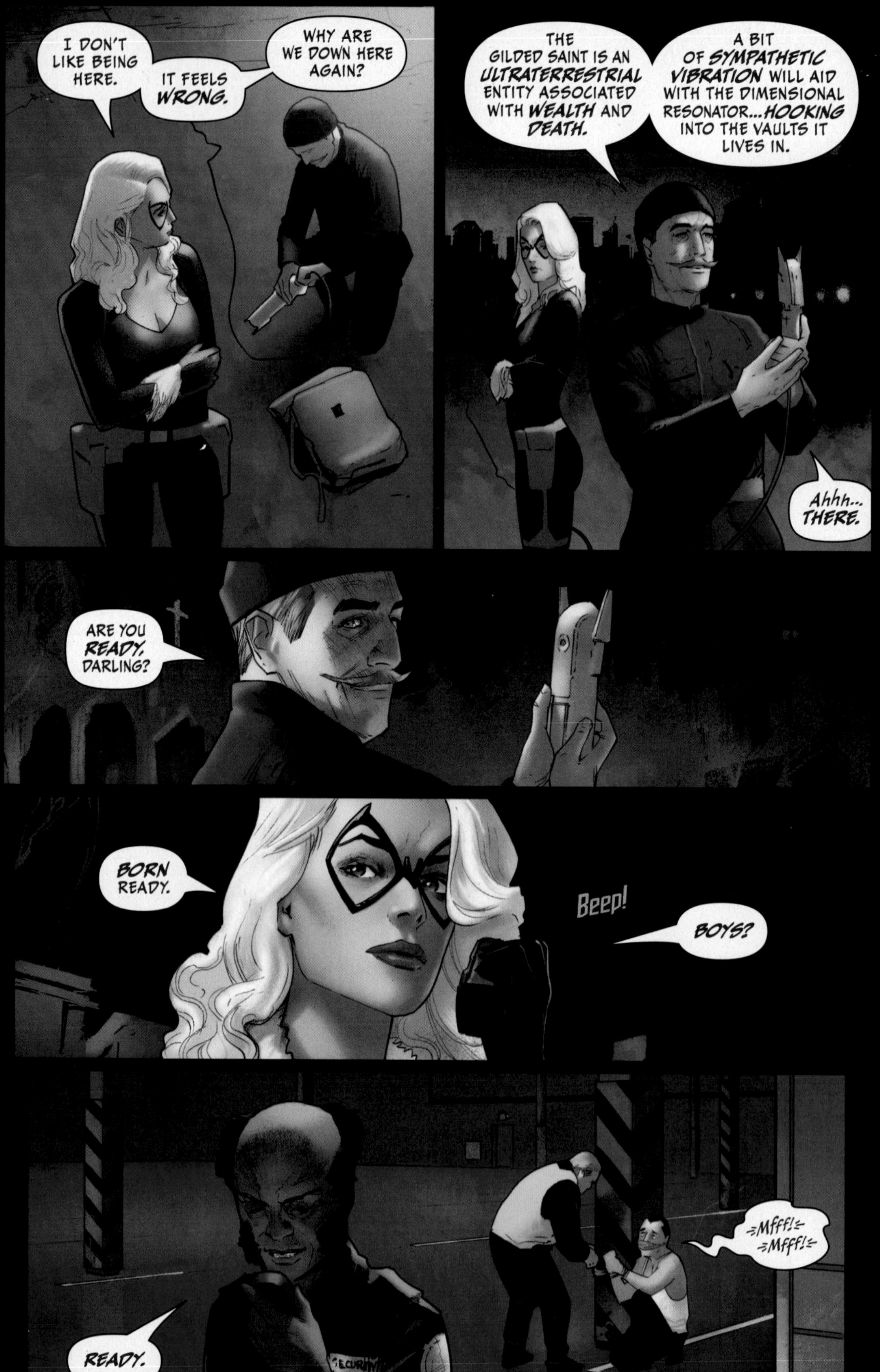
I DON'T LIKE BEING HERE.
IT FEELS WRONG.
WHY ARE WE DOWN HERE AGAIN?
THE GILDED SAINT IS AN ULTRATERRESTRIAL ENTITY ASSOCIATED WITH WEALTH AND DEATH.
A BIT OF SYMPATHETIC VIBRATION WILL AID WITH THE DIMENSIONAL RESONATOR...HOOKING INTO THE VAULTS IT LIVES IN.
Ahhh... THERE.
ARE YOU READY, DARLING?
BORN READY.
Beep!
BOYS?
READY.
=Mfff!=
=Mfff!=
SECURITY

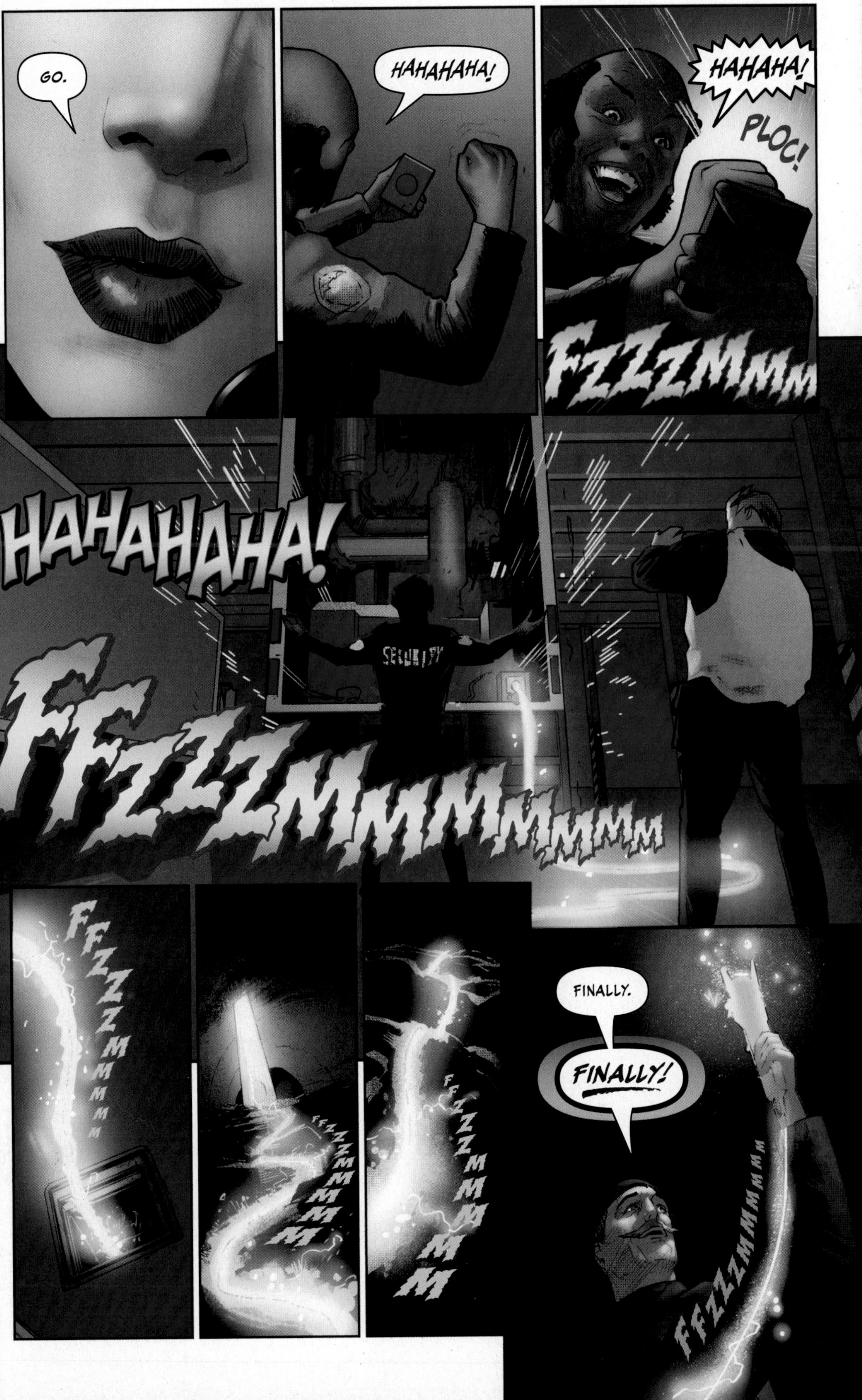
GO.
HAHAHAHA!
HAHAHA!
PLOC!
FZZZMMM
HAHAHAHA!
FFZZZMMMMMMMM
FFZZZZMMMMMM
FFZZZZMMMMMMM
FFZZZMMMMMM
FINALLY.
FINALLY!
FFZZZZMMMMMM

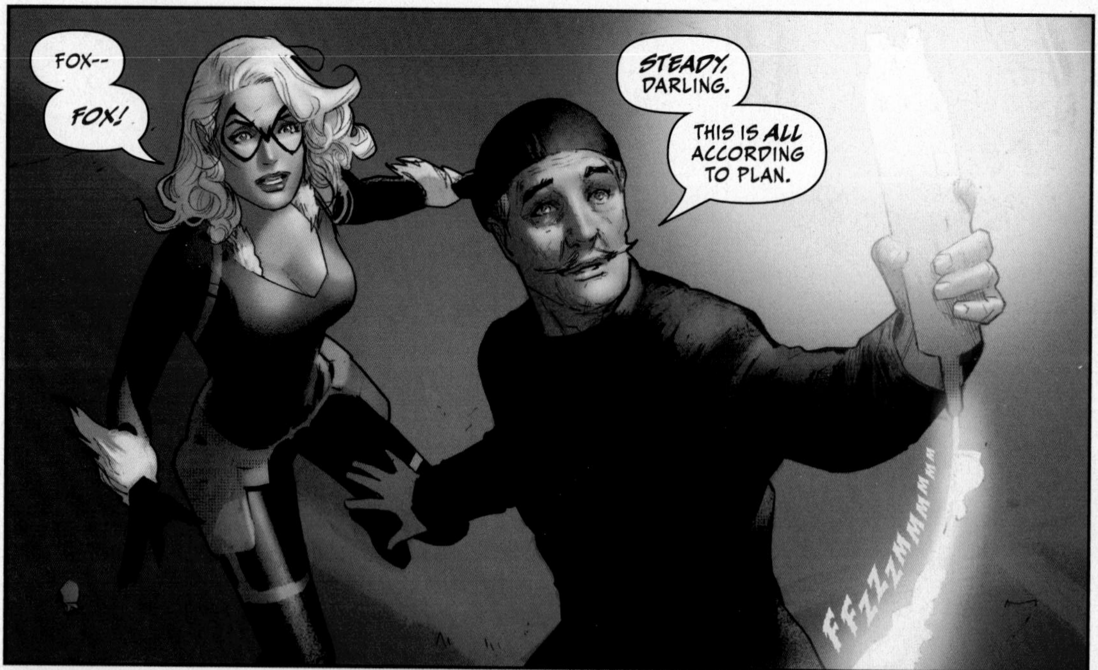
FOX--
FOX!
STEADY, DARLING.
THIS IS ALL ACCORDING TO PLAN.
FFZZZMMMMMM

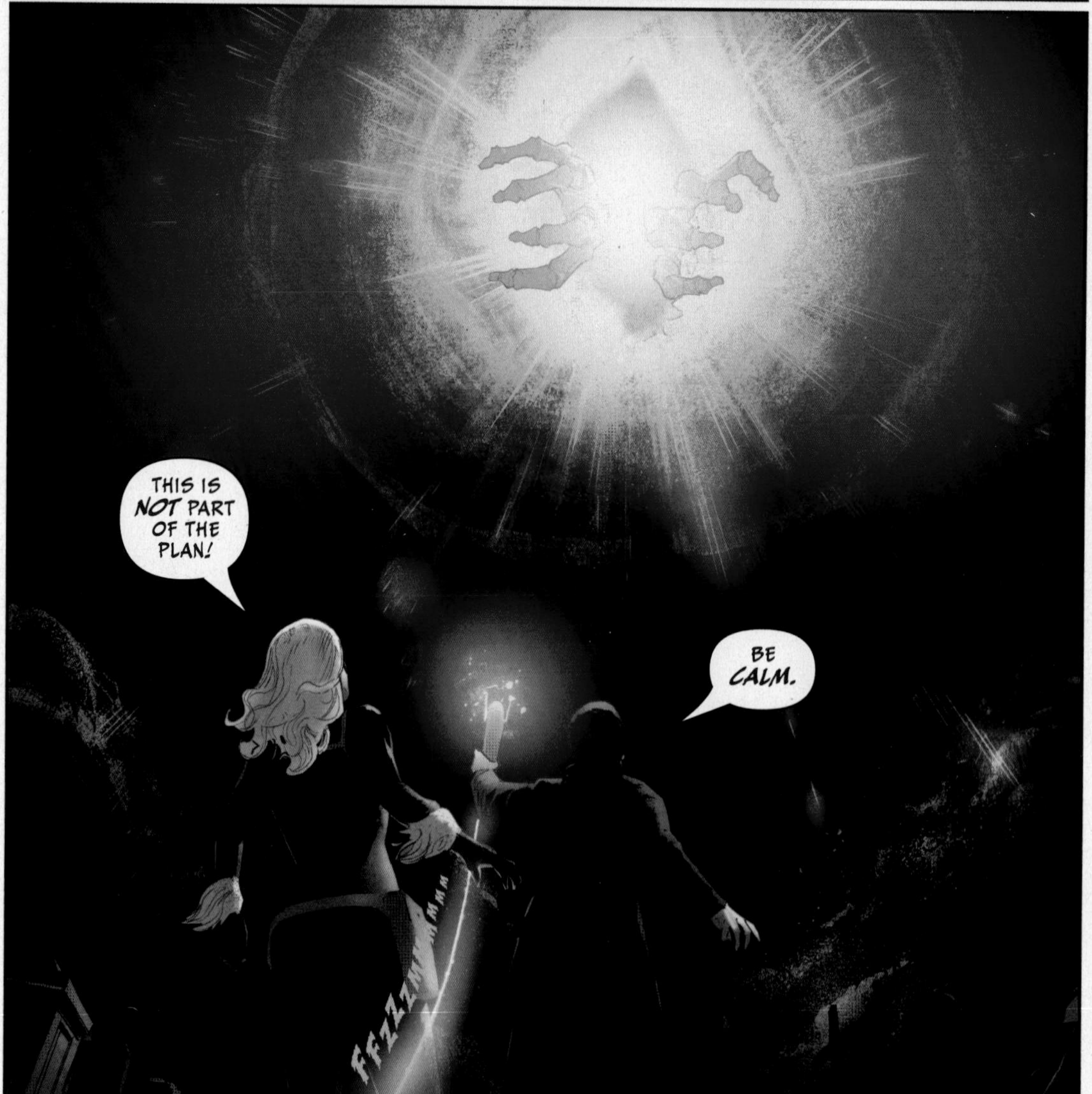
THIS IS NOT PART OF THE PLAN!
BE CALM.
FFZZZMMMMM

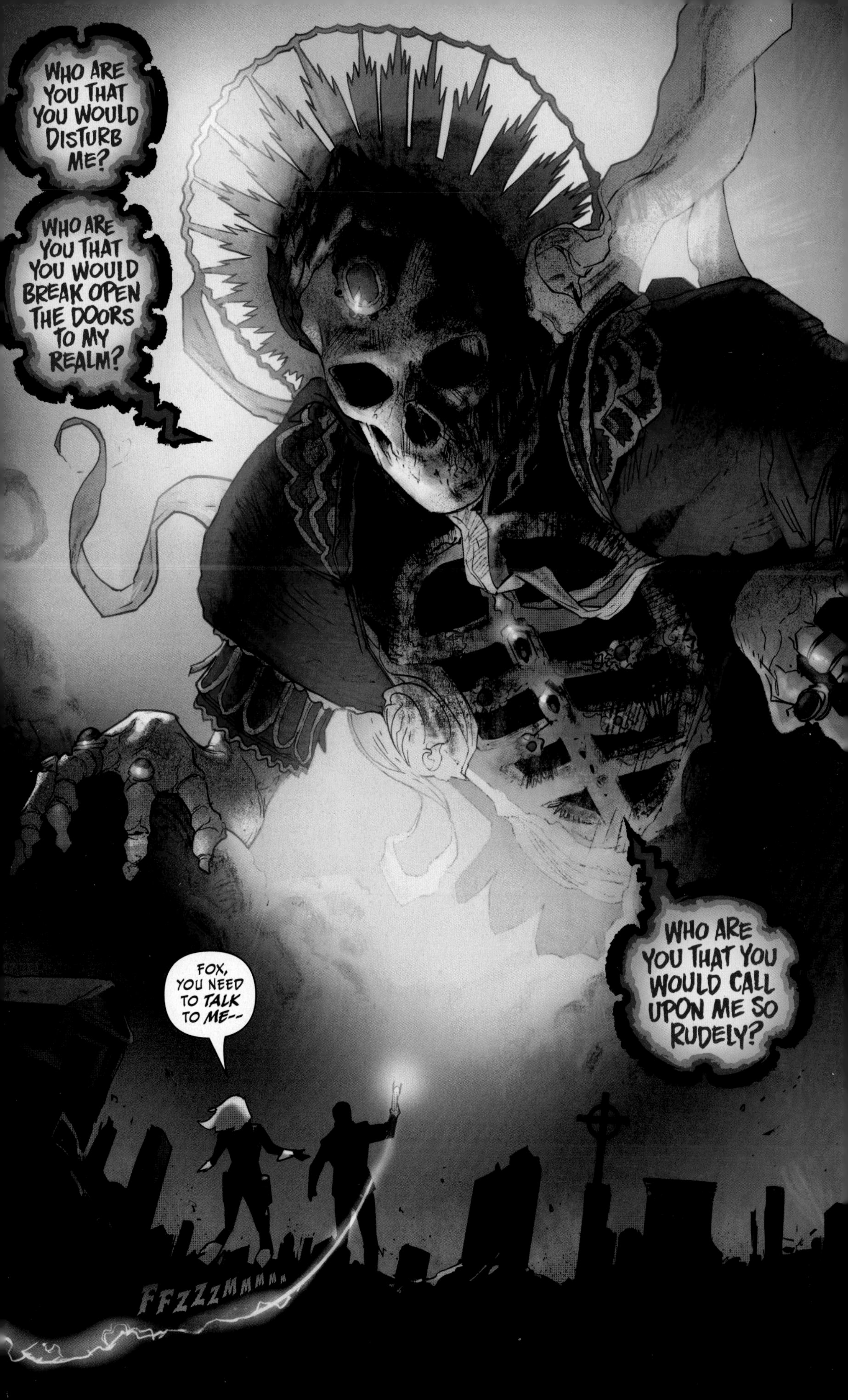
WHO ARE YOU THAT YOU WOULD DISTURB ME?
WHO ARE YOU THAT YOU WOULD BREAK OPEN THE DOORS TO MY REALM?
WHO ARE YOU THAT YOU WOULD CALL UPON ME SO RUDELY?
FOX, YOU NEED TO TALK TO ME--
FFZZZMMMMM

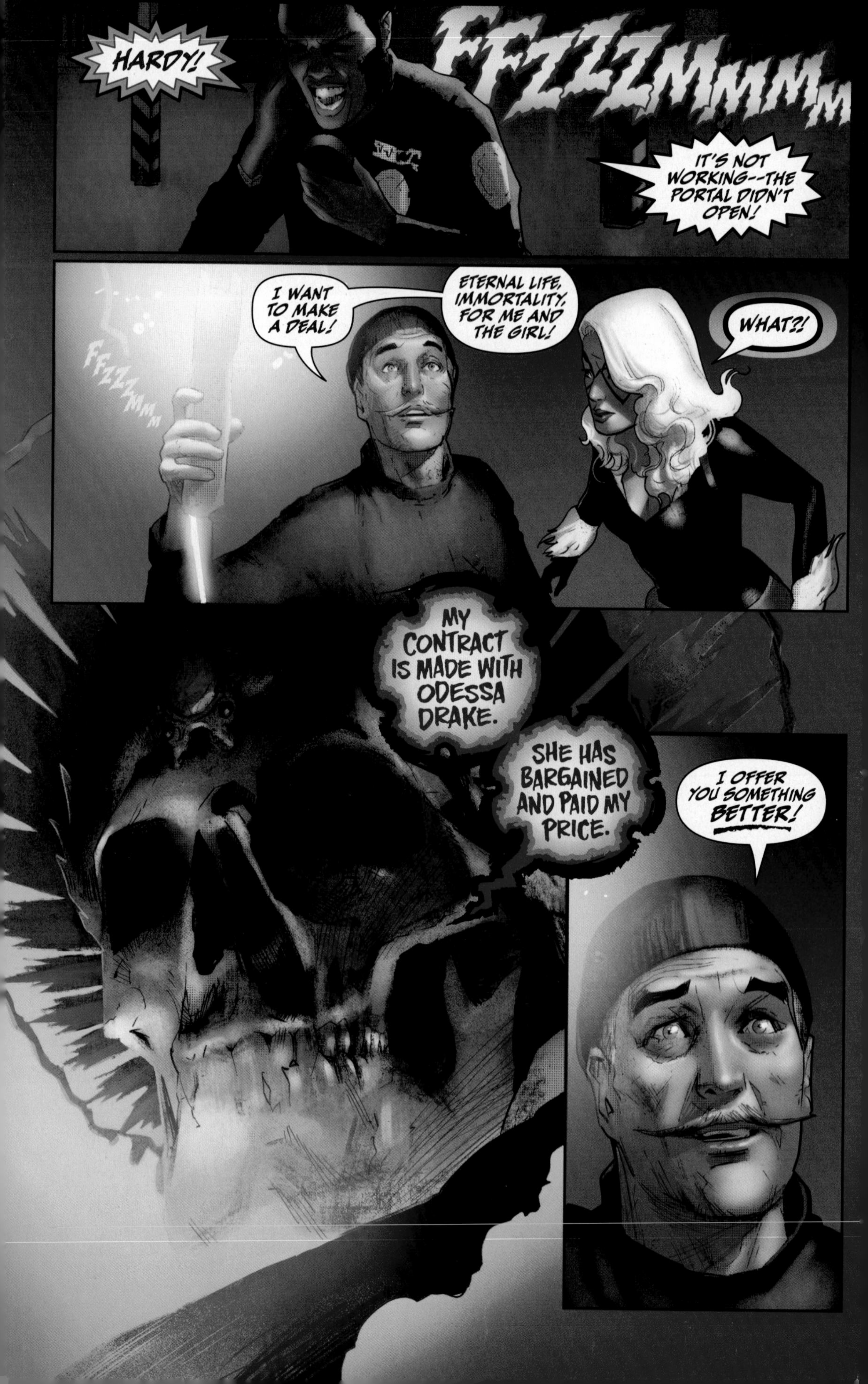
HARDY!
FFZZZMMMM
IT'S NOT WORKING--THE PORTAL DIDN'T OPEN!
I WANT TO MAKE A DEAL!
ETERNAL LIFE, IMMORTALITY, FOR ME AND THE GIRL!
WHAT?!
FFZZZMMM
MY CONTRACT IS MADE WITH ODESSA DRAKE.
SHE HAS BARGAINED AND PAID MY PRICE.
I OFFER YOU SOMETHING BETTER!

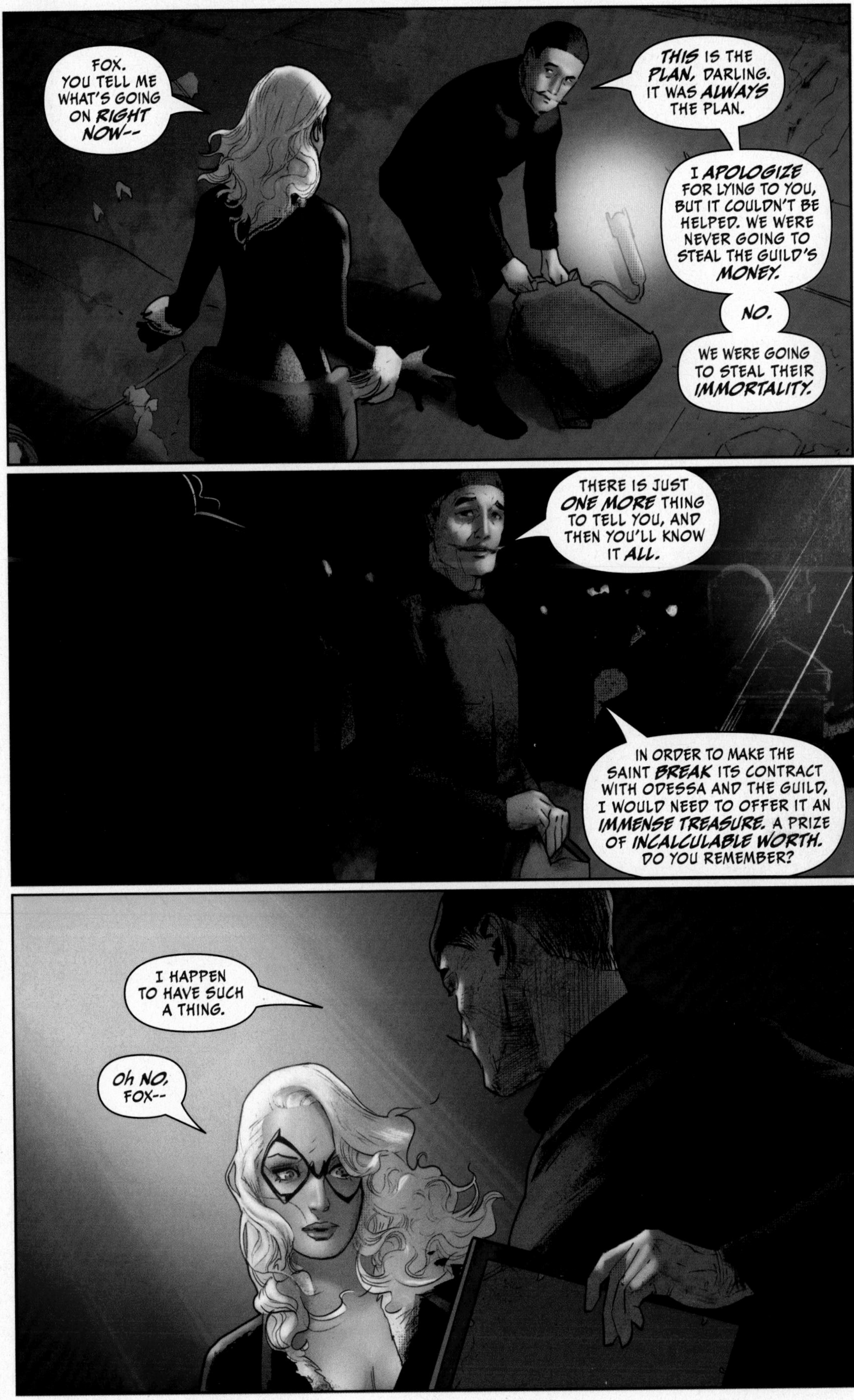
FOX. YOU TELL ME WHAT'S GOING ON RIGHT NOW--
THIS IS THE PLAN, DARLING. IT WAS ALWAYS THE PLAN.
I APOLOGIZE FOR LYING TO YOU, BUT IT COULDN'T BE HELPED. WE WERE NEVER GOING TO STEAL THE GUILD'S MONEY.
NO.
WE WERE GOING TO STEAL THEIR IMMORTALITY.
THERE IS JUST ONE MORE THING TO TELL YOU, AND THEN YOU'LL KNOW IT ALL.
IN ORDER TO MAKE THE SAINT BREAK ITS CONTRACT WITH ODESSA AND THE GUILD, I WOULD NEED TO OFFER IT AN IMMENSE TREASURE. A PRIZE OF INCALCULABLE WORTH. DO YOU REMEMBER?
I HAPPEN TO HAVE SUCH A THING.
Oh NO, FOX--

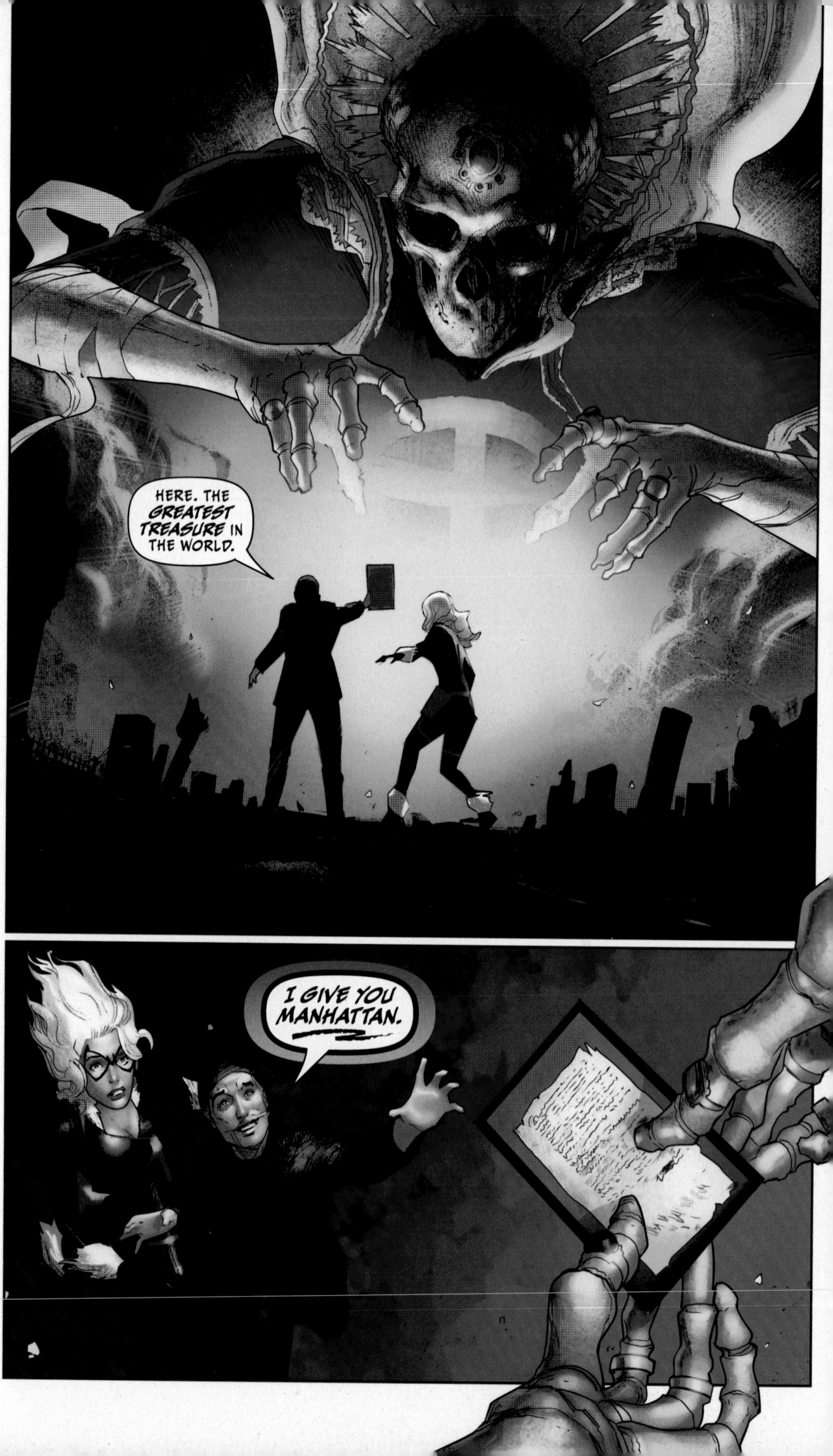
HERE. THE GREATEST TREASURE IN THE WORLD.
I GIVE YOU MANHATTAN.

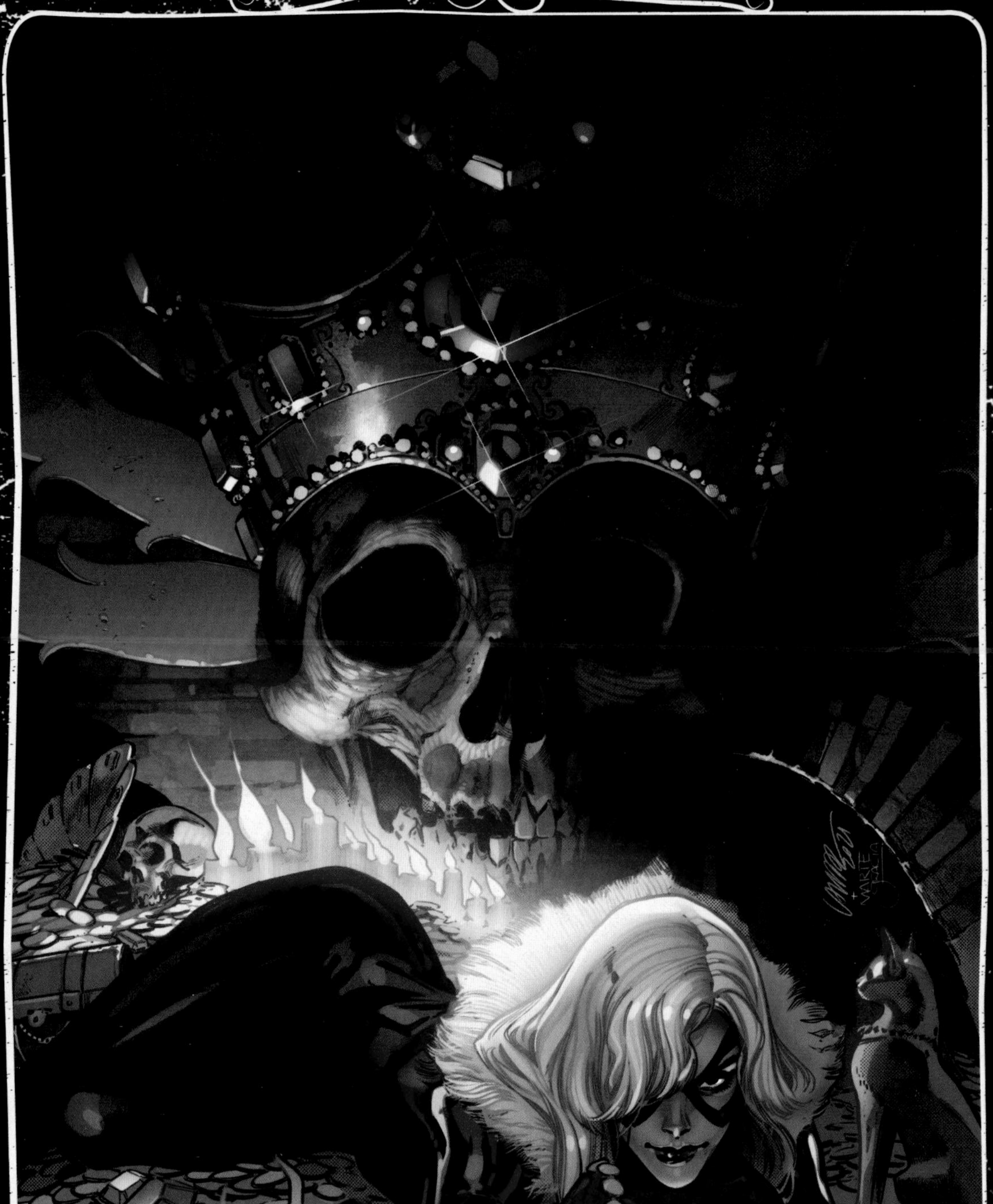

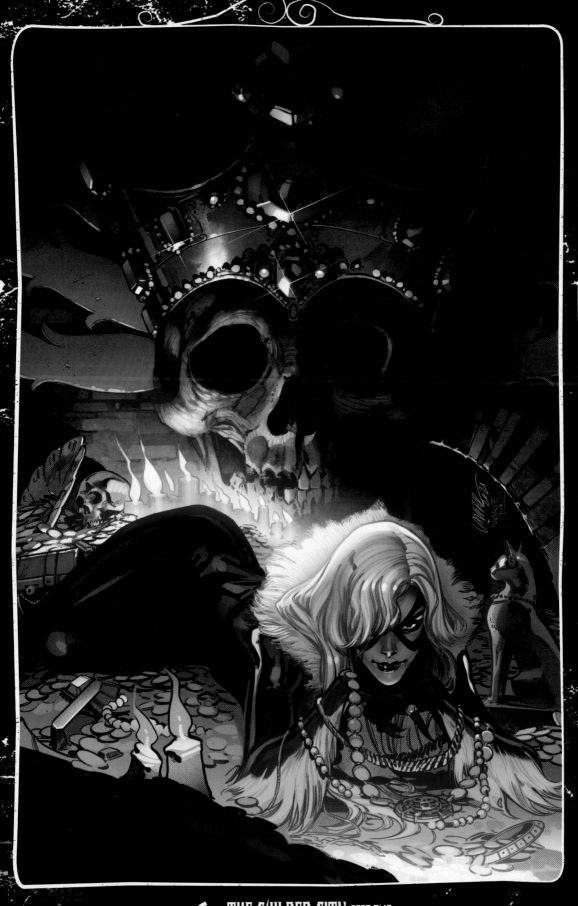

6 • THE GUILDED CITY PART TWO

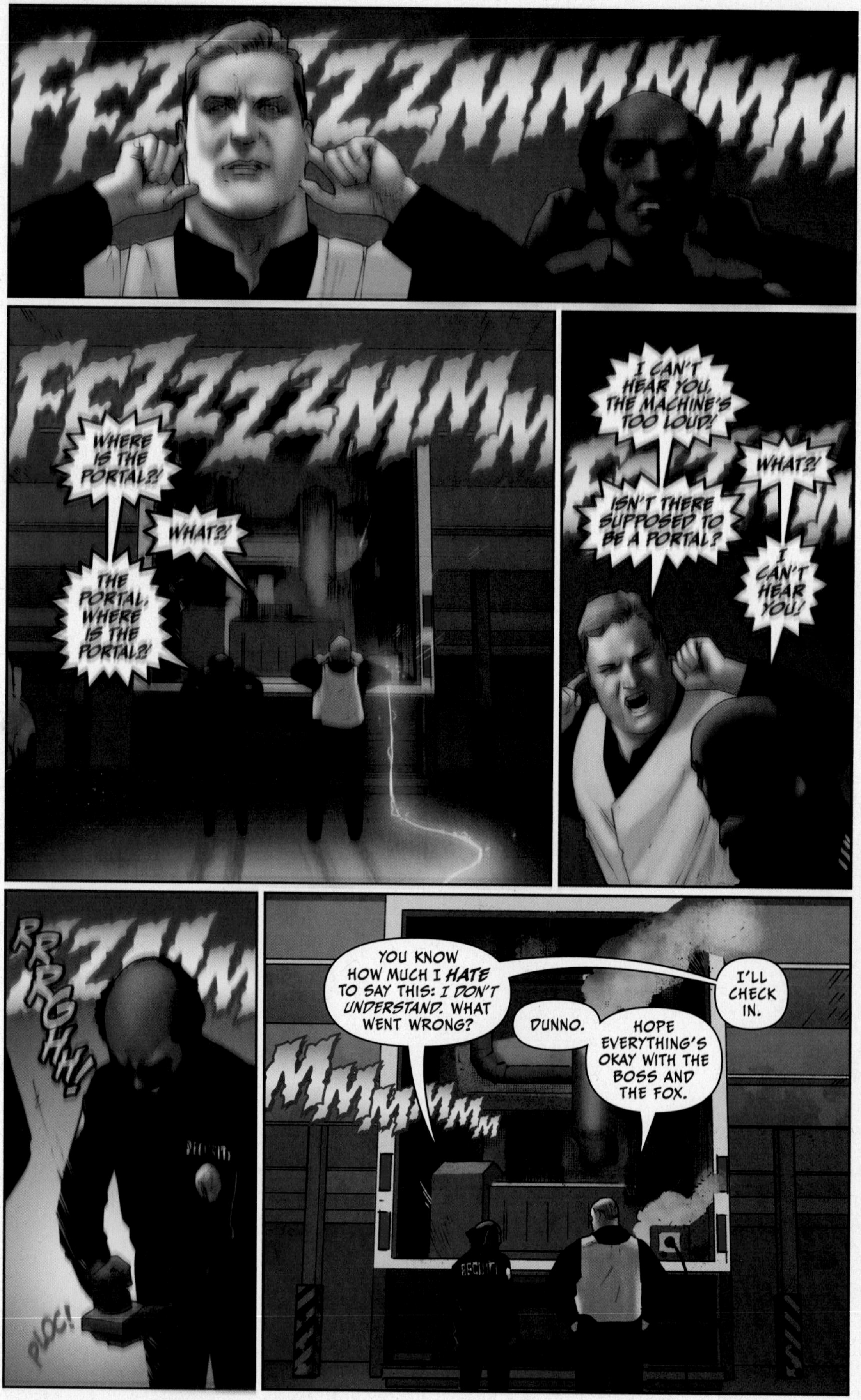

FFZZZZMMMMMM
FFZZZMMMM
WHERE IS THE PORTAL?!
WHAT?!
THE PORTAL, WHERE IS THE PORTAL?!
I CAN'T HEAR YOU, THE MACHINE'S TOO LOUD!
WHAT?!
ISN'T THERE SUPPOSED TO BE A PORTAL?
I CAN'T HEAR YOU!
ZZMM
RRRGHH!
PLOC!
MMMMMMm
YOU KNOW HOW MUCH I *HATE* TO SAY THIS: *I DON'T UNDERSTAND.* WHAT WENT WRONG?
I'LL CHECK IN.
DUNNO.
HOPE EVERYTHING'S OKAY WITH THE BOSS AND THE FOX.

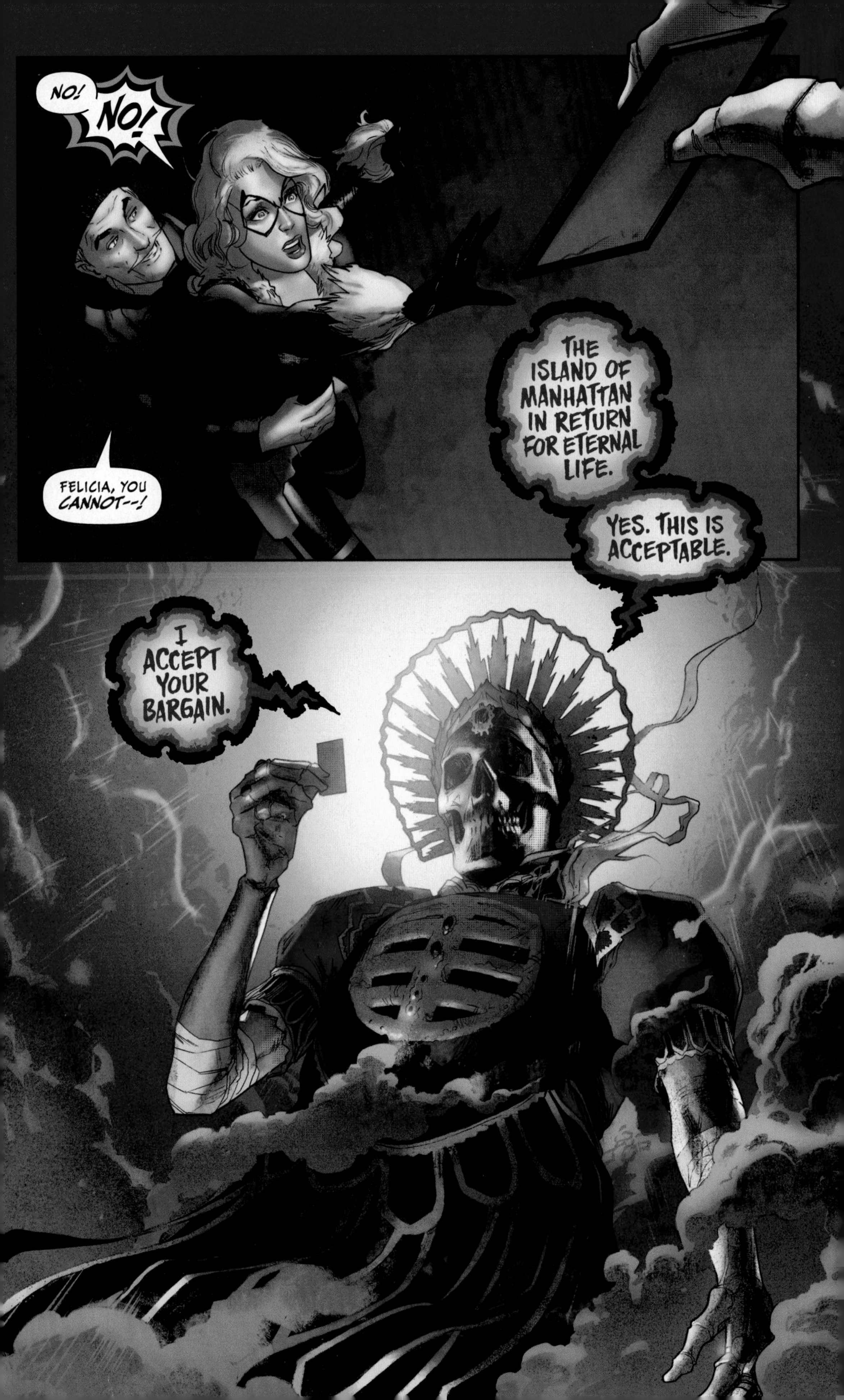
NO!
NO!
FELICIA, YOU CANNOT--!
THE ISLAND OF MANHATTAN IN RETURN FOR ETERNAL LIFE.
YES. THIS IS ACCEPTABLE.
I ACCEPT YOUR BARGAIN.

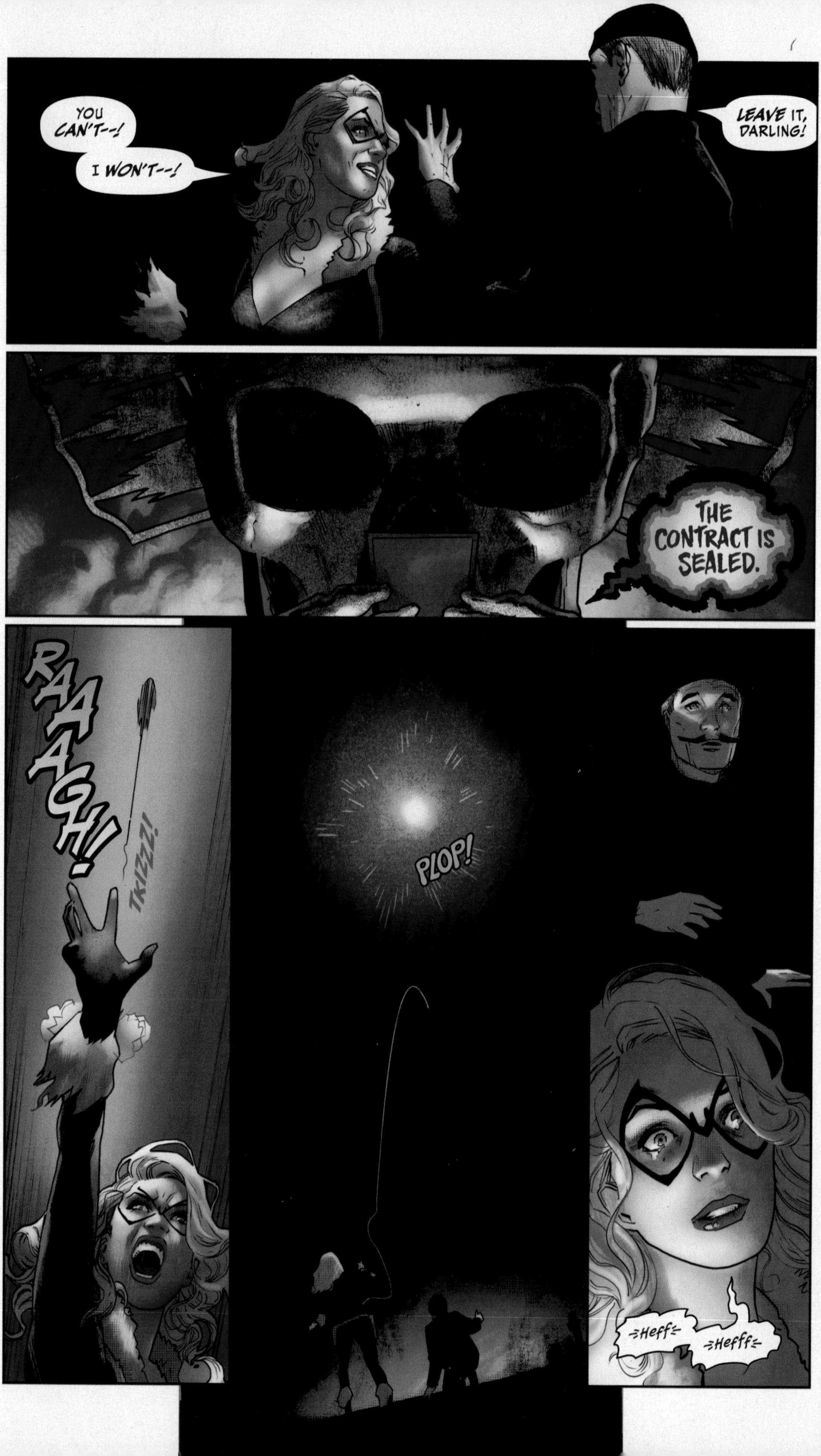
YOU CAN'T--!
I WON'T--!
LEAVE IT, DARLING!
THE CONTRACT IS SEALED.
RAAAGH!!
TKIZZZ!
PLOP!
≠Heff≠
≠Hefff≠

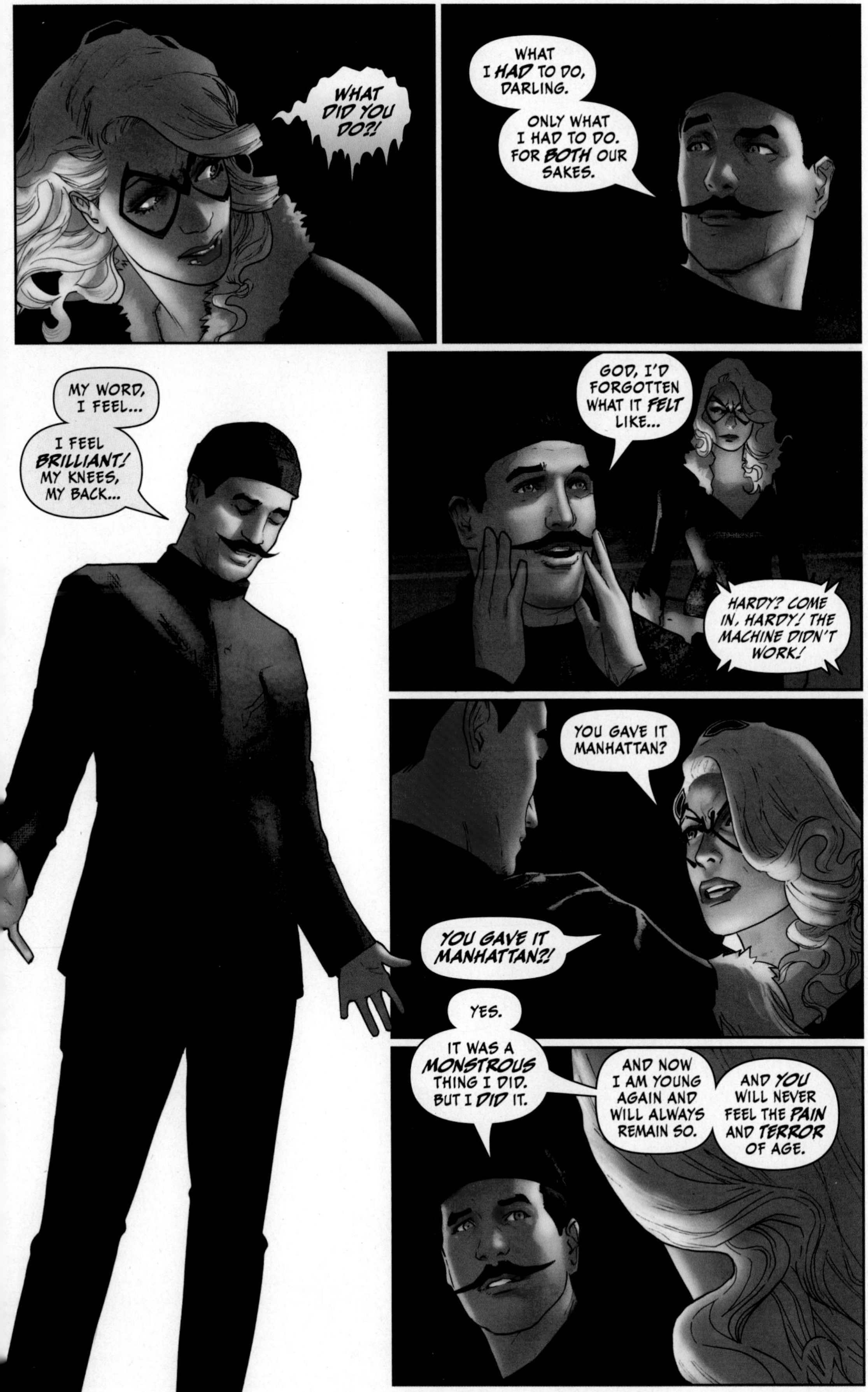
WHAT DID YOU DO?!
WHAT I HAD TO DO, DARLING.
ONLY WHAT I HAD TO DO. FOR BOTH OUR SAKES.
MY WORD, I FEEL...
I FEEL BRILLIANT! MY KNEES, MY BACK...
GOD, I'D FORGOTTEN WHAT IT FELT LIKE...
HARDY? COME IN, HARDY! THE MACHINE DIDN'T WORK!
YOU GAVE IT MANHATTAN?
YOU GAVE IT MANHATTAN?!
YES.
IT WAS A MONSTROUS THING I DID. BUT I DID IT.
AND NOW I AM YOUNG AGAIN AND WILL ALWAYS REMAIN SO.
AND YOU WILL NEVER FEEL THE PAIN AND TERROR OF AGE.

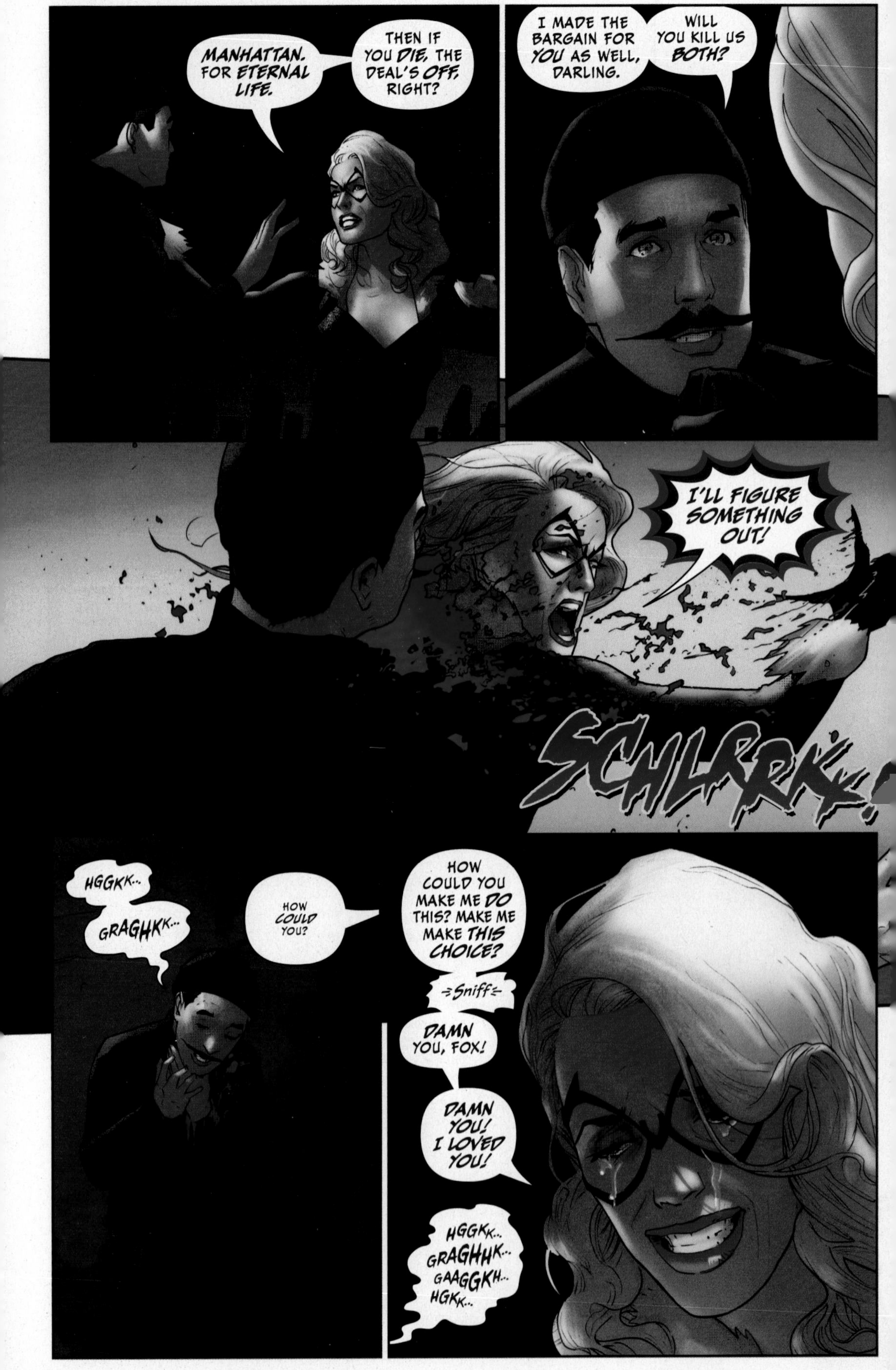

MANHATTAN. FOR ETERNAL LIFE.
THEN IF YOU DIE, THE DEAL'S OFF, RIGHT?
I MADE THE BARGAIN FOR YOU AS WELL, DARLING.
WILL YOU KILL US BOTH?
I'LL FIGURE SOMETHING OUT!
SCHLRRK!
HGGKK...
GRAGHKK...
HOW COULD YOU?
HOW COULD YOU MAKE ME DO THIS? MAKE ME MAKE THIS CHOICE?
Sniff
DAMN YOU, FOX!
DAMN YOU! I LOVED YOU!
HGGKK.. GRAGHHK.. GAAGGKH.. HGKK..

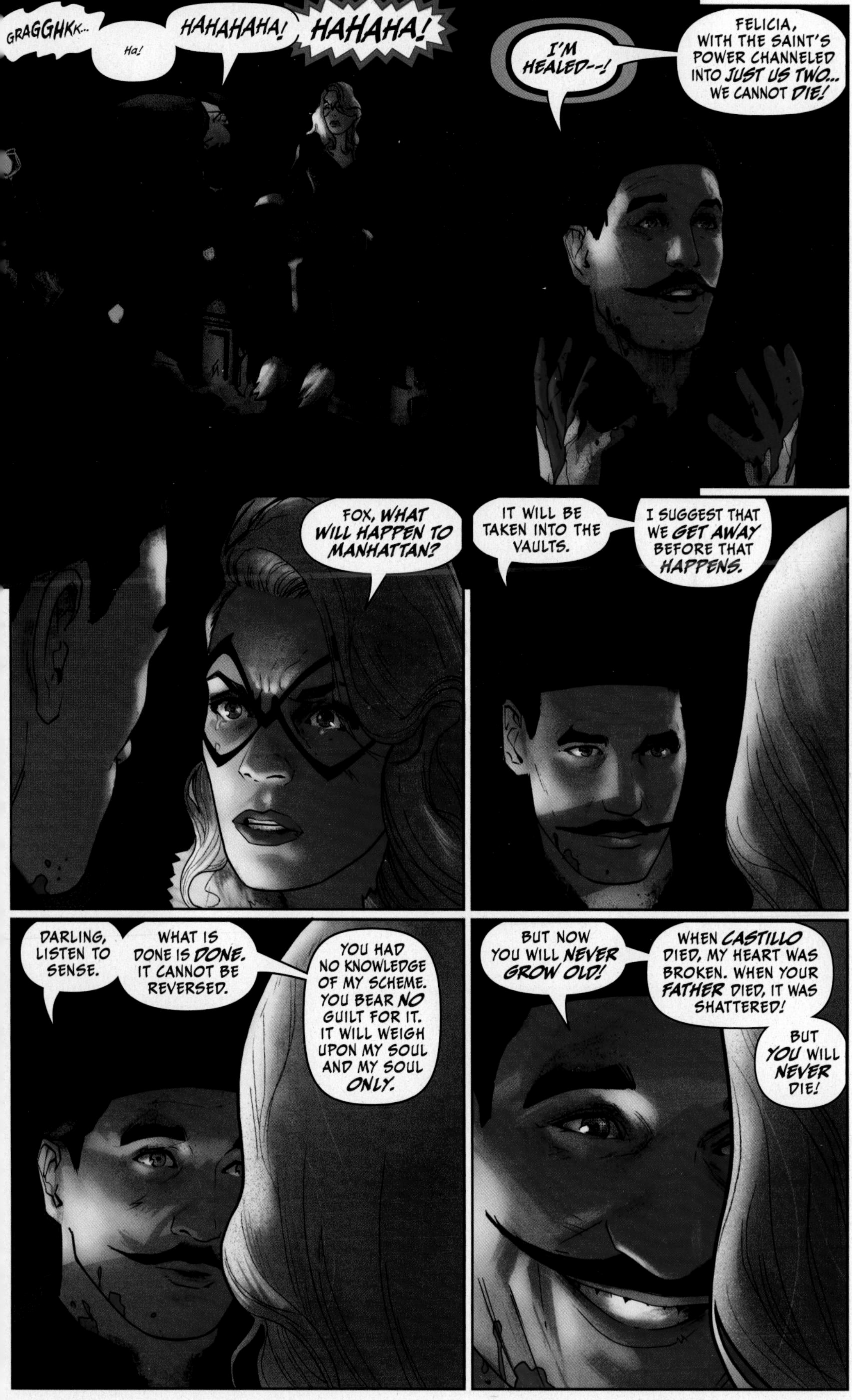
GRAGGHKK...
Ha!
HAHAHAHA!
HAHAHA!
I'M HEALED--!
FELICIA, WITH THE SAINT'S POWER CHANNELED INTO JUST US TWO... WE CANNOT DIE!
FOX, WHAT WILL HAPPEN TO MANHATTAN?
IT WILL BE TAKEN INTO THE VAULTS.
I SUGGEST THAT WE GET AWAY BEFORE THAT HAPPENS.
DARLING, LISTEN TO SENSE.
WHAT IS DONE IS DONE. IT CANNOT BE REVERSED.
YOU HAD NO KNOWLEDGE OF MY SCHEME. YOU BEAR NO GUILT FOR IT. IT WILL WEIGH UPON MY SOUL AND MY SOUL ONLY.
BUT NOW YOU WILL NEVER GROW OLD!
WHEN CASTILLO DIED, MY HEART WAS BROKEN. WHEN YOUR FATHER DIED, IT WAS SHATTERED!
BUT YOU WILL NEVER DIE!

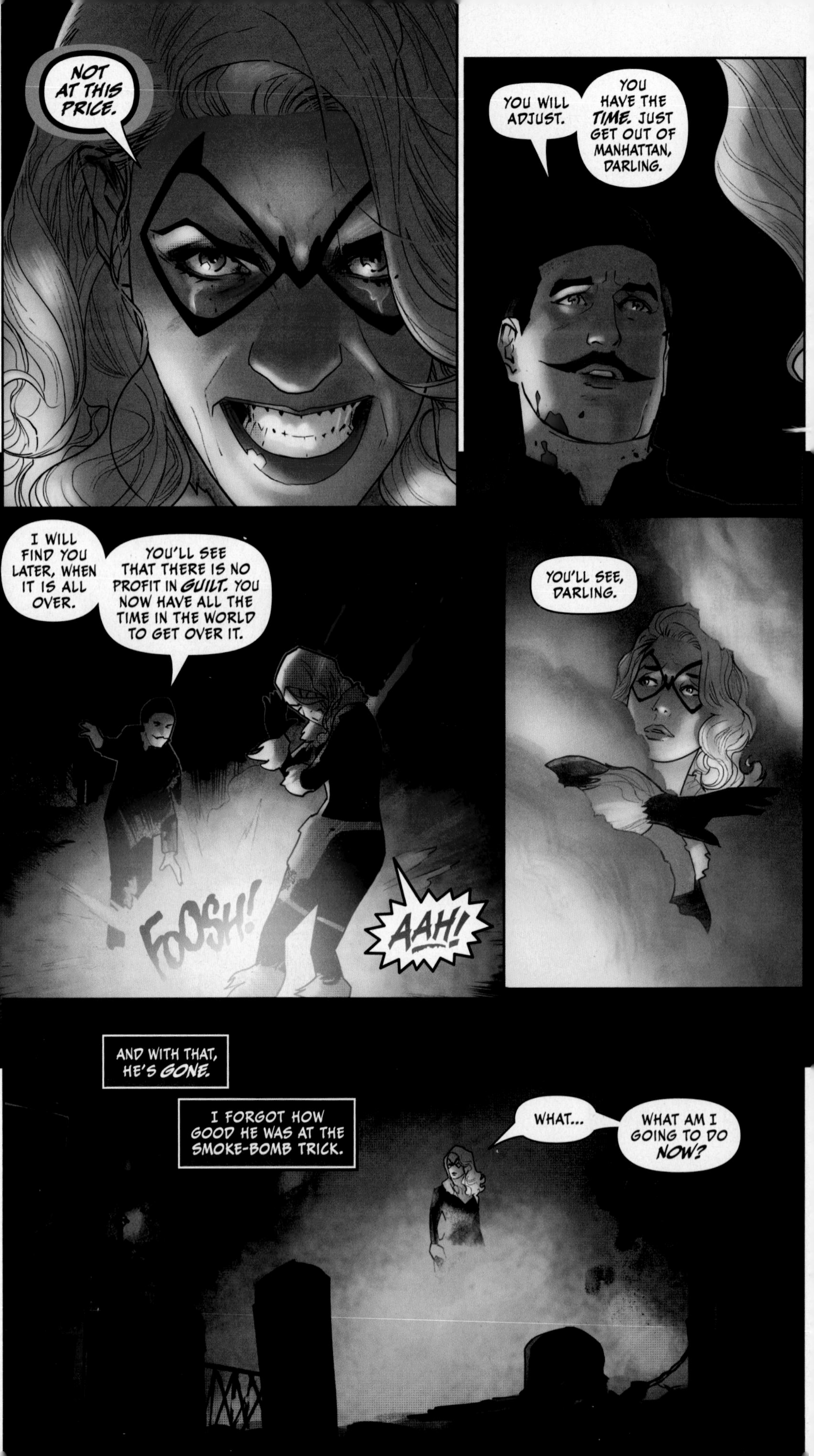
NOT AT THIS PRICE.
YOU WILL ADJUST.
YOU HAVE THE TIME. JUST GET OUT OF MANHATTAN, DARLING.
I WILL FIND YOU LATER, WHEN IT IS ALL OVER.
YOU'LL SEE THAT THERE IS NO PROFIT IN GUILT. YOU NOW HAVE ALL THE TIME IN THE WORLD TO GET OVER IT.
FOOSH!
AAH!
YOU'LL SEE, DARLING.
AND WITH THAT, HE'S GONE.
I FORGOT HOW GOOD HE WAS AT THE SMOKE-BOMB TRICK.
WHAT...
WHAT AM I GOING TO DO NOW?

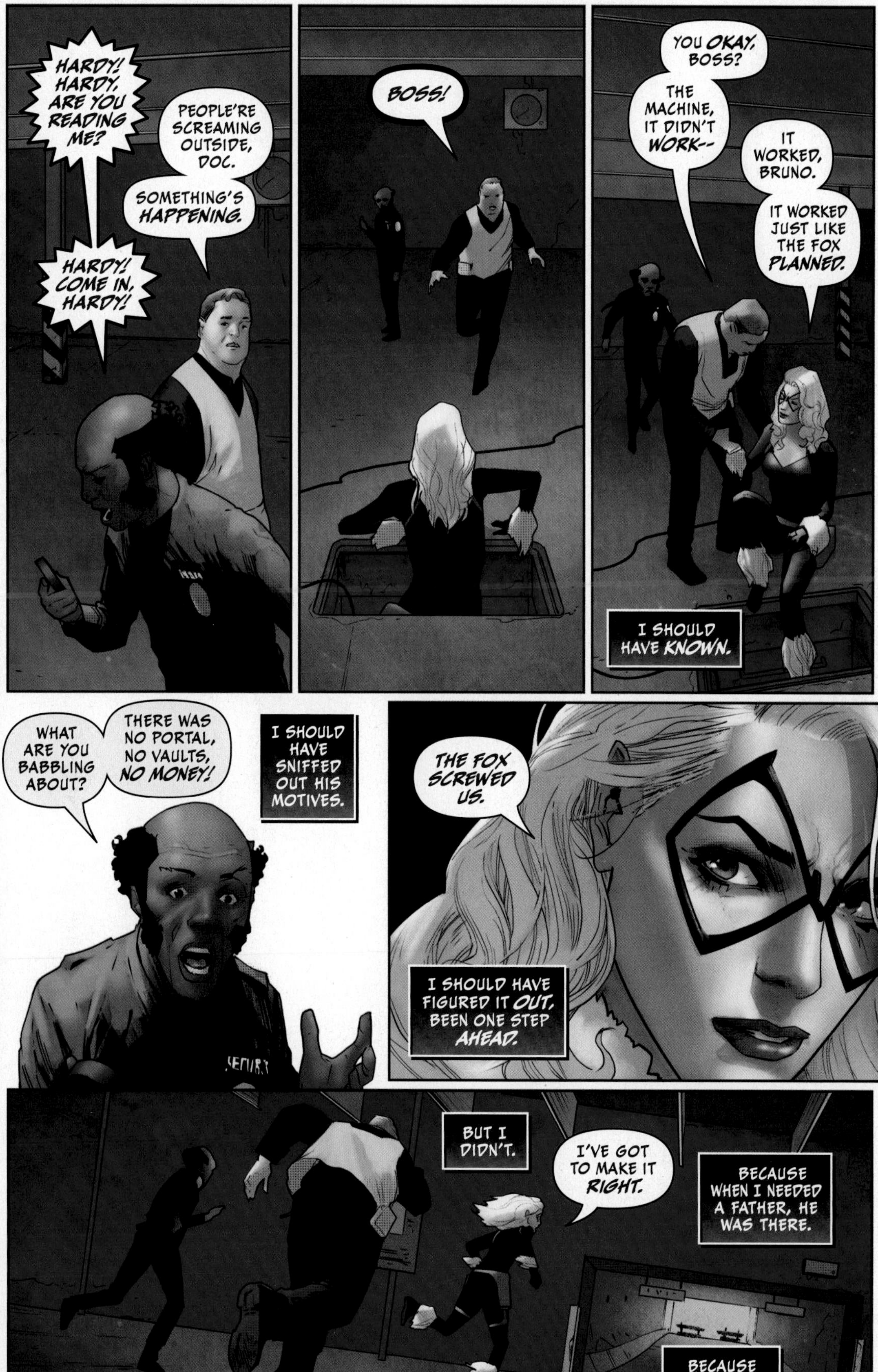

HARDY! HARDY, ARE YOU READING ME?
PEOPLE'RE SCREAMING OUTSIDE, DOC.
SOMETHING'S HAPPENING.
HARDY! COME IN, HARDY!
BOSS!
YOU OKAY, BOSS?
THE MACHINE, IT DIDN'T WORK--
IT WORKED, BRUNO.
IT WORKED JUST LIKE THE FOX PLANNED.
I SHOULD HAVE KNOWN.
WHAT ARE YOU BABBLING ABOUT?
THERE WAS NO PORTAL, NO VAULTS, NO MONEY!
I SHOULD HAVE SNIFFED OUT HIS MOTIVES.
THE FOX SCREWED US.
I SHOULD HAVE FIGURED IT OUT, BEEN ONE STEP AHEAD.
BUT I DIDN'T.
I'VE GOT TO MAKE IT RIGHT.
BECAUSE WHEN I NEEDED A FATHER, HE WAS THERE.
BECAUSE I LOVE HIM.

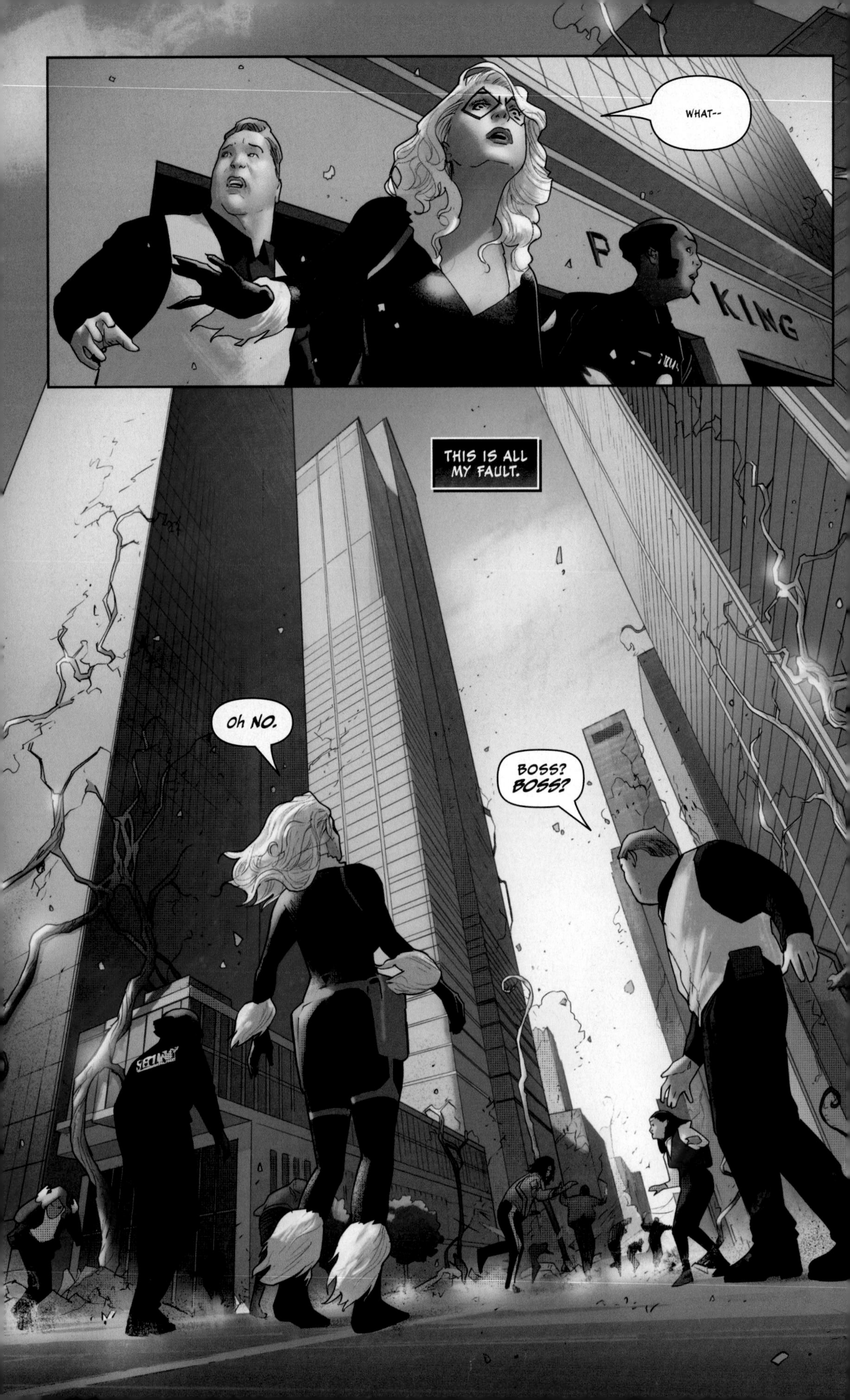

WHAT--
THIS IS ALL MY FAULT.
Oh NO.
BOSS? BOSS?

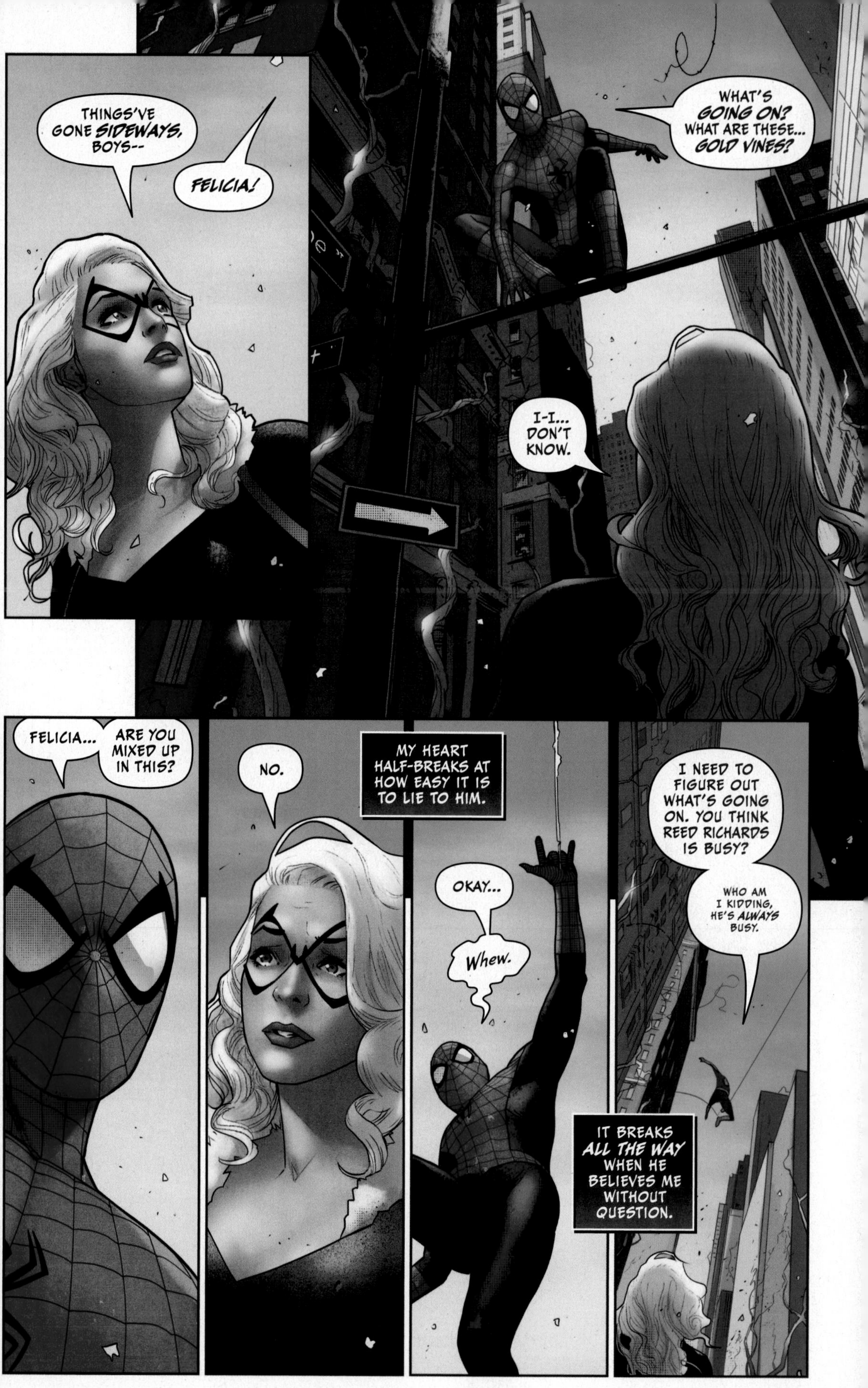
THINGS'VE GONE SIDEWAYS, BOYS--
FELICIA!
WHAT'S GOING ON? WHAT ARE THESE... GOLD VINES?
I-I... DON'T KNOW.
FELICIA...
ARE YOU MIXED UP IN THIS?
NO.
MY HEART HALF-BREAKS AT HOW EASY IT IS TO LIE TO HIM.
OKAY...
Whew.
I NEED TO FIGURE OUT WHAT'S GOING ON. YOU THINK REED RICHARDS IS BUSY?
WHO AM I KIDDING, HE'S ALWAYS BUSY.
IT BREAKS ALL THE WAY WHEN HE BELIEVES ME WITHOUT QUESTION.

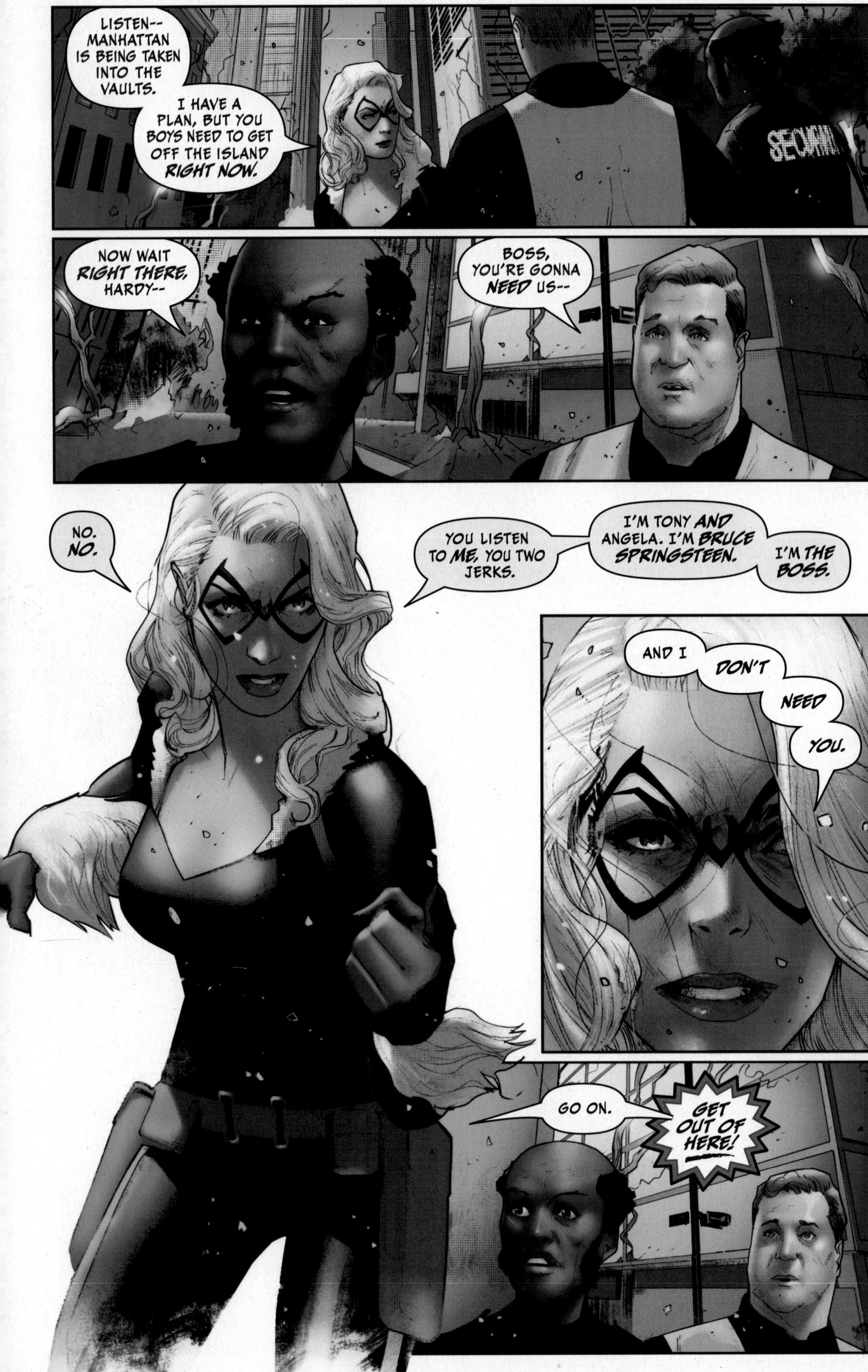
LISTEN-- MANHATTAN IS BEING TAKEN INTO THE VAULTS.
I HAVE A PLAN, BUT YOU BOYS NEED TO GET OFF THE ISLAND RIGHT NOW.
SECURITY
NOW WAIT RIGHT THERE, HARDY--
BOSS, YOU'RE GONNA NEED US--
NO. NO.
YOU LISTEN TO ME, YOU TWO JERKS.
I'M TONY AND ANGELA. I'M BRUCE SPRINGSTEEN.
I'M THE BOSS.
AND I
DON'T
NEED
YOU.
GO ON.
GET OUT OF HERE!

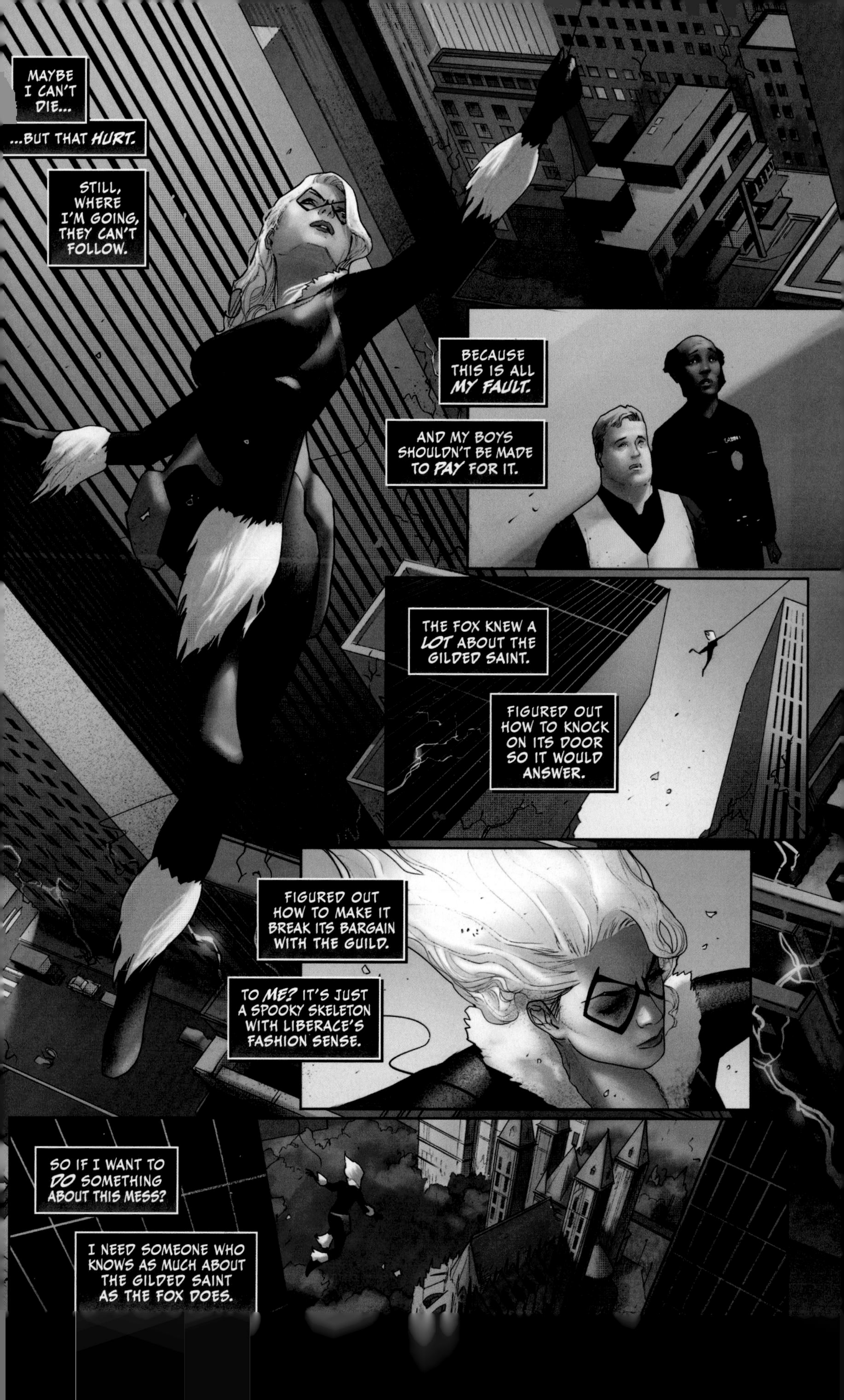
MAYBE I CAN'T DIE...
...BUT THAT HURT.
STILL, WHERE I'M GOING, THEY CAN'T FOLLOW.
BECAUSE THIS IS ALL MY FAULT.
AND MY BOYS SHOULDN'T BE MADE TO PAY FOR IT.
THE FOX KNEW A LOT ABOUT THE GILDED SAINT.
FIGURED OUT HOW TO KNOCK ON ITS DOOR SO IT WOULD ANSWER.
FIGURED OUT HOW TO MAKE IT BREAK ITS BARGAIN WITH THE GUILD.
TO ME? IT'S JUST A SPOOKY SKELETON WITH LIBERACE'S FASHION SENSE.
SO IF I WANT TO DO SOMETHING ABOUT THIS MESS?
I NEED SOMEONE WHO KNOWS AS MUCH ABOUT THE GILDED SAINT AS THE FOX DOES.

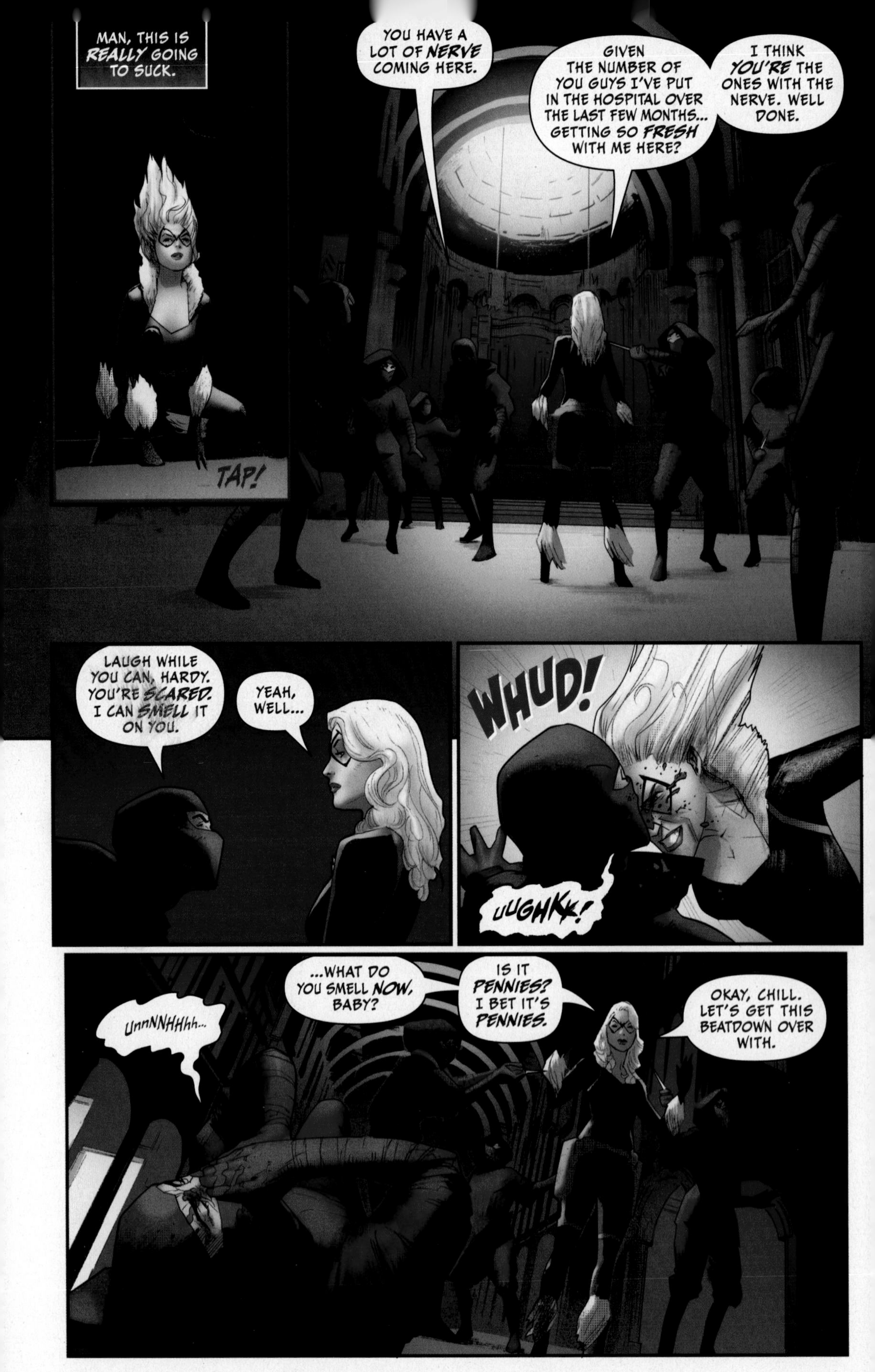
MAN, THIS IS REALLY GOING TO SUCK.
TAP!
YOU HAVE A LOT OF NERVE COMING HERE.
GIVEN THE NUMBER OF YOU GUYS I'VE PUT IN THE HOSPITAL OVER THE LAST FEW MONTHS... GETTING SO FRESH WITH ME HERE?
I THINK YOU'RE THE ONES WITH THE NERVE. WELL DONE.
LAUGH WHILE YOU CAN, HARDY. YOU'RE SCARED. I CAN SMELL IT ON YOU.
YEAH, WELL...
WHUD!
UUGHKK!
UnnNNHHhh...
...WHAT DO YOU SMELL NOW, BABY?
IS IT PENNIES? I BET IT'S PENNIES.
OKAY, CHILL. LET'S GET THIS BEATDOWN OVER WITH.

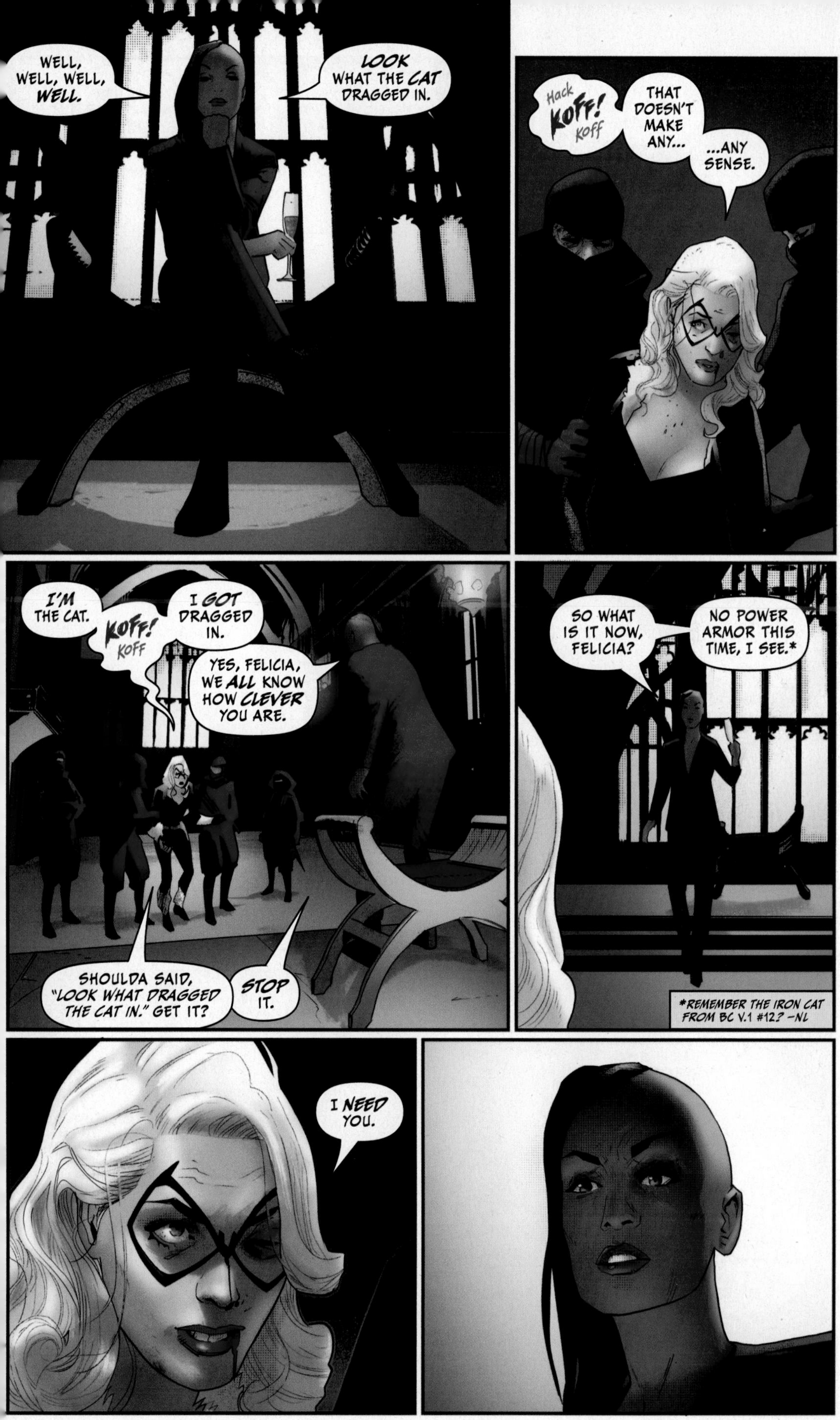
WELL, WELL, WELL, WELL.
LOOK WHAT THE CAT DRAGGED IN.
Hack KOFF! Koff
THAT DOESN'T MAKE ANY...
...ANY SENSE.
I'M THE CAT.
KOFF! KOFF
I GOT DRAGGED IN.
YES, FELICIA, WE ALL KNOW HOW CLEVER YOU ARE.
SHOULDA SAID, "LOOK WHAT DRAGGED THE CAT IN." GET IT?
STOP IT.
SO WHAT IS IT NOW, FELICIA?
NO POWER ARMOR THIS TIME, I SEE.*
*REMEMBER THE IRON CAT FROM BC V.1 #12? –NL
I NEED YOU.

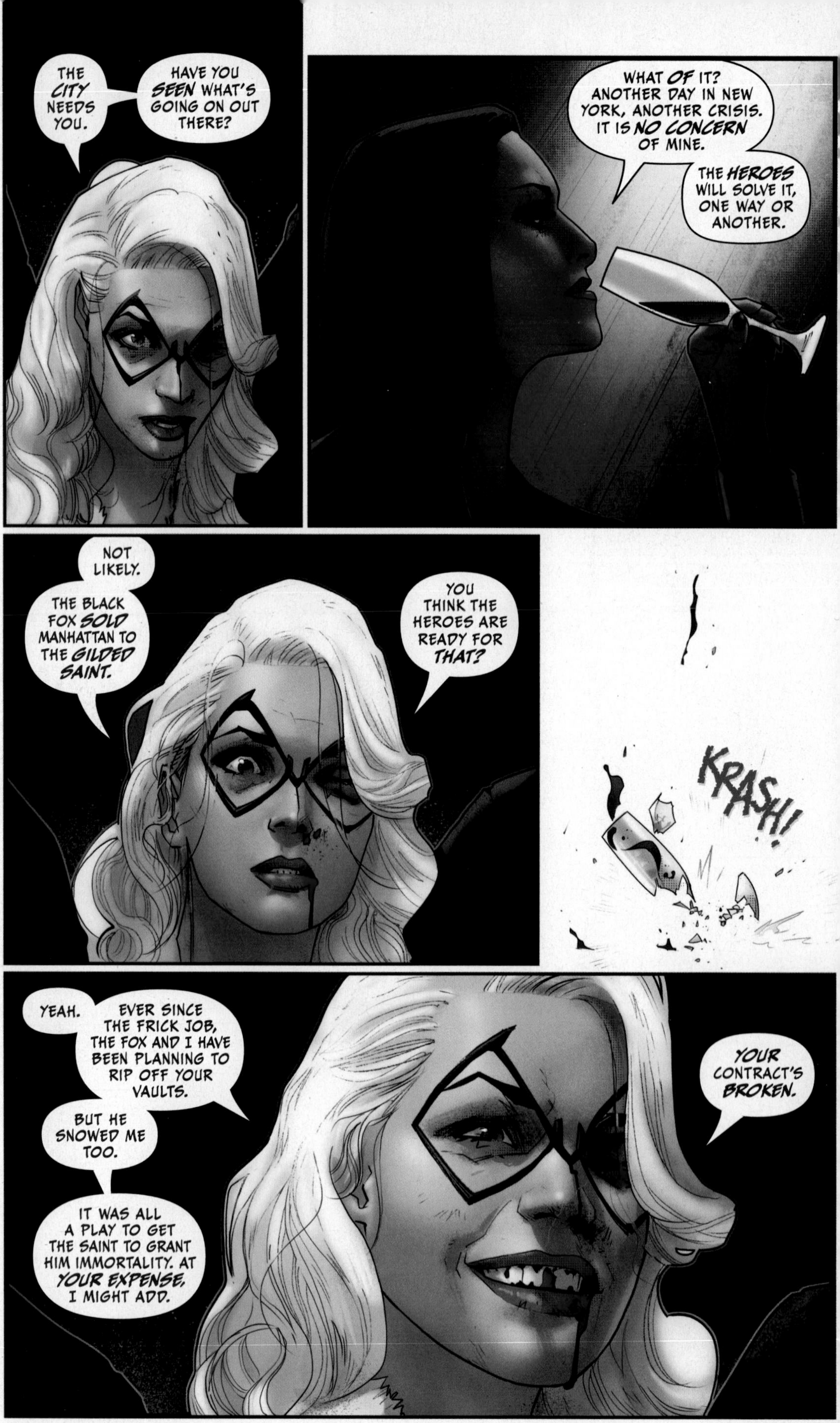
THE CITY NEEDS YOU.
HAVE YOU SEEN WHAT'S GOING ON OUT THERE?
WHAT OF IT? ANOTHER DAY IN NEW YORK, ANOTHER CRISIS. IT IS NO CONCERN OF MINE.
THE HEROES WILL SOLVE IT, ONE WAY OR ANOTHER.
NOT LIKELY.
THE BLACK FOX SOLD MANHATTAN TO THE GILDED SAINT.
YOU THINK THE HEROES ARE READY FOR THAT?
KRASH!
YEAH.
EVER SINCE THE FRICK JOB, THE FOX AND I HAVE BEEN PLANNING TO RIP OFF YOUR VAULTS.
BUT HE SNOWED ME TOO.
IT WAS ALL A PLAY TO GET THE SAINT TO GRANT HIM IMMORTALITY. AT YOUR EXPENSE, I MIGHT ADD.
YOUR CONTRACT'S BROKEN.

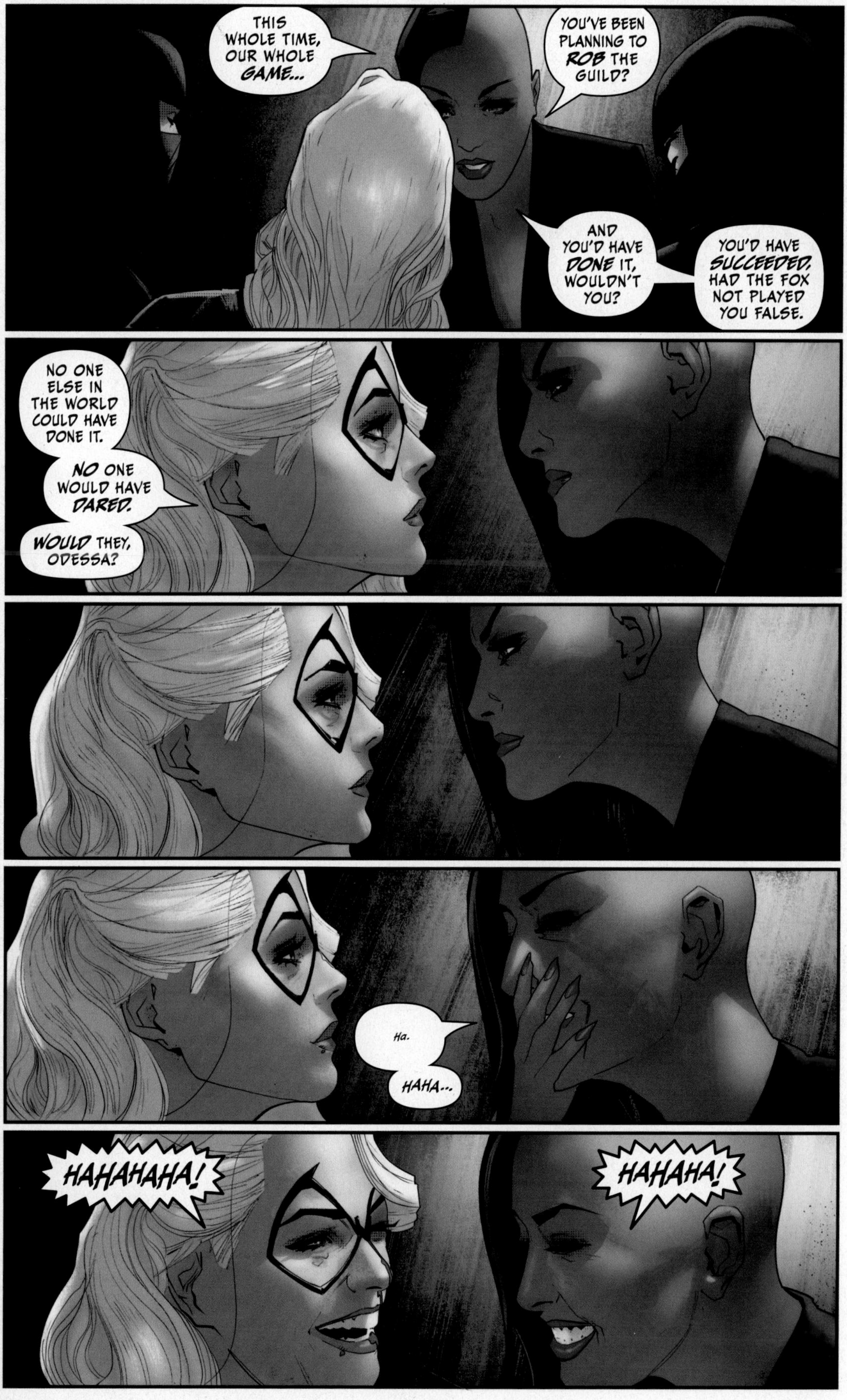

THIS WHOLE TIME, OUR WHOLE GAME...
YOU'VE BEEN PLANNING TO ROB THE GUILD?
AND YOU'D HAVE DONE IT, WOULDN'T YOU?
YOU'D HAVE SUCCEEDED, HAD THE FOX NOT PLAYED YOU FALSE.
NO ONE ELSE IN THE WORLD COULD HAVE DONE IT.
NO ONE WOULD HAVE DARED.
WOULD THEY, ODESSA?
Ha.
HAHA...
HAHAHAHA!
HAHAHA!

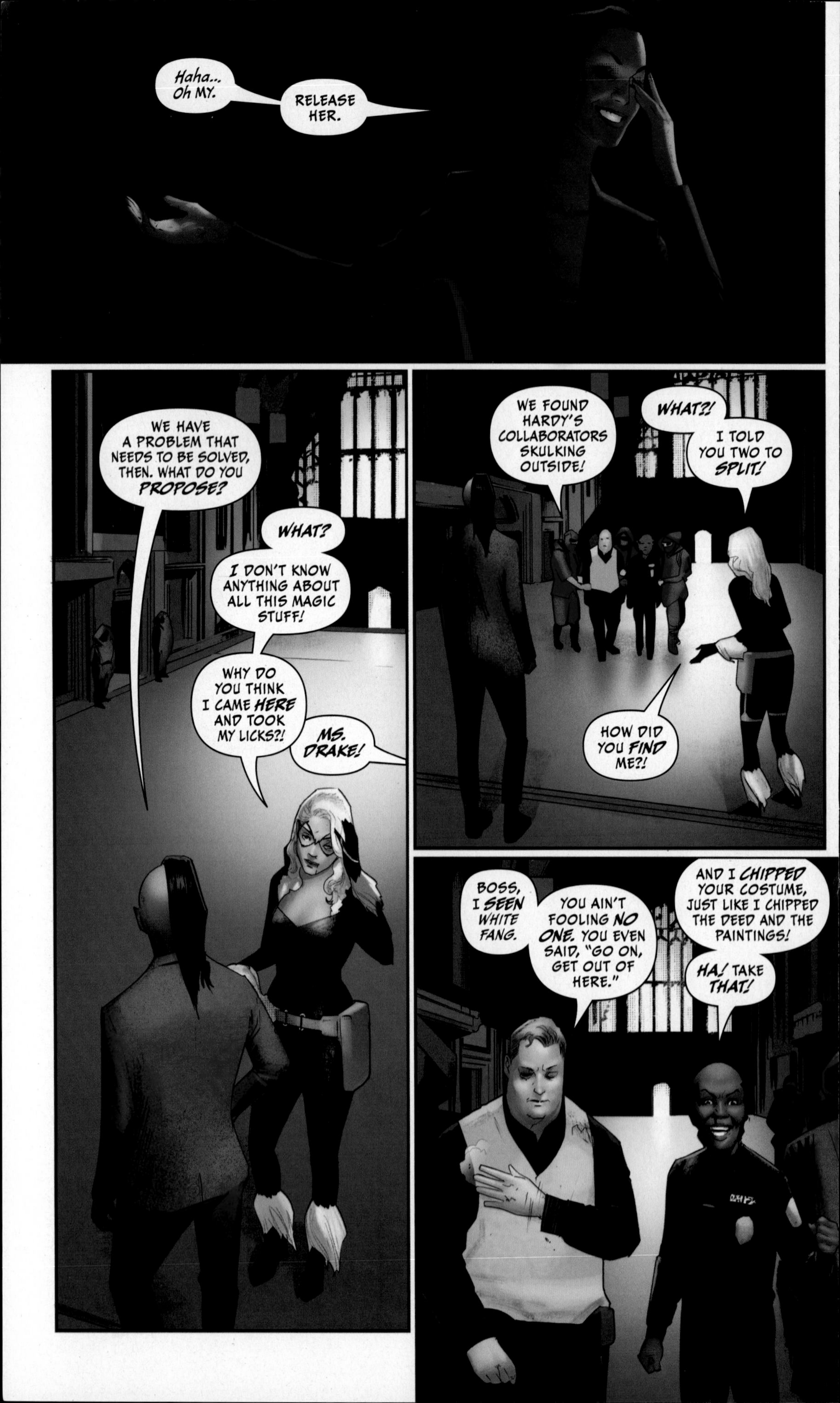
Haha... Oh MY.
RELEASE HER.
WE HAVE A PROBLEM THAT NEEDS TO BE SOLVED, THEN. WHAT DO YOU PROPOSE?
WHAT?
I DON'T KNOW ANYTHING ABOUT ALL THIS MAGIC STUFF!
WHY DO YOU THINK I CAME HERE AND TOOK MY LICKS?!
MS. DRAKE!
WE FOUND HARDY'S COLLABORATORS SKULKING OUTSIDE!
WHAT?!
I TOLD YOU TWO TO SPLIT!
HOW DID YOU FIND ME?!
BOSS, I SEEN WHITE FANG.
YOU AIN'T FOOLING NO ONE. YOU EVEN SAID, "GO ON, GET OUT OF HERE."
AND I CHIPPED YOUR COSTUME, JUST LIKE I CHIPPED THE DEED AND THE PAINTINGS!
HA! TAKE THAT!

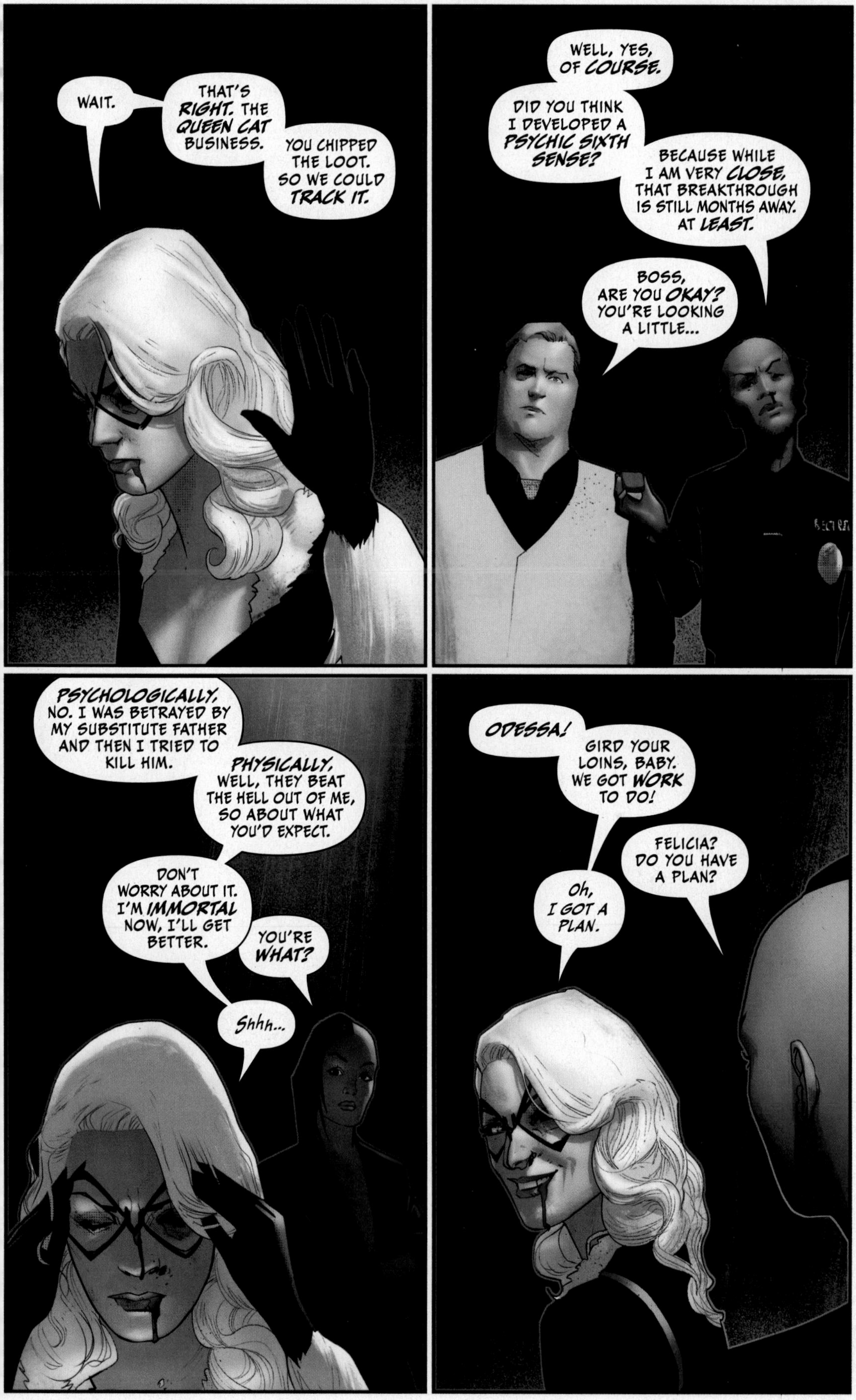

WAIT.
THAT'S RIGHT. THE QUEEN CAT BUSINESS.
YOU CHIPPED THE LOOT. SO WE COULD TRACK IT.
WELL, YES, OF COURSE.
DID YOU THINK I DEVELOPED A PSYCHIC SIXTH SENSE?
BECAUSE WHILE I AM VERY CLOSE, THAT BREAKTHROUGH IS STILL MONTHS AWAY. AT LEAST.
BOSS, ARE YOU OKAY? YOU'RE LOOKING A LITTLE...
PSYCHOLOGICALLY, NO. I WAS BETRAYED BY MY SUBSTITUTE FATHER AND THEN I TRIED TO KILL HIM.
PHYSICALLY, WELL, THEY BEAT THE HELL OUT OF ME, SO ABOUT WHAT YOU'D EXPECT.
DON'T WORRY ABOUT IT. I'M IMMORTAL NOW, I'LL GET BETTER.
YOU'RE WHAT?
Shhh...
ODESSA!
GIRD YOUR LOINS, BABY. WE GOT WORK TO DO!
FELICIA? DO YOU HAVE A PLAN?
Oh, I GOT A PLAN.

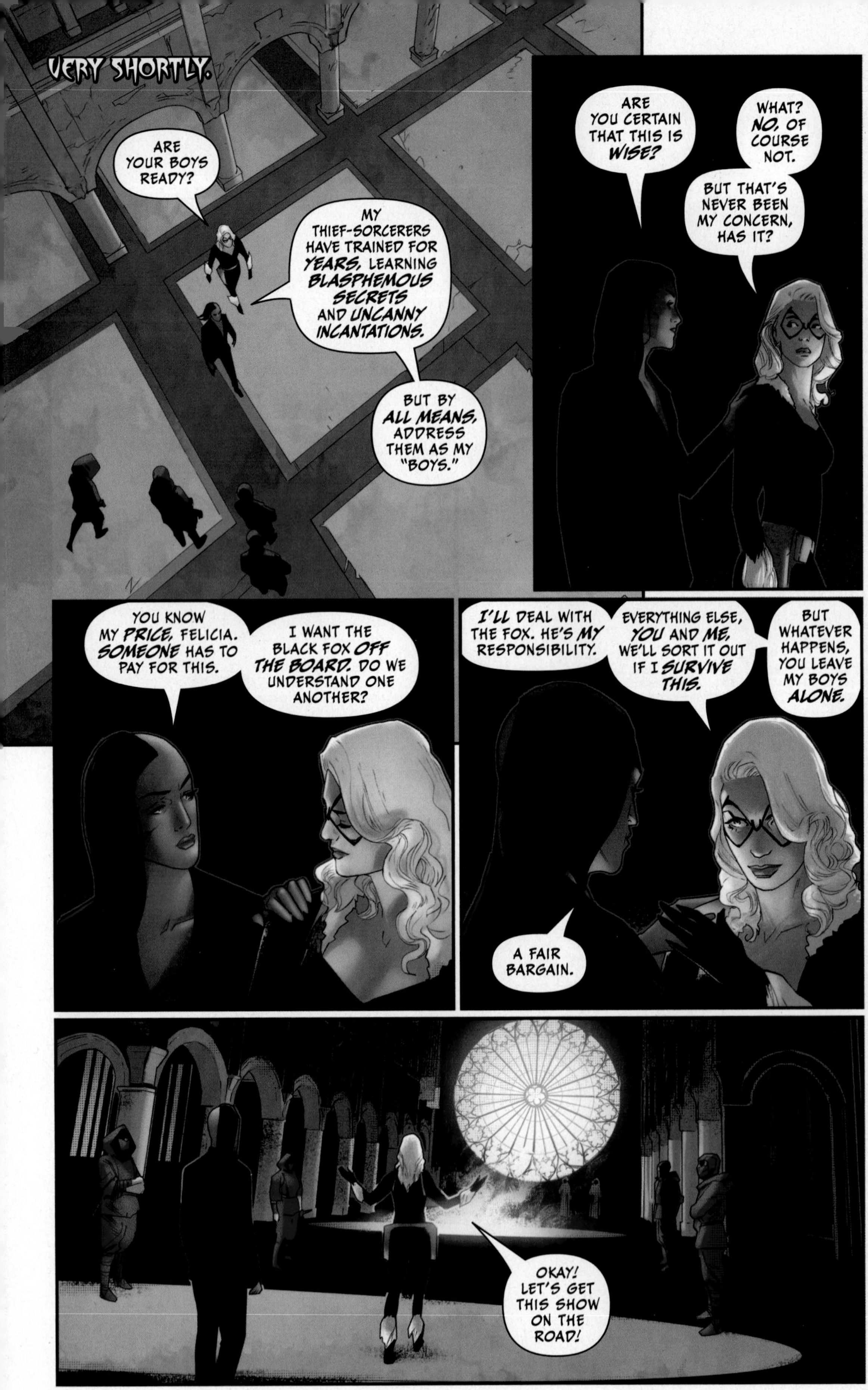
VERY SHORTLY.
ARE YOUR BOYS READY?
MY THIEF-SORCERERS HAVE TRAINED FOR YEARS, LEARNING BLASPHEMOUS SECRETS AND UNCANNY INCANTATIONS.
BUT BY ALL MEANS, ADDRESS THEM AS MY "BOYS."
ARE YOU CERTAIN THAT THIS IS WISE?
WHAT? NO, OF COURSE NOT.
BUT THAT'S NEVER BEEN MY CONCERN, HAS IT?
YOU KNOW MY PRICE, FELICIA. SOMEONE HAS TO PAY FOR THIS.
I WANT THE BLACK FOX OFF THE BOARD. DO WE UNDERSTAND ONE ANOTHER?
I'LL DEAL WITH THE FOX. HE'S MY RESPONSIBILITY.
EVERYTHING ELSE, YOU AND ME, WE'LL SORT IT OUT IF I SURVIVE THIS.
BUT WHATEVER HAPPENS, YOU LEAVE MY BOYS ALONE.
A FAIR BARGAIN.
OKAY! LET'S GET THIS SHOW ON THE ROAD!

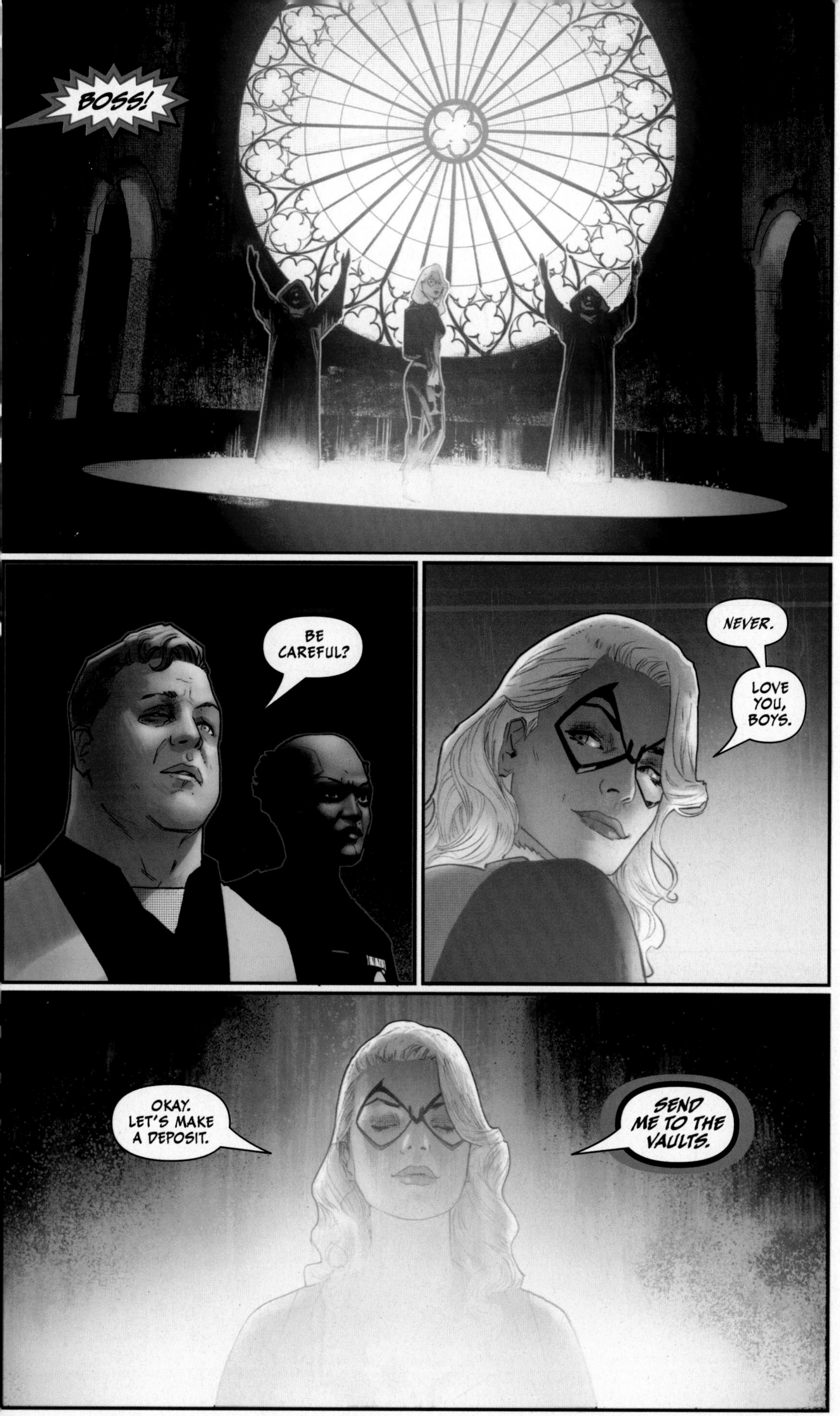
BOSS!
BE CAREFUL?
NEVER.
LOVE YOU, BOYS.
OKAY. LET'S MAKE A DEPOSIT.
SEND ME TO THE VAULTS.

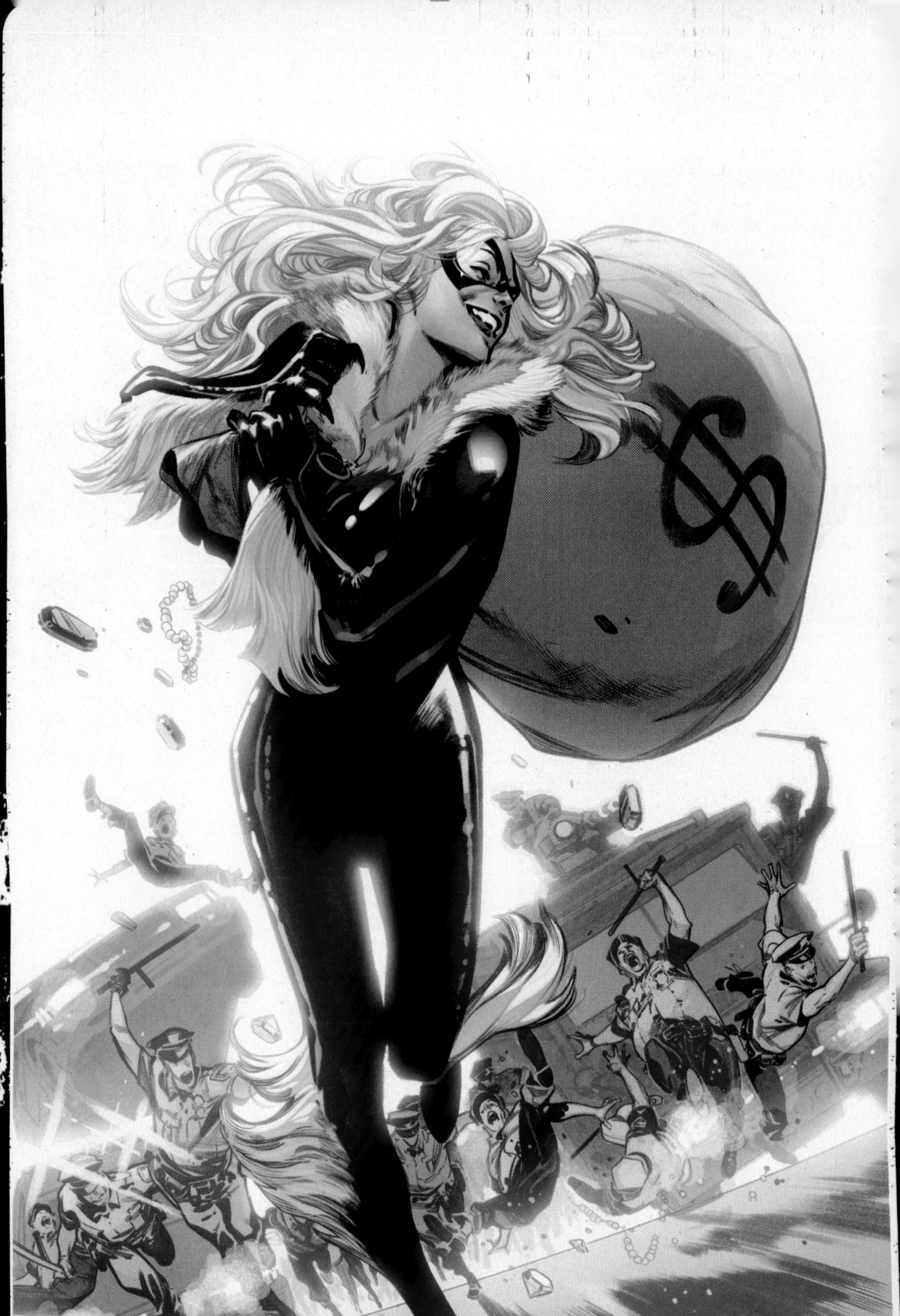

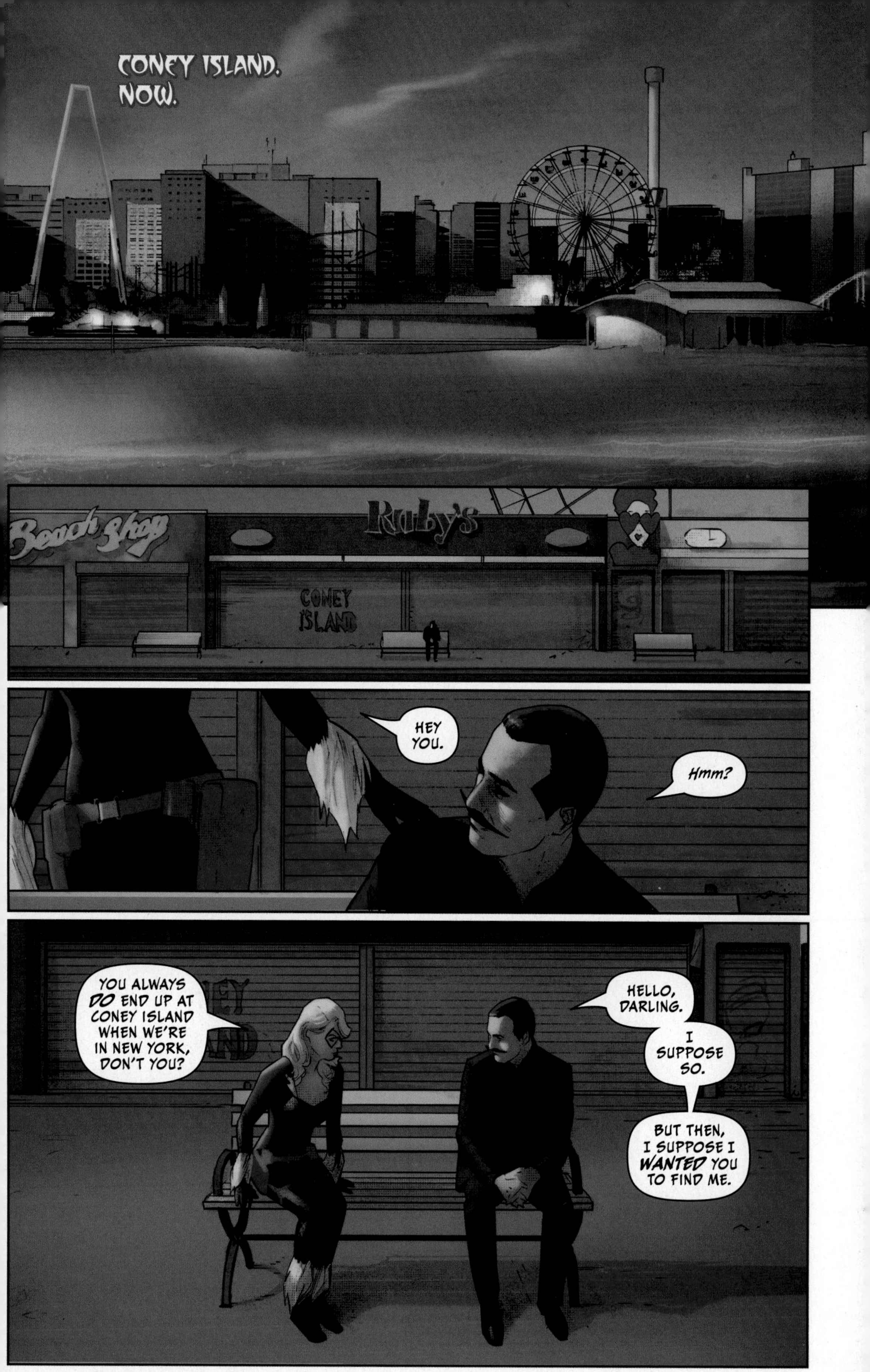
CONEY ISLAND. NOW.
Beach Shop
Ruby's
CONEY ISLAND
HEY YOU.
Hmm?
YOU ALWAYS DO END UP AT CONEY ISLAND WHEN WE'RE IN NEW YORK, DON'T YOU?
HELLO, DARLING.
I SUPPOSE SO.
BUT THEN, I SUPPOSE I WANTED YOU TO FIND ME.

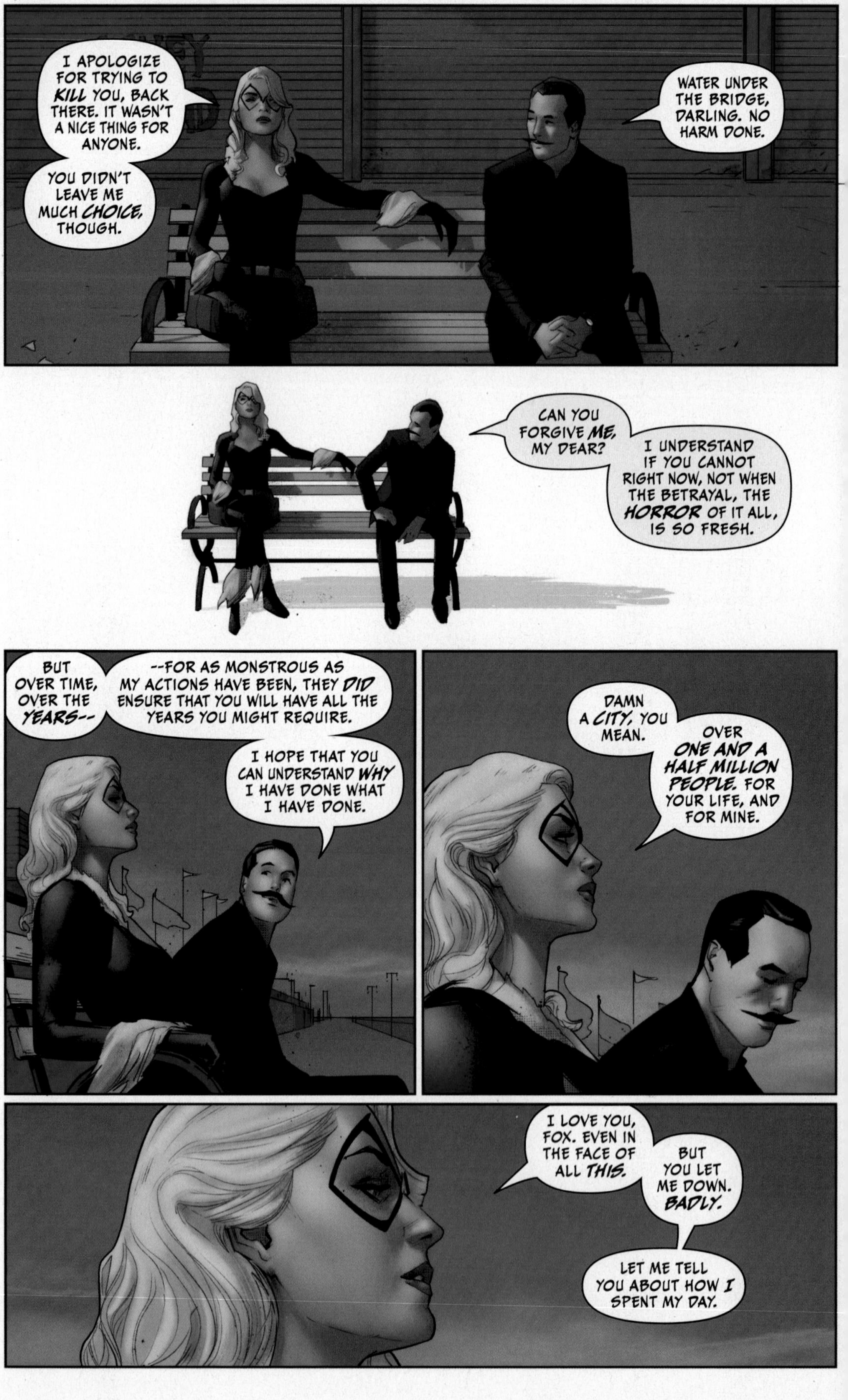

I APOLOGIZE FOR TRYING TO KILL YOU, BACK THERE. IT WASN'T A NICE THING FOR ANYONE.
YOU DIDN'T LEAVE ME MUCH CHOICE, THOUGH.
WATER UNDER THE BRIDGE, DARLING. NO HARM DONE.
CAN YOU FORGIVE ME, MY DEAR?
I UNDERSTAND IF YOU CANNOT RIGHT NOW, NOT WHEN THE BETRAYAL, THE HORROR OF IT ALL, IS SO FRESH.
BUT OVER TIME, OVER THE YEARS--
--FOR AS MONSTROUS AS MY ACTIONS HAVE BEEN, THEY DID ENSURE THAT YOU WILL HAVE ALL THE YEARS YOU MIGHT REQUIRE.
I HOPE THAT YOU CAN UNDERSTAND WHY I HAVE DONE WHAT I HAVE DONE.
DAMN A CITY, YOU MEAN.
OVER ONE AND A HALF MILLION PEOPLE. FOR YOUR LIFE, AND FOR MINE.
I LOVE YOU, FOX. EVEN IN THE FACE OF ALL THIS.
BUT YOU LET ME DOWN. BADLY.
LET ME TELL YOU ABOUT HOW I SPENT MY DAY.

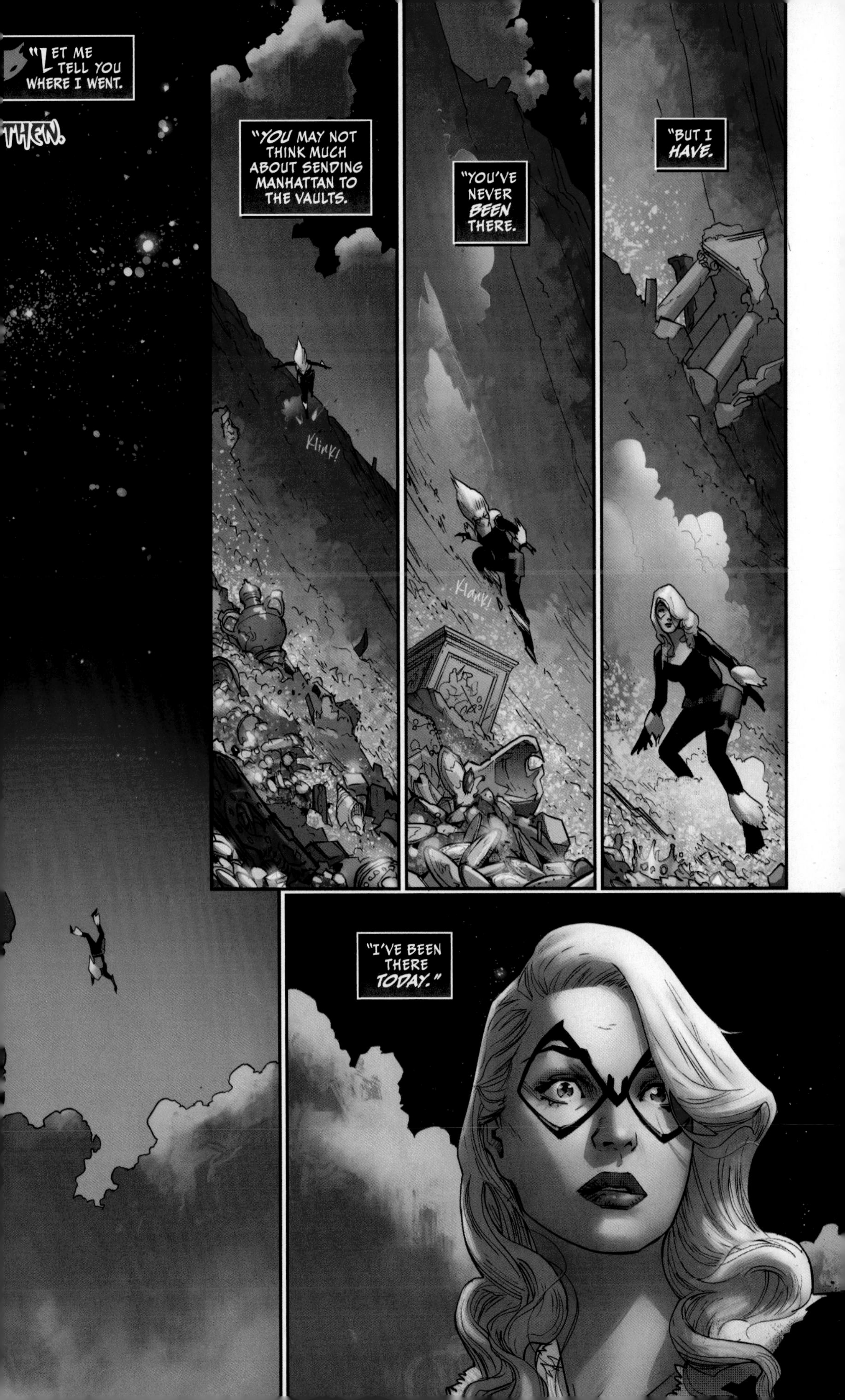

"LET ME TELL YOU WHERE I WENT.
THEN.
"YOU MAY NOT THINK MUCH ABOUT SENDING MANHATTAN TO THE VAULTS.
Klink!
"YOU'VE NEVER BEEN THERE.
Klank!
"BUT I HAVE.
"I'VE BEEN THERE TODAY."

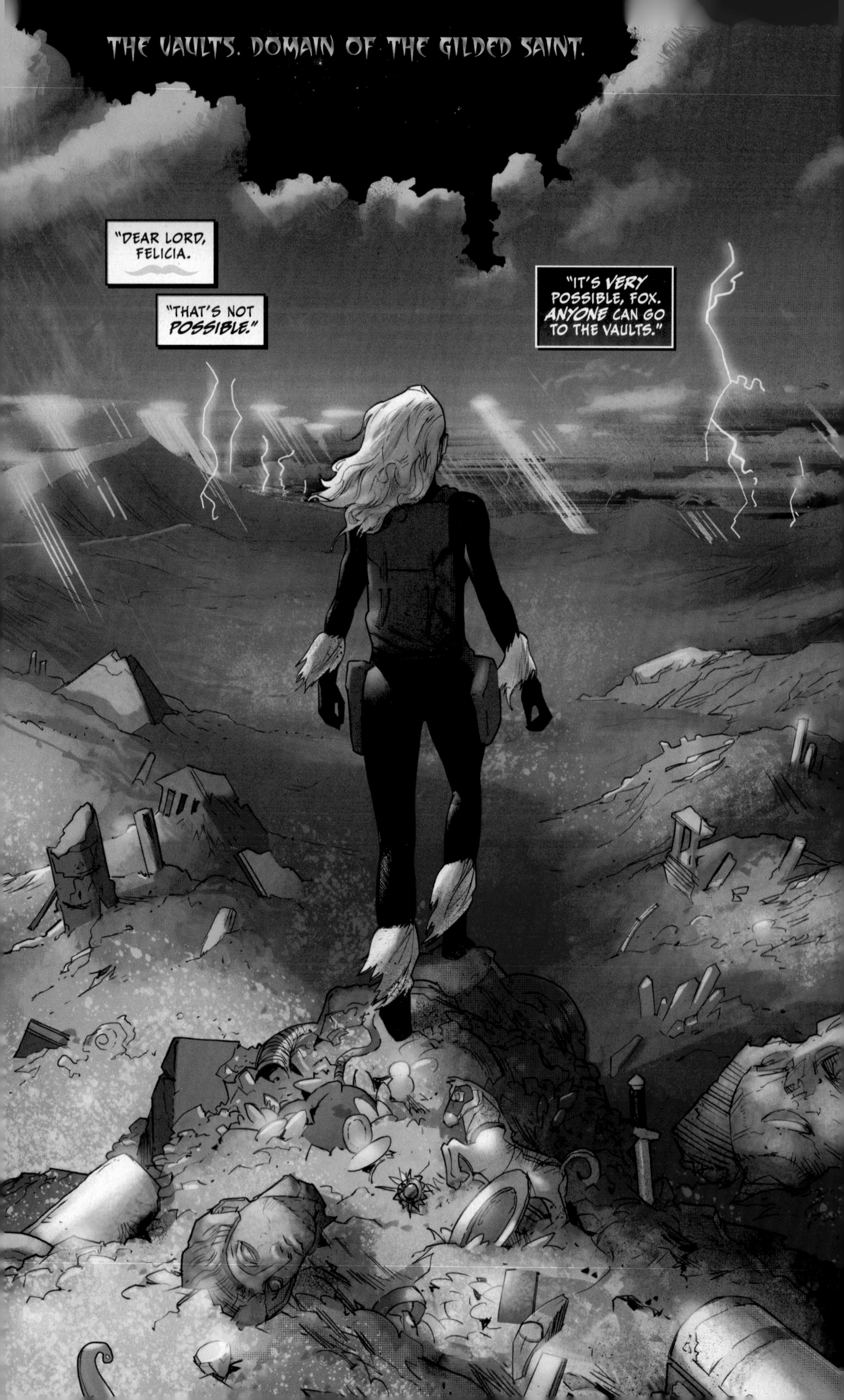
THE VAULTS. DOMAIN OF THE GILDED SAINT.
"DEAR LORD, FELICIA.
"THAT'S NOT POSSIBLE."
"IT'S VERY POSSIBLE, FOX. ANYONE CAN GO TO THE VAULTS."

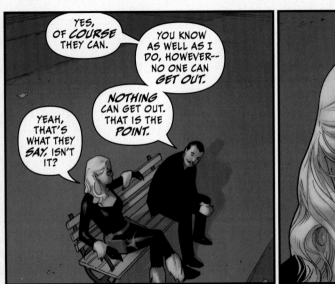

YES, OF *COURSE* THEY CAN.

YOU KNOW AS WELL AS I DO, HOWEVER-- NO ONE CAN *GET OUT.*

NOTHING CAN GET OUT. THAT IS THE *POINT.*

YEAH, THAT'S WHAT THEY *SAY,* ISN'T IT?

YOU SHOULD *SEE* IT, FOX.

WEALTH, AS FAR AS THE EYE CAN *SEE.*

"PEOPLE HAVE BEEN SACRIFICING TREASURE TO THE GILDED SAINT FOR A *LOT LONGER* THAN YOU'D THINK.

"I FOUND COINS THERE FROM ANCIENT CHINA. GREECE. MESOPOTAMIA.

"*SEASHELLS,* EVEN. FROM BEFORE PEOPLE EVEN *USED* COIN."

BUT IT'S NOT EXCITING, LIKE YOU'D *THINK.*

THERE'S NO *THRILL* TO ALL THAT LOOT.

"THE VAULTS ARE A DESERT. *DEAD.*

"NOTHING LIVES THERE. NOTHING *CAN.*"

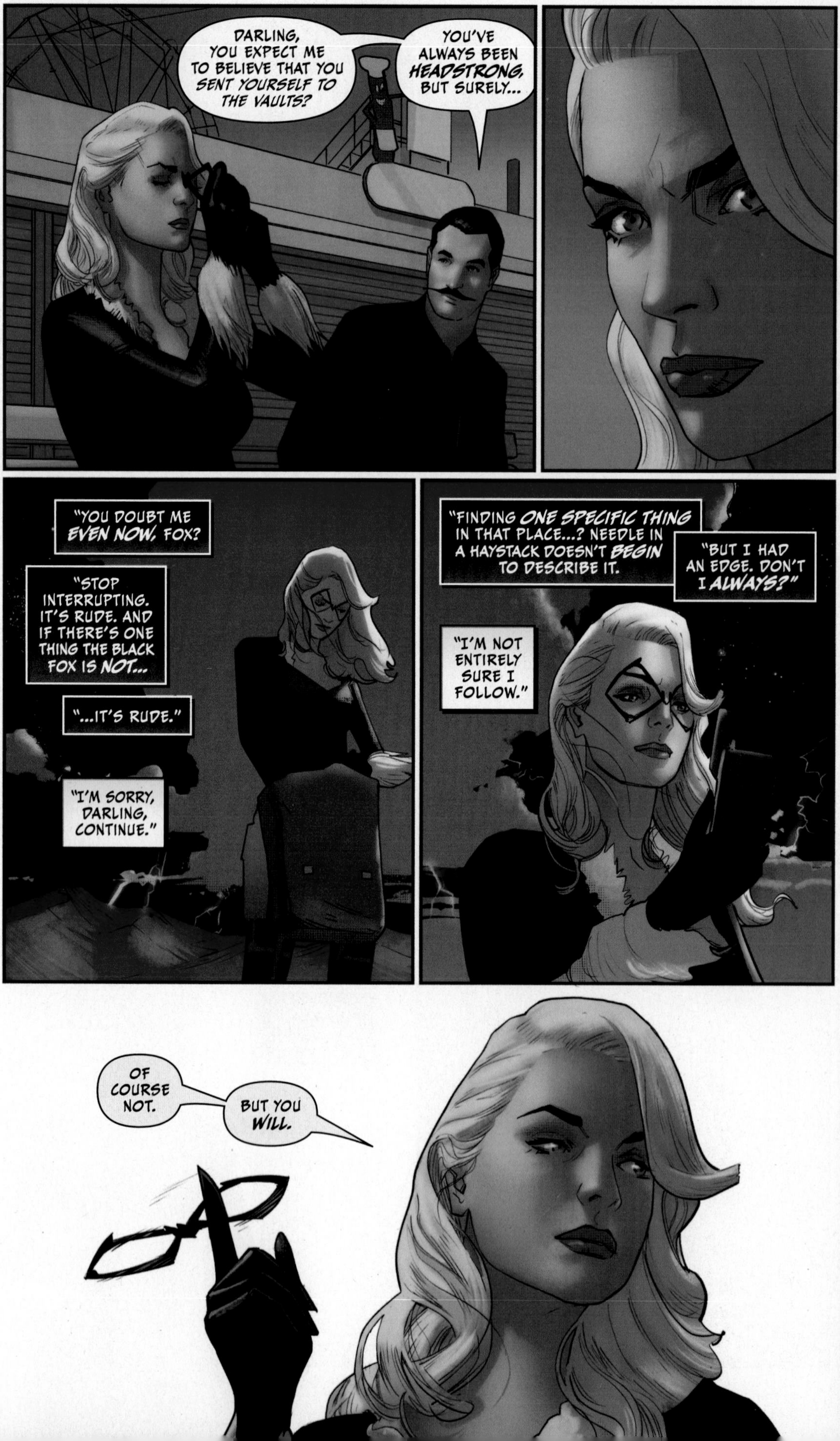
DARLING, YOU EXPECT ME TO BELIEVE THAT YOU SENT *YOURSELF* TO THE VAULTS?
YOU'VE ALWAYS BEEN *HEADSTRONG,* BUT SURELY...
"YOU DOUBT ME *EVEN NOW,* FOX?
"STOP INTERRUPTING. IT'S RUDE. AND IF THERE'S ONE THING THE BLACK FOX IS *NOT...*
"...IT'S RUDE."
"I'M SORRY, DARLING, CONTINUE."
"FINDING *ONE SPECIFIC THING* IN THAT PLACE...? NEEDLE IN A HAYSTACK DOESN'T *BEGIN* TO DESCRIBE IT.
"BUT I HAD AN EDGE. DON'T I *ALWAYS?"*
"I'M NOT ENTIRELY SURE I FOLLOW."
OF COURSE NOT.
BUT YOU *WILL.*

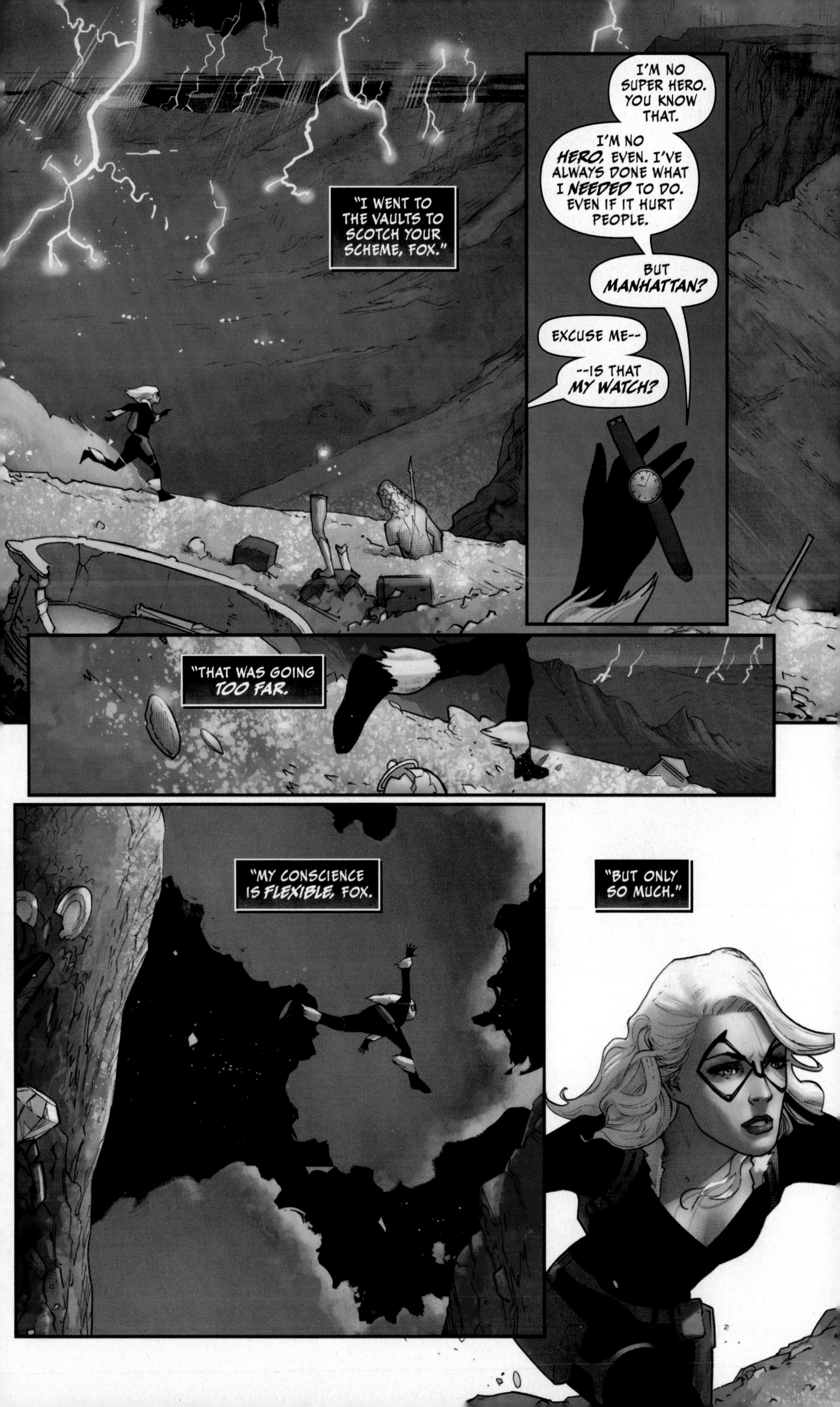
"I WENT TO THE VAULTS TO SCOTCH YOUR SCHEME, FOX."
I'M NO SUPER HERO. YOU KNOW THAT.
I'M NO HERO, EVEN. I'VE ALWAYS DONE WHAT I NEEDED TO DO. EVEN IF IT HURT PEOPLE.
BUT MANHATTAN?
EXCUSE ME--
--IS THAT MY WATCH?
"THAT WAS GOING TOO FAR.
"MY CONSCIENCE IS FLEXIBLE, FOX.
"BUT ONLY SO MUCH."

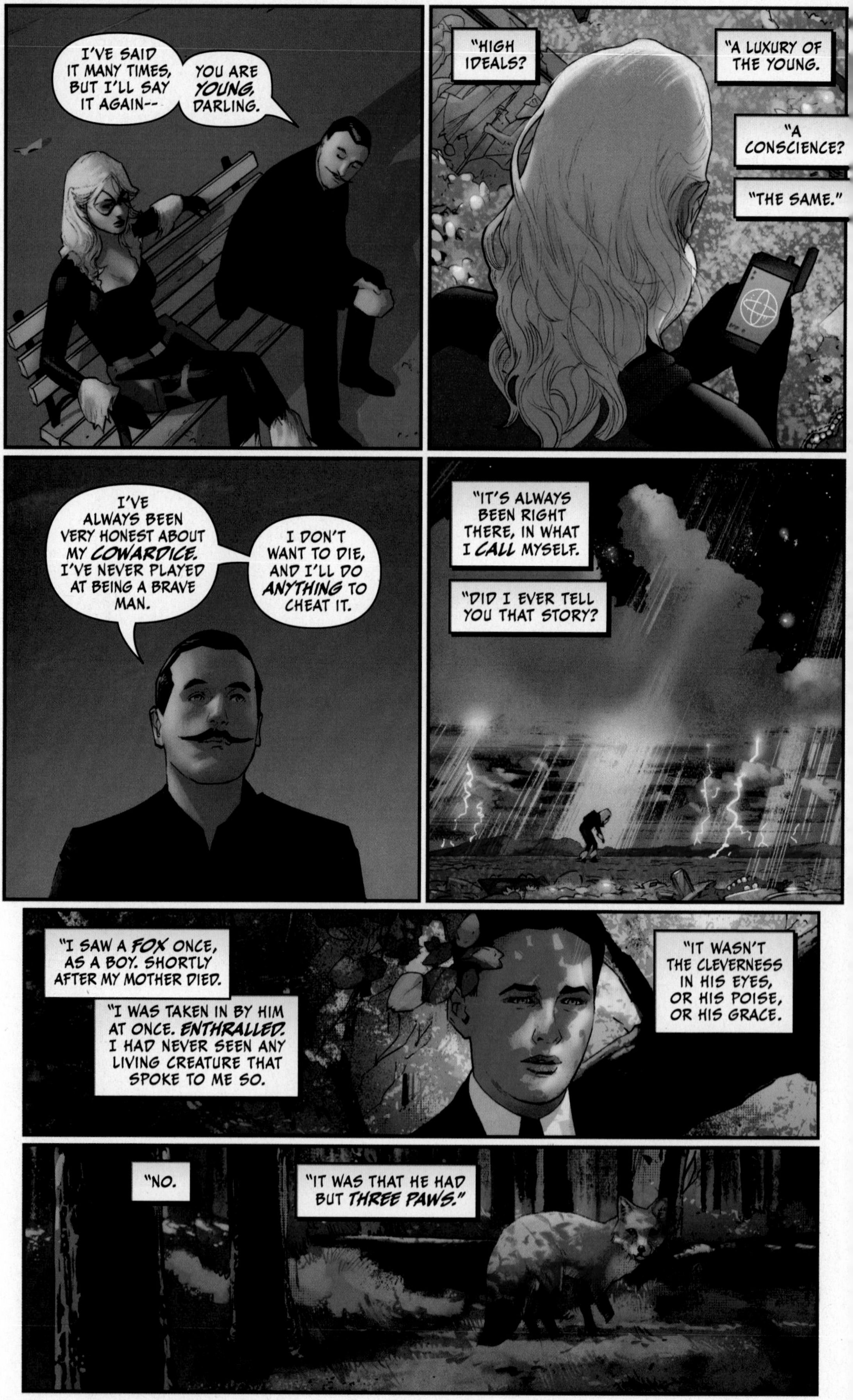

I'VE SAID IT MANY TIMES, BUT I'LL SAY IT AGAIN--
YOU ARE YOUNG, DARLING.
"HIGH IDEALS?
"A LUXURY OF THE YOUNG.
"A CONSCIENCE?
"THE SAME."
I'VE ALWAYS BEEN VERY HONEST ABOUT MY COWARDICE. I'VE NEVER PLAYED AT BEING A BRAVE MAN.
I DON'T WANT TO DIE, AND I'LL DO ANYTHING TO CHEAT IT.
"IT'S ALWAYS BEEN RIGHT THERE, IN WHAT I CALL MYSELF.
"DID I EVER TELL YOU THAT STORY?
"I SAW A FOX ONCE, AS A BOY. SHORTLY AFTER MY MOTHER DIED.
"I WAS TAKEN IN BY HIM AT ONCE. ENTHRALLED. I HAD NEVER SEEN ANY LIVING CREATURE THAT SPOKE TO ME SO.
"IT WASN'T THE CLEVERNESS IN HIS EYES, OR HIS POISE, OR HIS GRACE.
"NO.
"IT WAS THAT HE HAD BUT THREE PAWS."

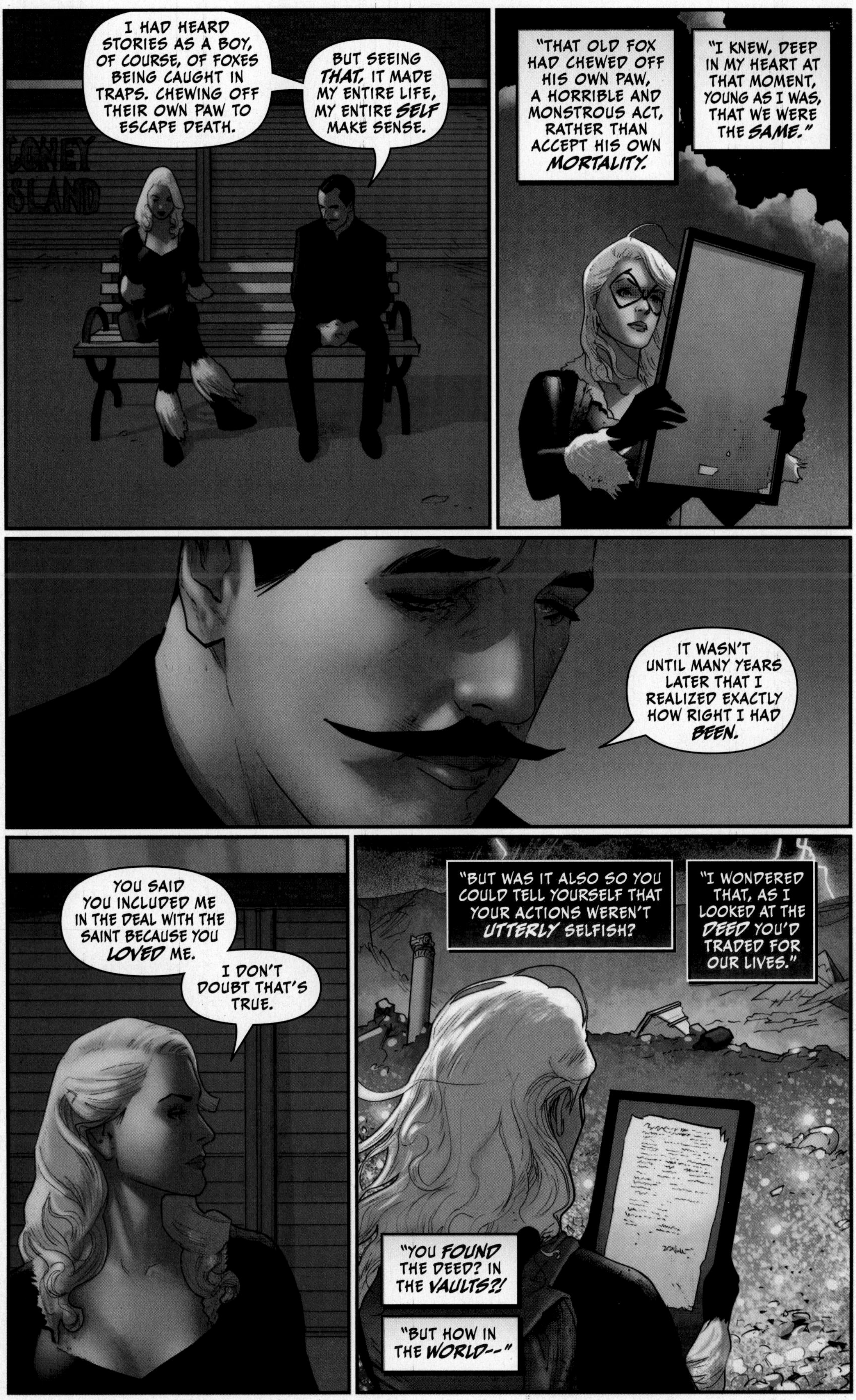
I HAD HEARD STORIES AS A BOY, OF COURSE, OF FOXES BEING CAUGHT IN TRAPS. CHEWING OFF THEIR OWN PAW TO ESCAPE DEATH.
BUT SEEING THAT, IT MADE MY ENTIRE LIFE, MY ENTIRE SELF MAKE SENSE.
CONEY ISLAND
"THAT OLD FOX HAD CHEWED OFF HIS OWN PAW, A HORRIBLE AND MONSTROUS ACT, RATHER THAN ACCEPT HIS OWN MORTALITY.
"I KNEW, DEEP IN MY HEART AT THAT MOMENT, YOUNG AS I WAS, THAT WE WERE THE SAME."
IT WASN'T UNTIL MANY YEARS LATER THAT I REALIZED EXACTLY HOW RIGHT I HAD BEEN.
YOU SAID YOU INCLUDED ME IN THE DEAL WITH THE SAINT BECAUSE YOU LOVED ME.
I DON'T DOUBT THAT'S TRUE.
"BUT WAS IT ALSO SO YOU COULD TELL YOURSELF THAT YOUR ACTIONS WEREN'T UTTERLY SELFISH?
"I WONDERED THAT, AS I LOOKED AT THE DEED YOU'D TRADED FOR OUR LIVES."
"YOU FOUND THE DEED? IN THE VAULTS?!
"BUT HOW IN THE WORLD--"

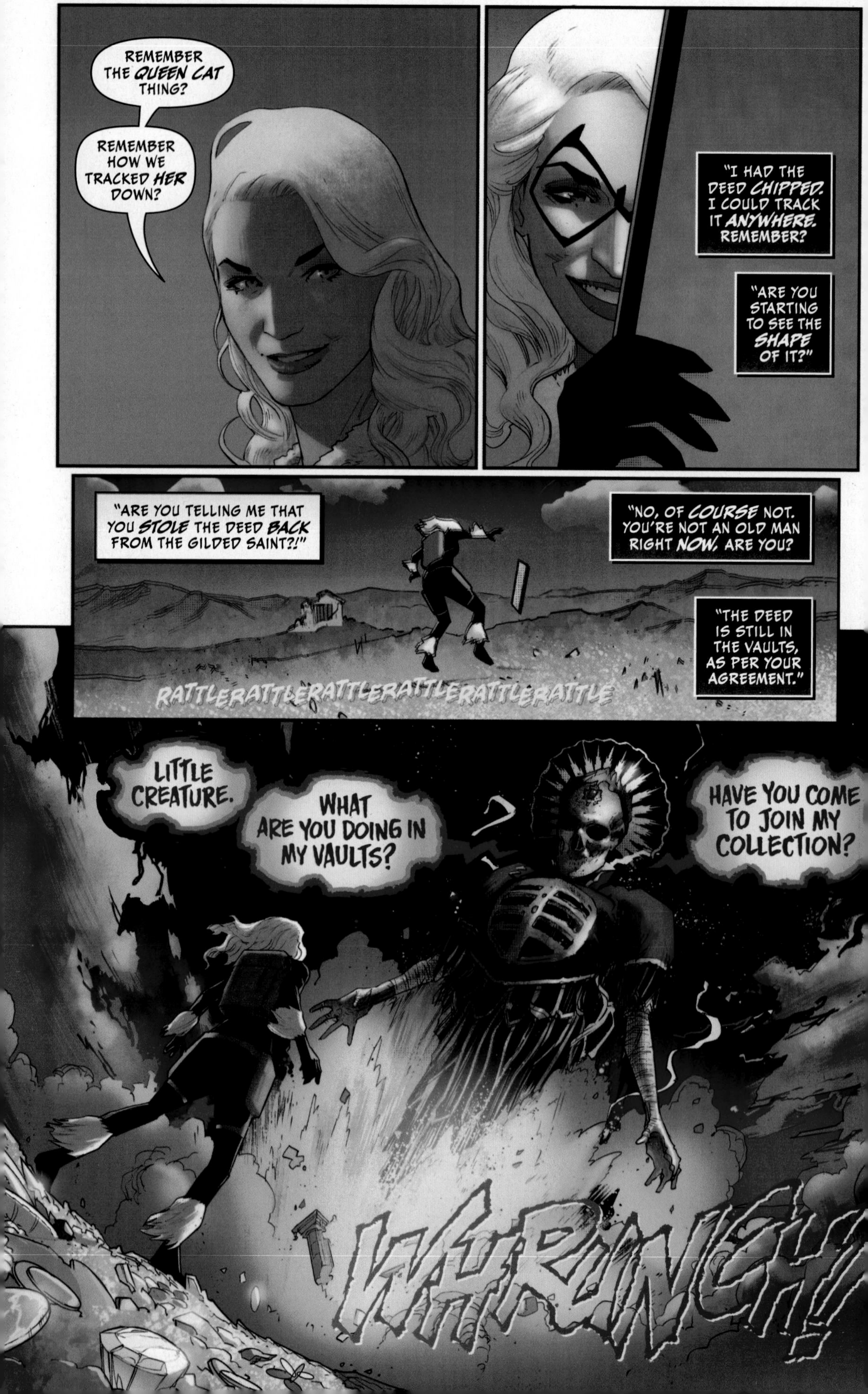

REMEMBER THE QUEEN CAT THING?
REMEMBER HOW WE TRACKED HER DOWN?
"I HAD THE DEED CHIPPED. I COULD TRACK IT ANYWHERE. REMEMBER?
"ARE YOU STARTING TO SEE THE SHAPE OF IT?"
"ARE YOU TELLING ME THAT YOU STOLE THE DEED BACK FROM THE GILDED SAINT?!"
"NO, OF COURSE NOT. YOU'RE NOT AN OLD MAN RIGHT NOW, ARE YOU?
"THE DEED IS STILL IN THE VAULTS, AS PER YOUR AGREEMENT."
RATTLERATTLERATTLERATTLERATTLERATTLE
LITTLE CREATURE.
WHAT ARE YOU DOING IN MY VAULTS?
HAVE YOU COME TO JOIN MY COLLECTION?
WHRUNCH!

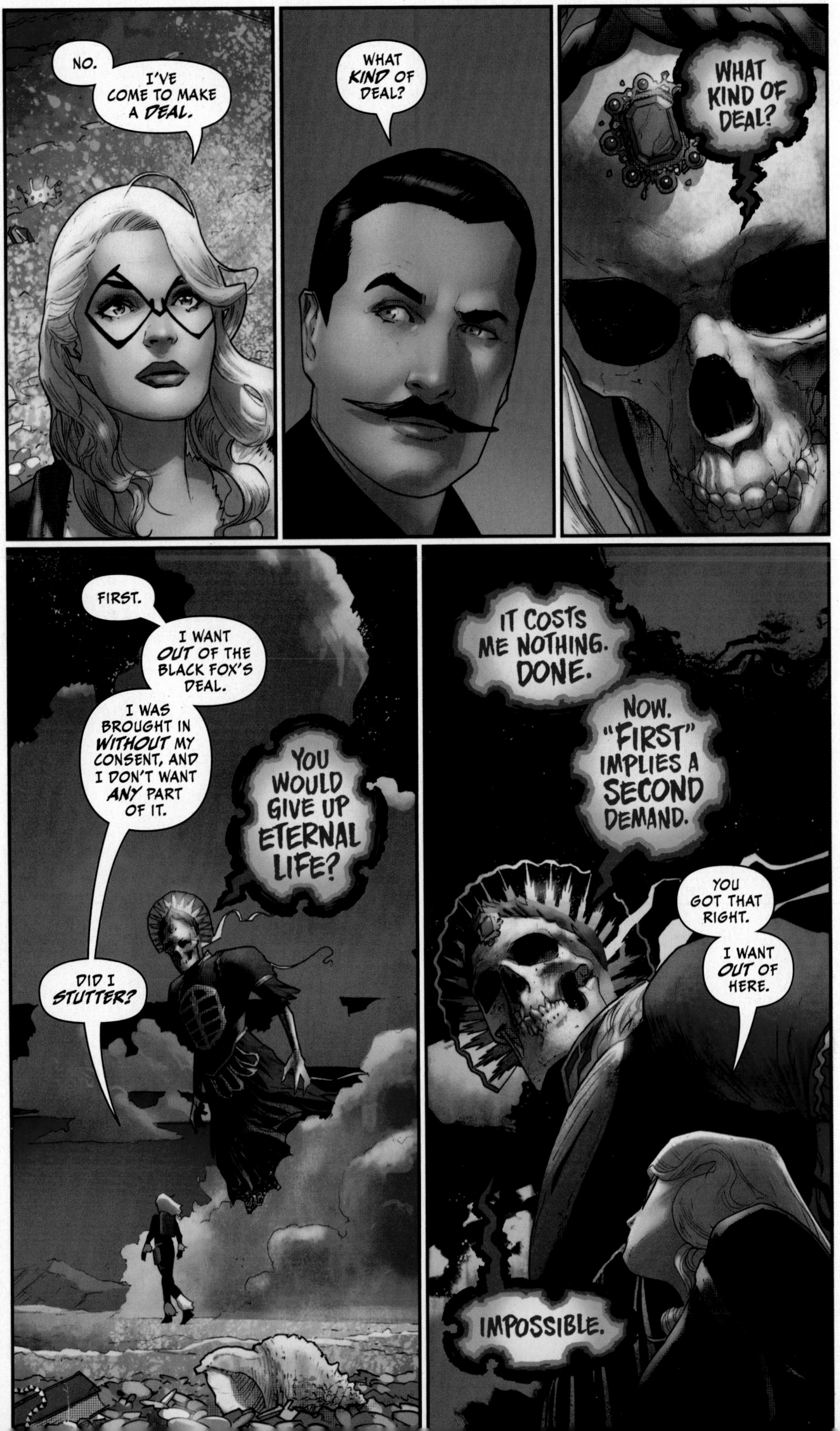
NO.
I'VE COME TO MAKE A DEAL.
WHAT KIND OF DEAL?
WHAT KIND OF DEAL?
FIRST.
I WANT OUT OF THE BLACK FOX'S DEAL.
I WAS BROUGHT IN WITHOUT MY CONSENT, AND I DON'T WANT ANY PART OF IT.
YOU WOULD GIVE UP ETERNAL LIFE?
DID I STUTTER?
IT COSTS ME NOTHING. DONE.
NOW. "FIRST" IMPLIES A SECOND DEMAND.
YOU GOT THAT RIGHT.
I WANT OUT OF HERE.
IMPOSSIBLE.

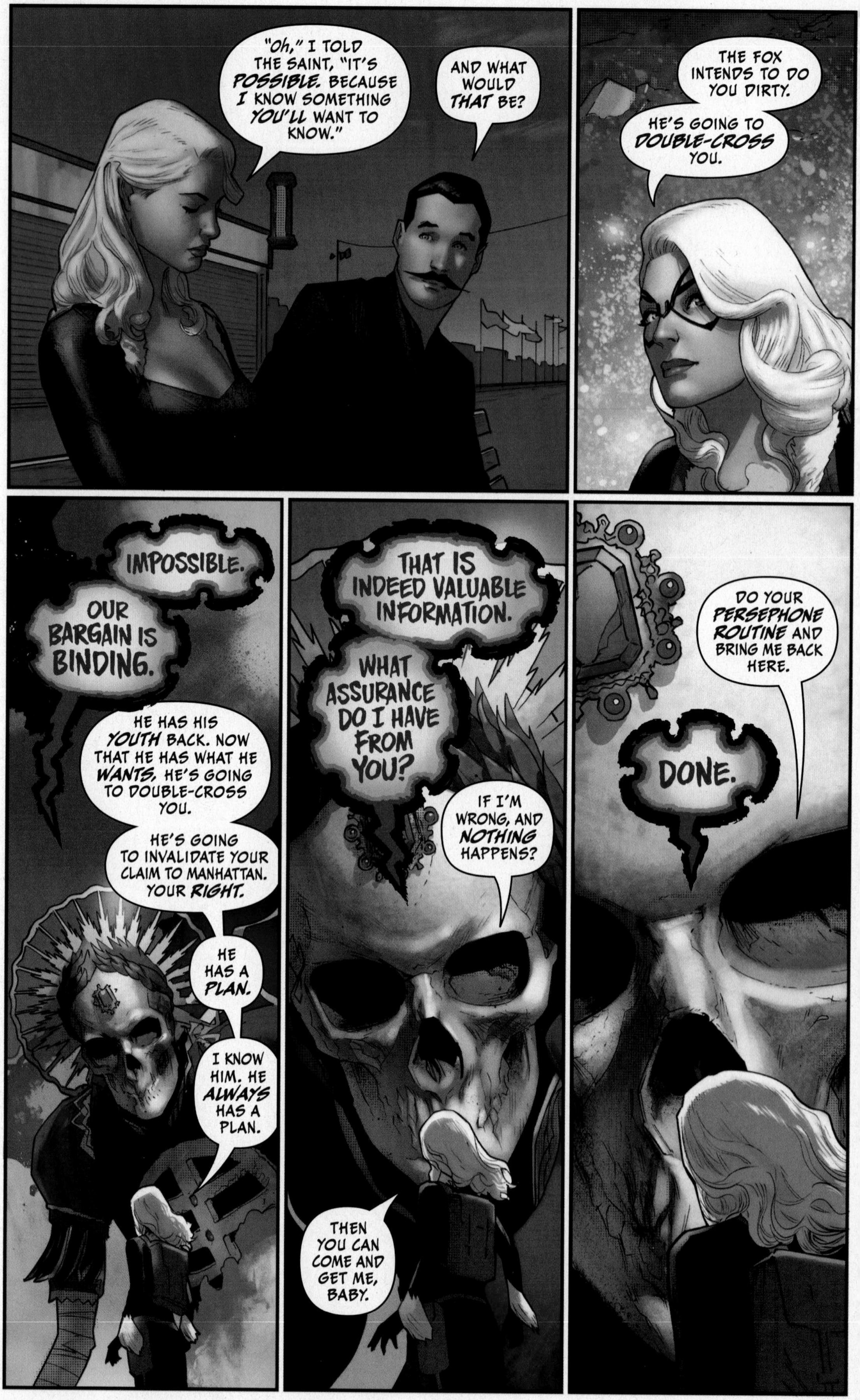
"Oh," I TOLD THE SAINT, "IT'S POSSIBLE. BECAUSE I KNOW SOMETHING YOU'LL WANT TO KNOW."
AND WHAT WOULD THAT BE?
THE FOX INTENDS TO DO YOU DIRTY.
HE'S GOING TO DOUBLE-CROSS YOU.
IMPOSSIBLE.
OUR BARGAIN IS BINDING.
HE HAS HIS YOUTH BACK. NOW THAT HE HAS WHAT HE WANTS, HE'S GOING TO DOUBLE-CROSS YOU.
HE'S GOING TO INVALIDATE YOUR CLAIM TO MANHATTAN. YOUR RIGHT.
HE HAS A PLAN.
I KNOW HIM. HE ALWAYS HAS A PLAN.
THAT IS INDEED VALUABLE INFORMATION.
WHAT ASSURANCE DO I HAVE FROM YOU?
IF I'M WRONG, AND NOTHING HAPPENS?
THEN YOU CAN COME AND GET ME, BABY.
DO YOUR PERSEPHONE ROUTINE AND BRING ME BACK HERE.
DONE.

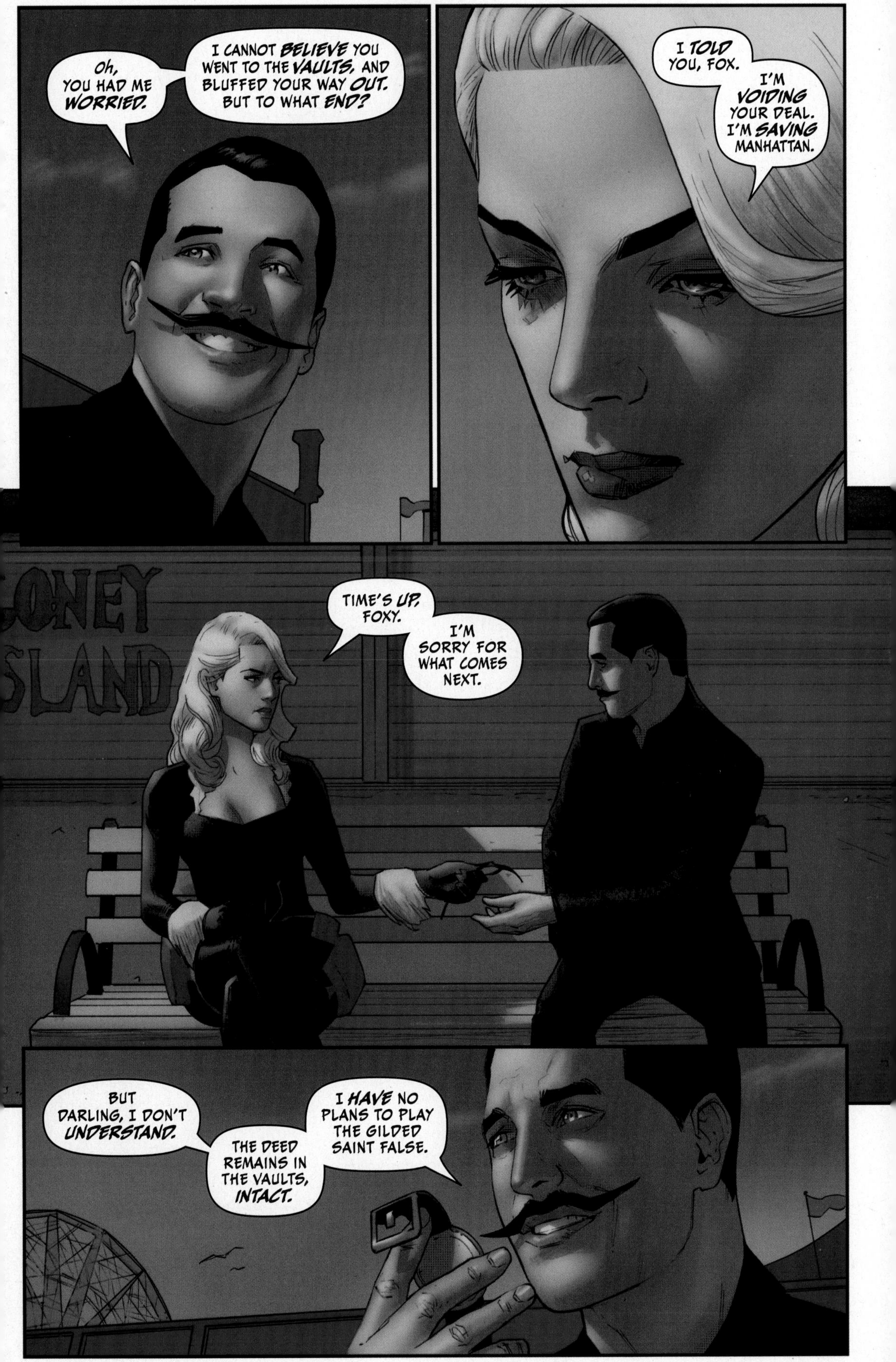

Oh, YOU HAD ME WORRIED.
I CANNOT BELIEVE YOU WENT TO THE VAULTS, AND BLUFFED YOUR WAY OUT. BUT TO WHAT END?
I TOLD YOU, FOX.
I'M VOIDING YOUR DEAL. I'M SAVING MANHATTAN.
CONEY ISLAND
TIME'S UP, FOXY.
I'M SORRY FOR WHAT COMES NEXT.
BUT DARLING, I DON'T UNDERSTAND.
THE DEED REMAINS IN THE VAULTS, INTACT.
I HAVE NO PLANS TO PLAY THE GILDED SAINT FALSE.

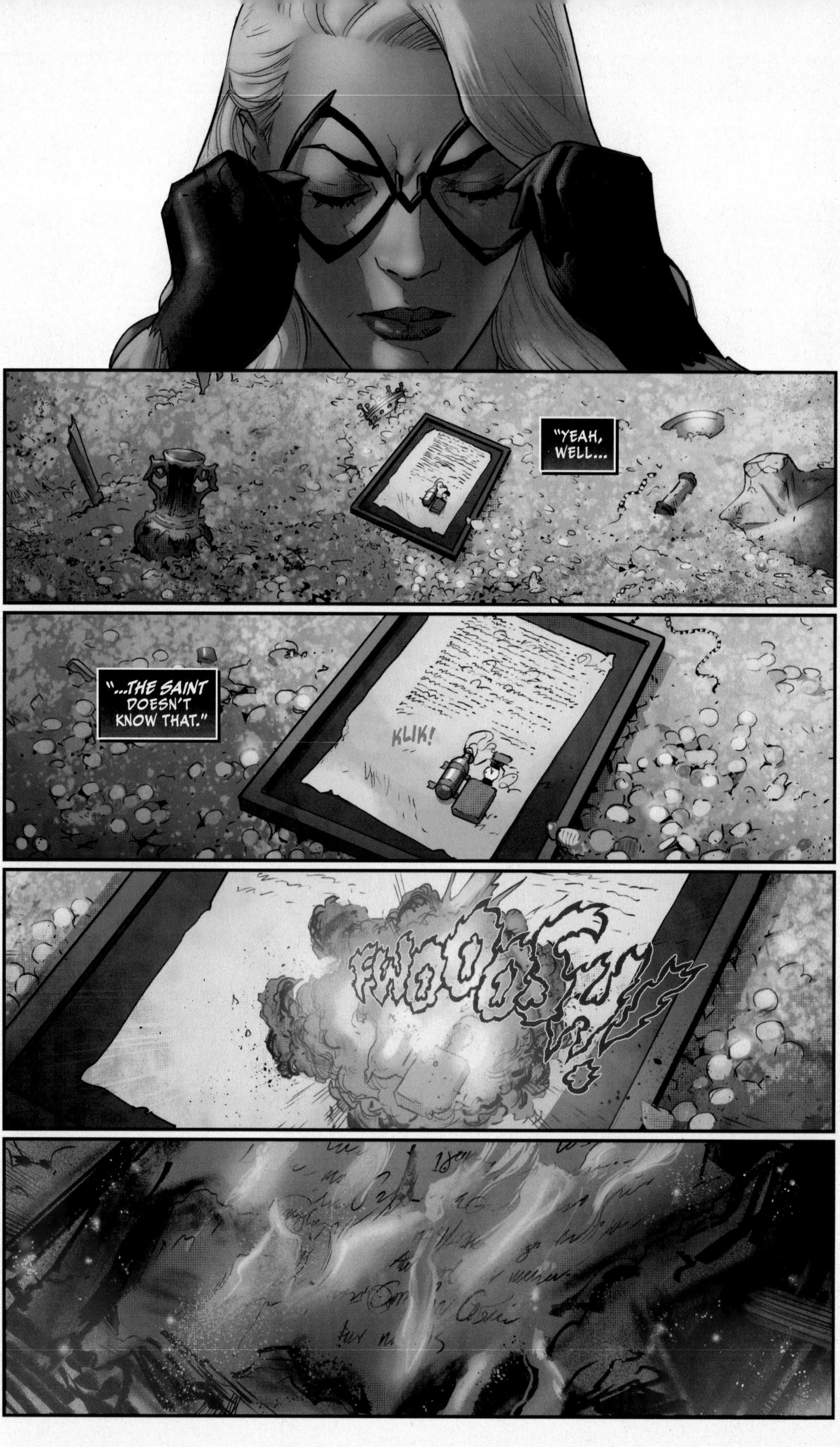
"YEAH, WELL...
"...THE SAINT DOESN'T KNOW THAT."
KLIK!
FWOOOSH!

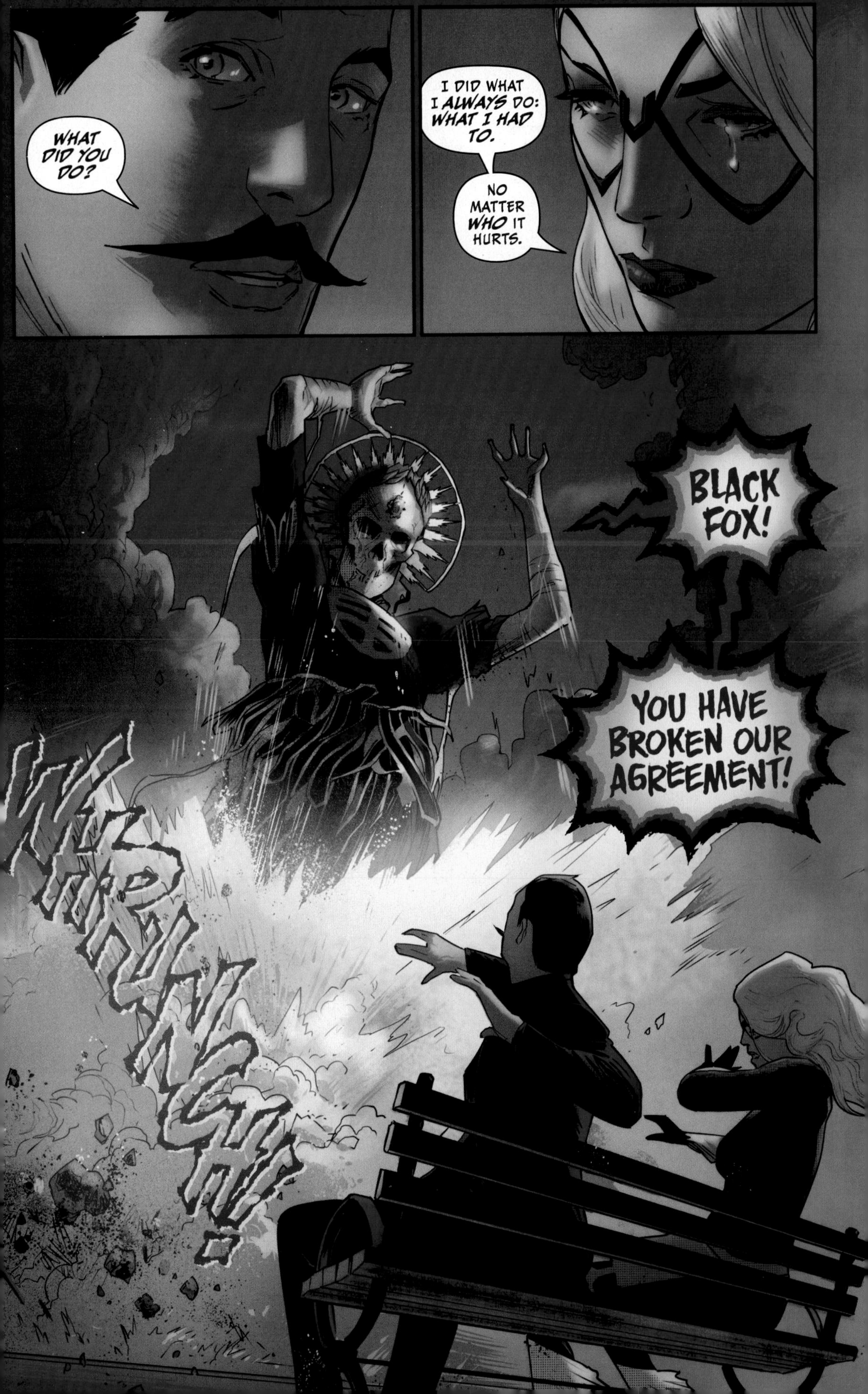
WHAT DID YOU DO?
I DID WHAT I ALWAYS DO: WHAT I HAD TO.
NO MATTER WHO IT HURTS.
BLACK FOX!
YOU HAVE BROKEN OUR AGREEMENT!

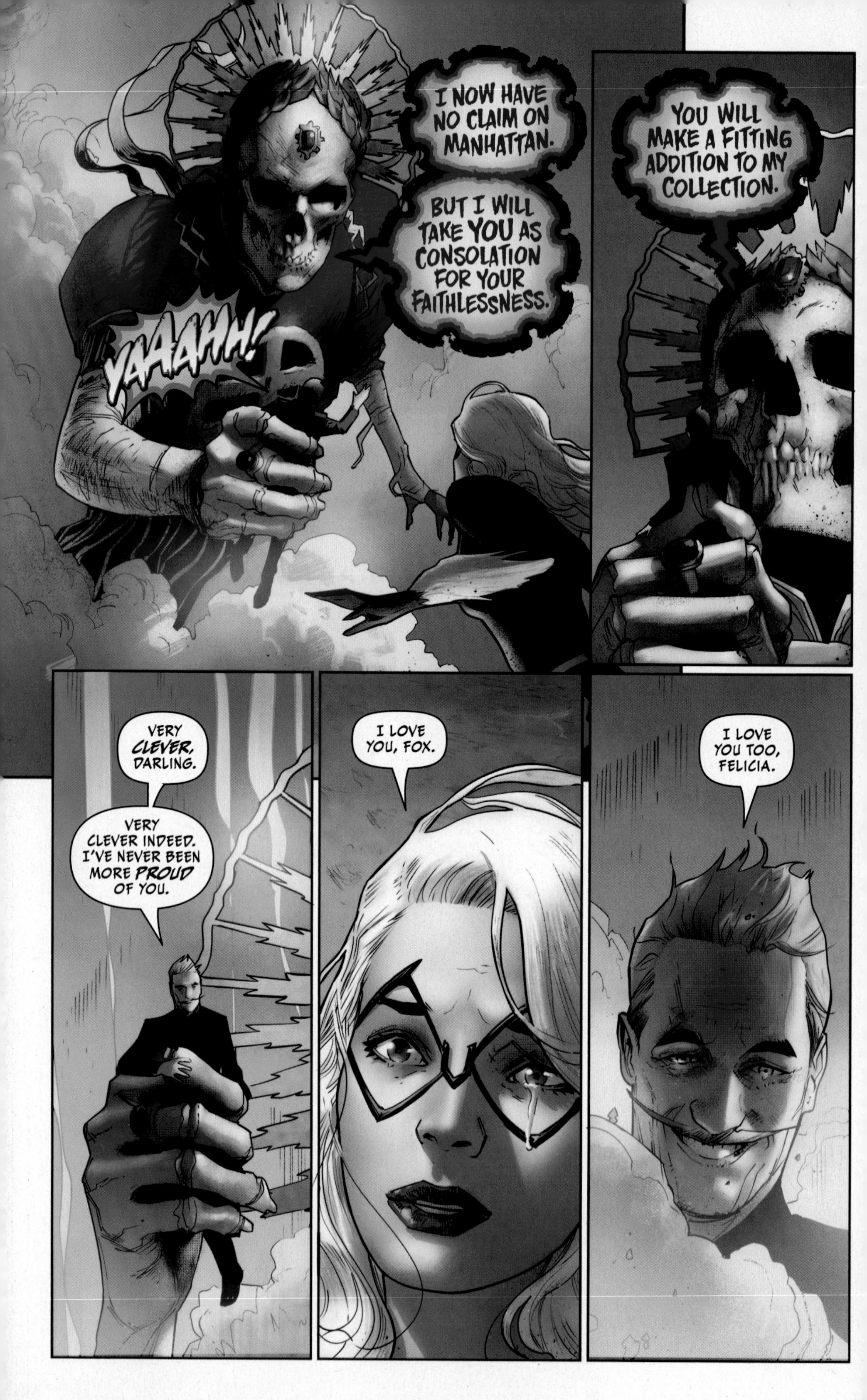
I NOW HAVE NO CLAIM ON MANHATTAN.
BUT I WILL TAKE YOU AS CONSOLATION FOR YOUR FAITHLESSNESS.
YAAAHH!
YOU WILL MAKE A FITTING ADDITION TO MY COLLECTION.
VERY CLEVER, DARLING.
VERY CLEVER INDEED. I'VE NEVER BEEN MORE PROUD OF YOU.
I LOVE YOU, FOX.
I LOVE YOU TOO, FELICIA.

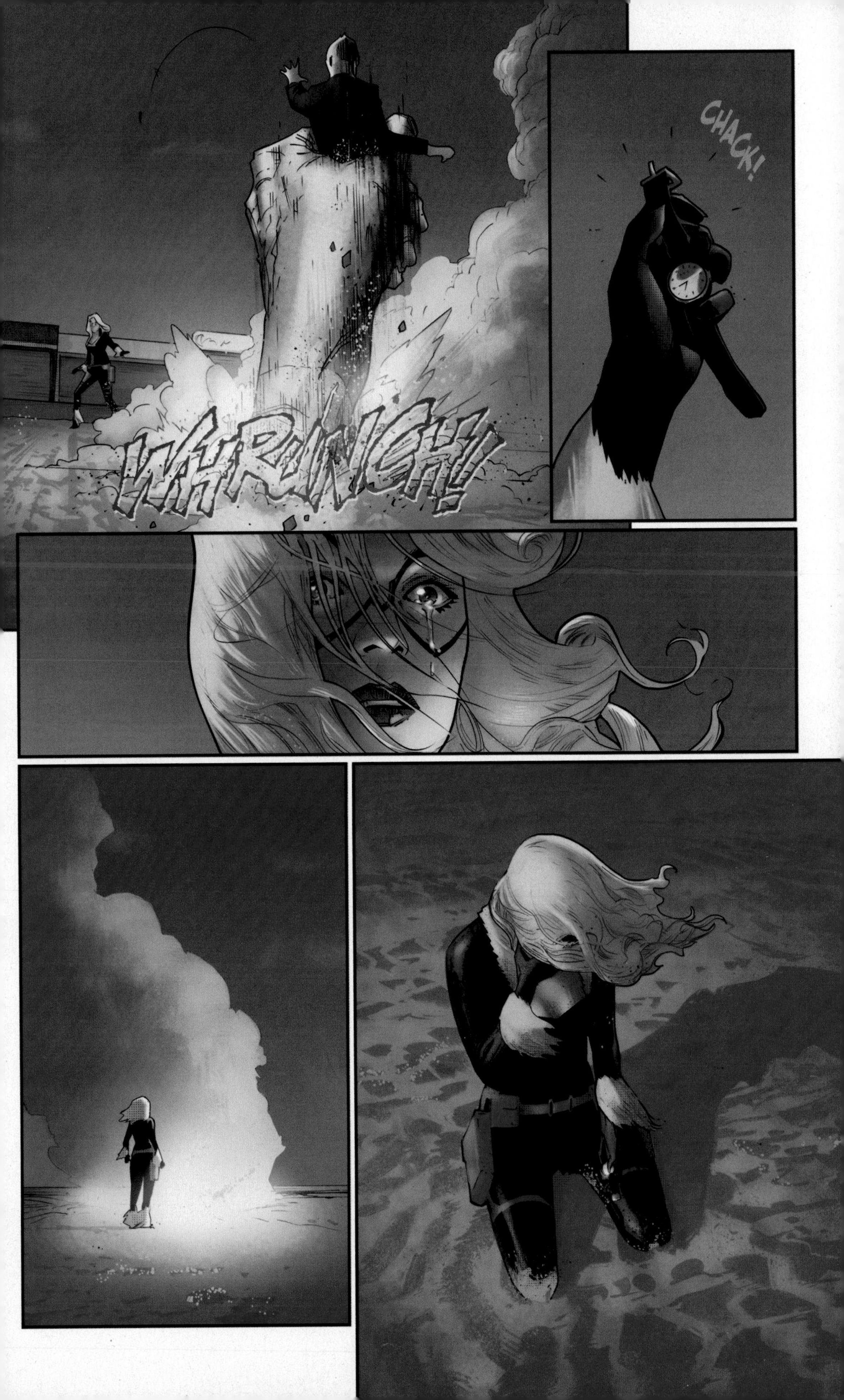
WHRINCH!
CHACK!

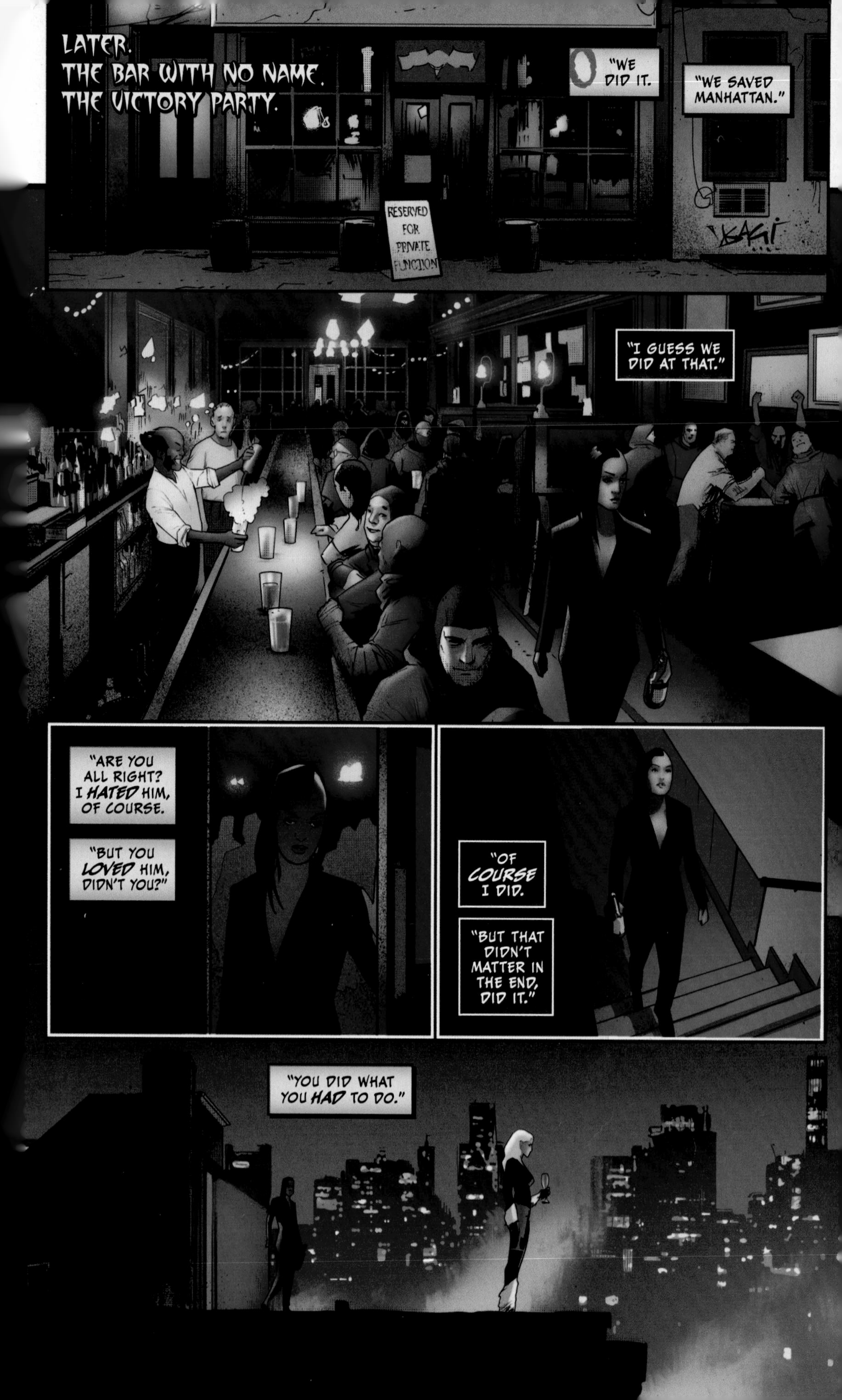
LATER.
THE BAR WITH NO NAME.
THE VICTORY PARTY.
"WE DID IT.
"WE SAVED MANHATTAN."
RESERVED FOR PRIVATE FUNCTION
"I GUESS WE DID AT THAT."
"ARE YOU ALL RIGHT? I HATED HIM, OF COURSE.
"BUT YOU LOVED HIM, DIDN'T YOU?"
"OF COURSE I DID.
"BUT THAT DIDN'T MATTER IN THE END, DID IT."
"YOU DID WHAT YOU HAD TO DO."

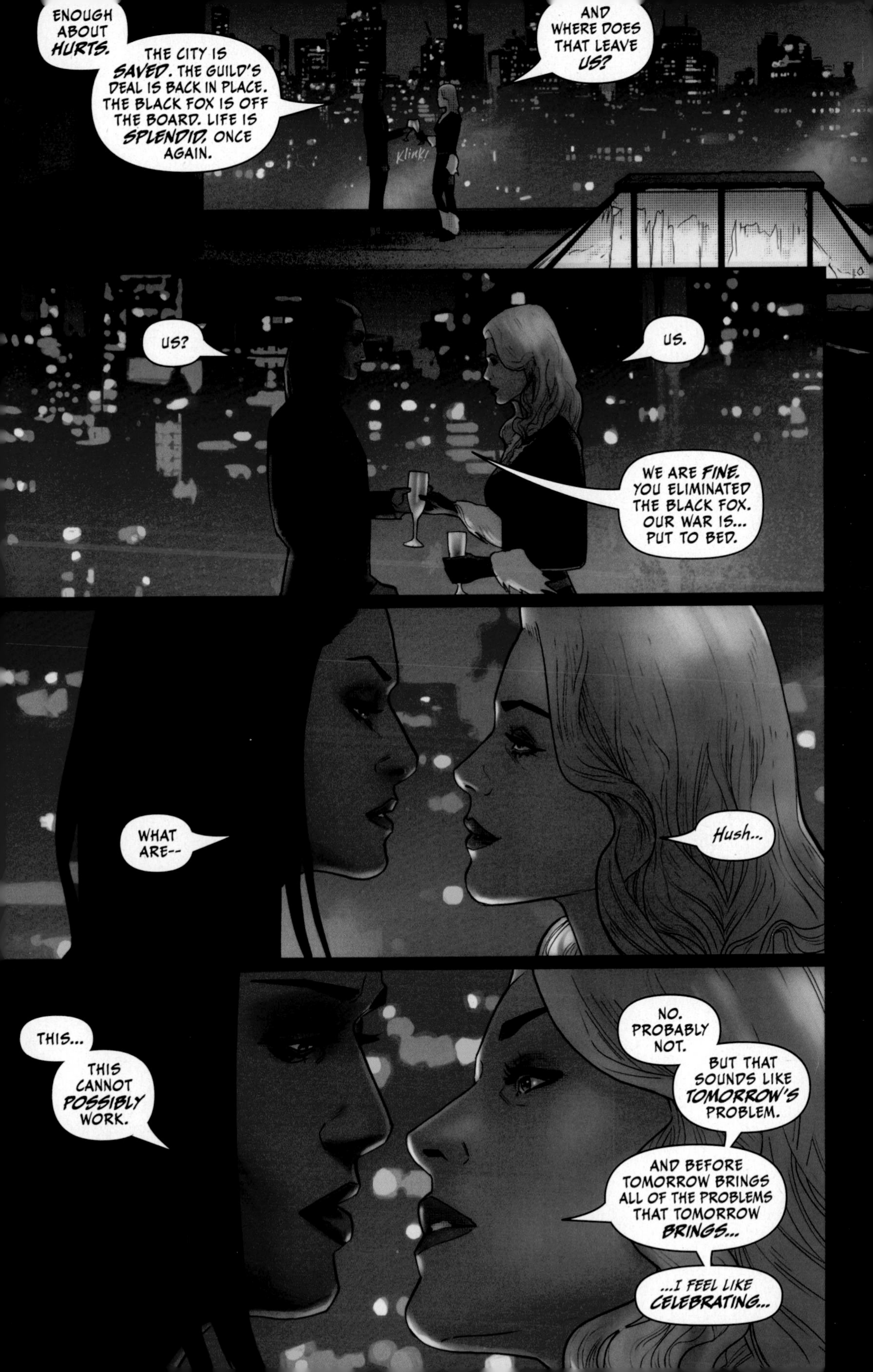
ENOUGH ABOUT HURTS.
THE CITY IS SAVED. THE GUILD'S DEAL IS BACK IN PLACE. THE BLACK FOX IS OFF THE BOARD. LIFE IS SPLENDID, ONCE AGAIN.
Klink!
AND WHERE DOES THAT LEAVE US?
US?
US.
WE ARE FINE. YOU ELIMINATED THE BLACK FOX. OUR WAR IS... PUT TO BED.
WHAT ARE--
Hush...
THIS...
THIS CANNOT POSSIBLY WORK.
NO. PROBABLY NOT.
BUT THAT SOUNDS LIKE TOMORROW'S PROBLEM.
AND BEFORE TOMORROW BRINGS ALL OF THE PROBLEMS THAT TOMORROW BRINGS...
...I FEEL LIKE CELEBRATING...

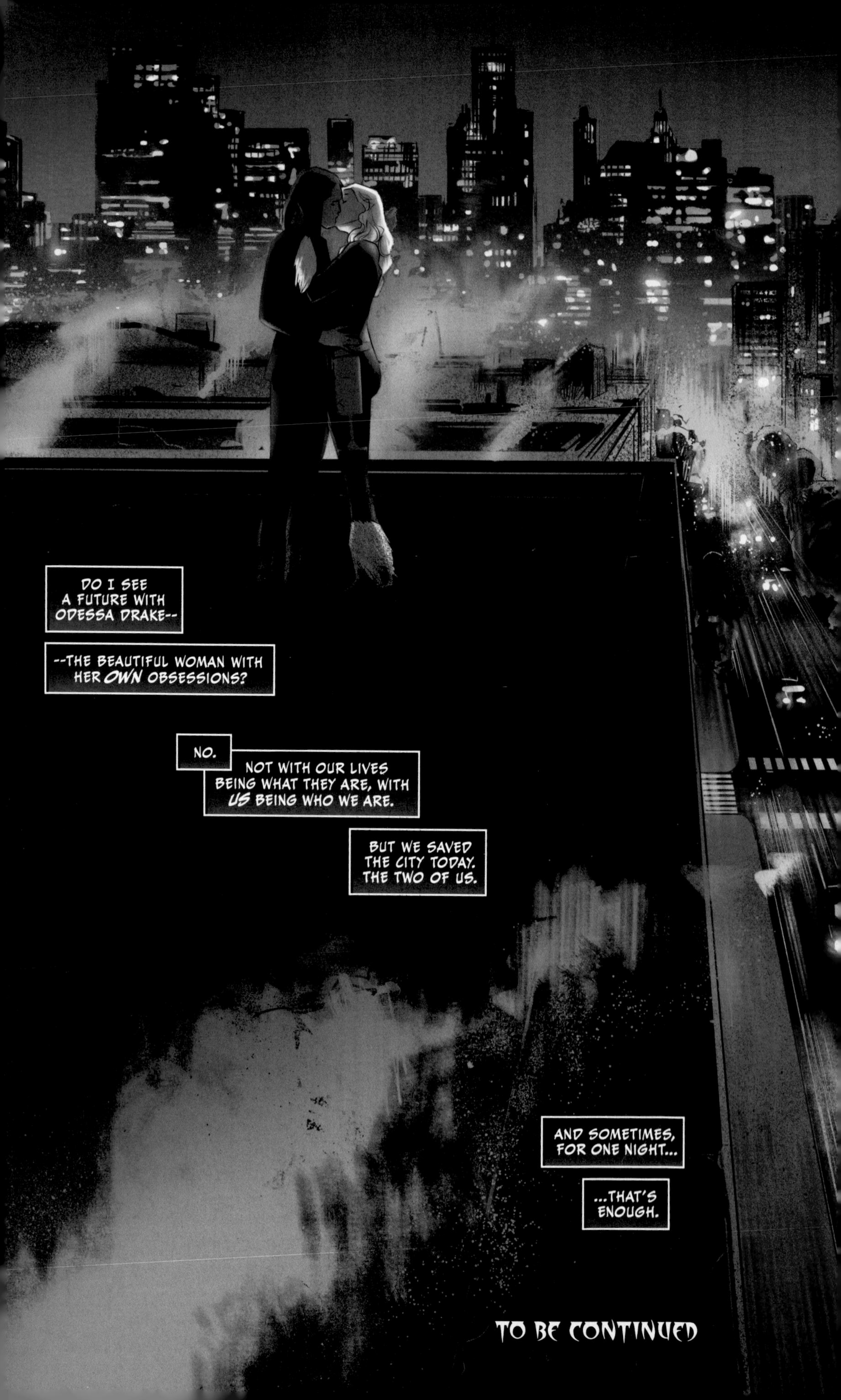
DO I SEE A FUTURE WITH ODESSA DRAKE--
--THE BEAUTIFUL WOMAN WITH HER OWN OBSESSIONS?
NO.
NOT WITH OUR LIVES BEING WHAT THEY ARE, WITH US BEING WHO WE ARE.
BUT WE SAVED THE CITY TODAY. THE TWO OF US.
AND SOMETIMES, FOR ONE NIGHT...
...THAT'S ENOUGH.
TO BE CONTINUED

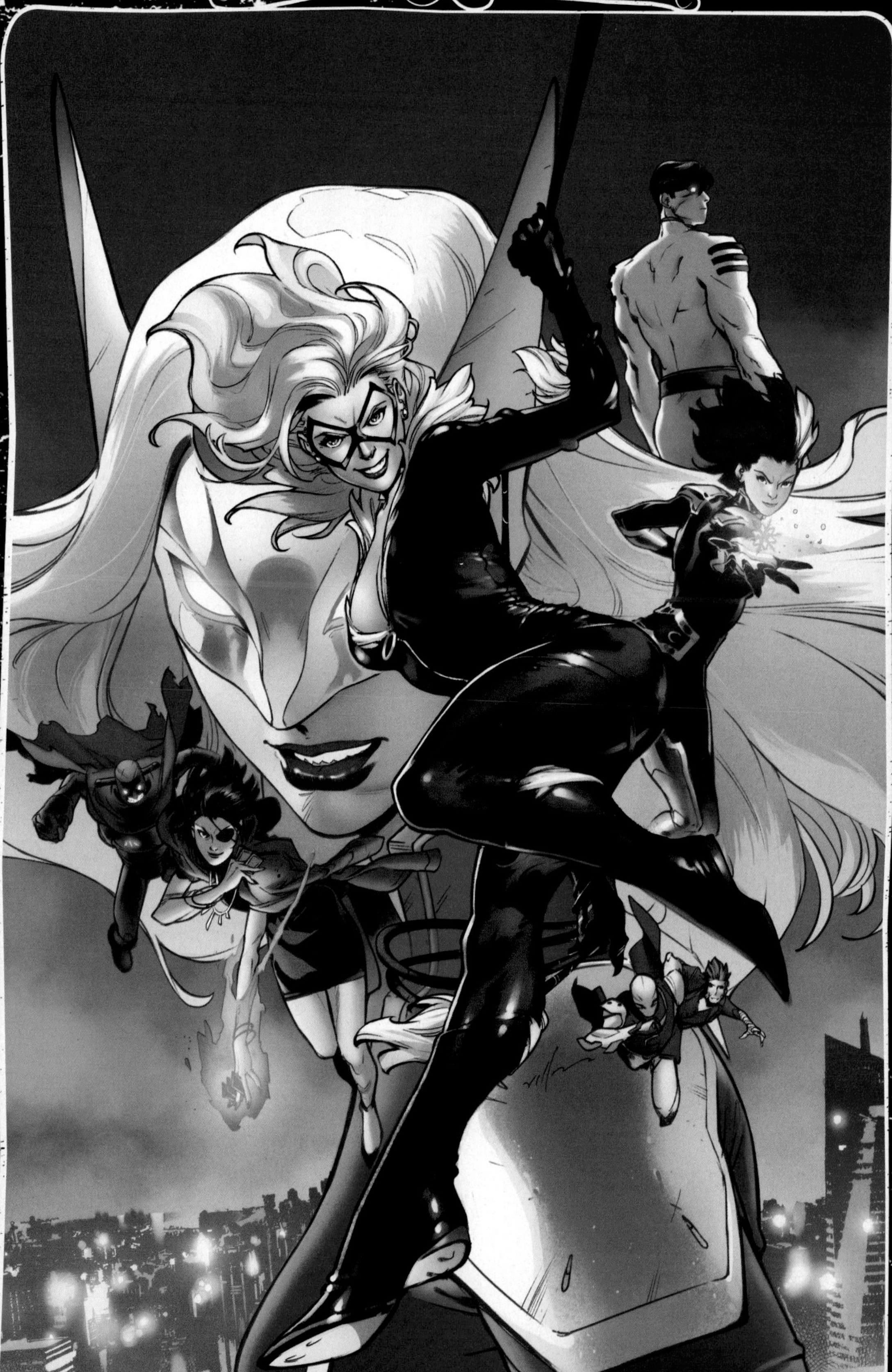

ANNUAL #1

FELICIA HARDY IS THE GREATEST CAT BURGLER IN THE WORLD. MEOW. WITH THE HELP OF HER CREW—BRUNO &
DOCTOR KORPSE—FELICIA SPENDS HER NINE LIVES FLEECING THE WORLD OVER AS THE ONE AND ONLY...

BLACK CAT

INFINITE DESTINIES

Born from the remains of an omnipotent being, the six Infinity Stones, when gathered, grant untold power. They have wiped out half the life in the universe and resurrected it, they have threatened and saved the Multiverse... and now they have been sent out to bond with individuals... No one knows why the Stones bond with each bearer... nor what will happen if they are gathered. Will the story you are about to read reveal another Stone-Bearer or give a clue to the cosmically mysterious intentions of the most powerful artifacts in the universe?

Read on, True Believer!

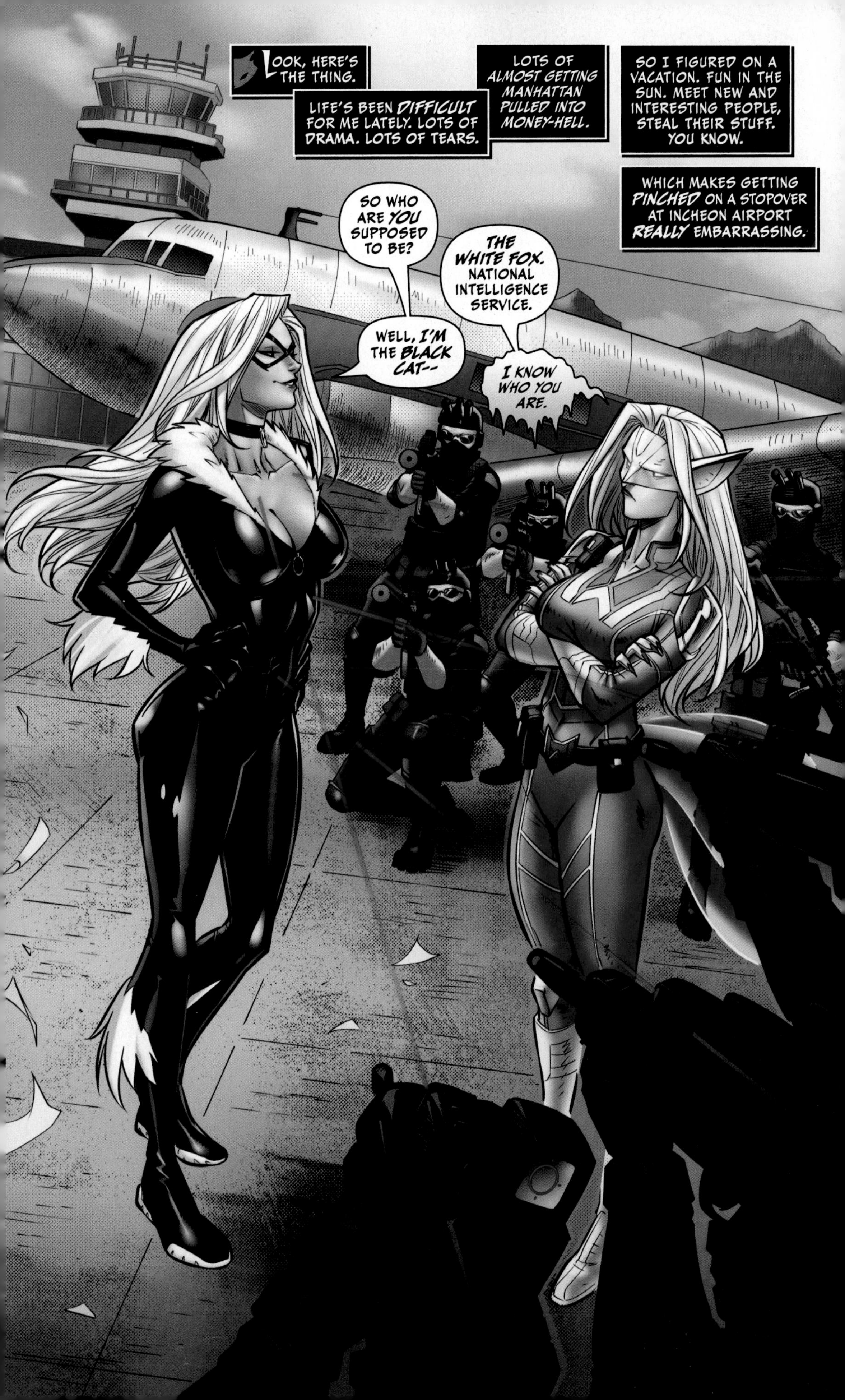
LOOK, HERE'S THE THING.
LIFE'S BEEN DIFFICULT FOR ME LATELY. LOTS OF DRAMA. LOTS OF TEARS.
LOTS OF ALMOST GETTING MANHATTAN PULLED INTO MONEY-HELL.
SO I FIGURED ON A VACATION. FUN IN THE SUN. MEET NEW AND INTERESTING PEOPLE, STEAL THEIR STUFF. YOU KNOW.
WHICH MAKES GETTING PINCHED ON A STOPOVER AT INCHEON AIRPORT REALLY EMBARRASSING.
SO WHO ARE YOU SUPPOSED TO BE?
WELL, I'M THE BLACK CAT--
THE WHITE FOX. NATIONAL INTELLIGENCE SERVICE.
I KNOW WHO YOU ARE.

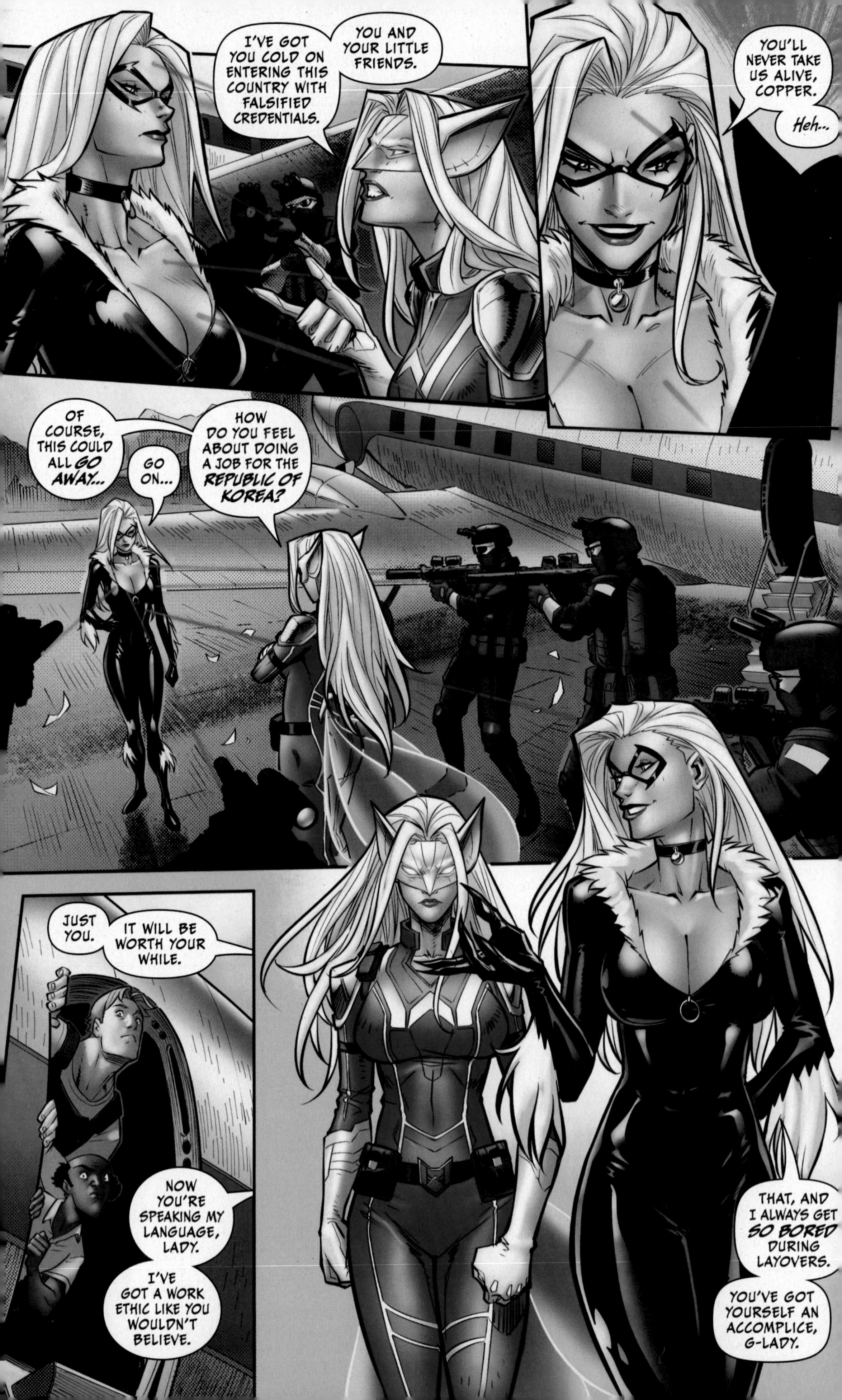
I'VE GOT YOU COLD ON ENTERING THIS COUNTRY WITH FALSIFIED CREDENTIALS.
YOU AND YOUR LITTLE FRIENDS.
YOU'LL NEVER TAKE US ALIVE, COPPER.
Heh...
OF COURSE, THIS COULD ALL GO AWAY...
GO ON...
HOW DO YOU FEEL ABOUT DOING A JOB FOR THE REPUBLIC OF KOREA?
JUST YOU.
IT WILL BE WORTH YOUR WHILE.
NOW YOU'RE SPEAKING MY LANGUAGE, LADY.
I'VE GOT A WORK ETHIC LIKE YOU WOULDN'T BELIEVE.
THAT, AND I ALWAYS GET SO BORED DURING LAYOVERS.
YOU'VE GOT YOURSELF AN ACCOMPLICE, G-LADY.

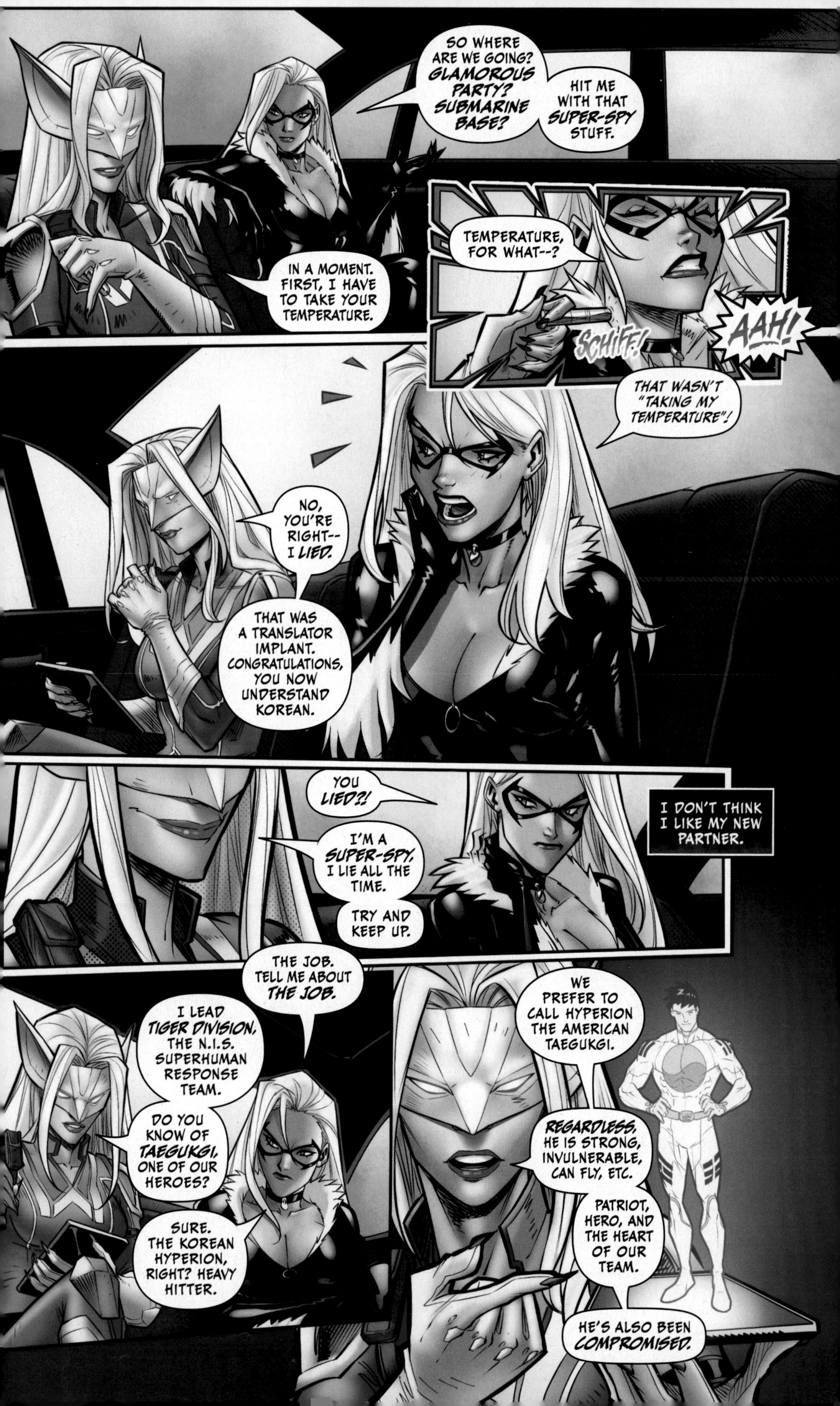
SO WHERE ARE WE GOING? GLAMOROUS PARTY? SUBMARINE BASE?
HIT ME WITH THAT SUPER-SPY STUFF.
IN A MOMENT. FIRST, I HAVE TO TAKE YOUR TEMPERATURE.
TEMPERATURE, FOR WHAT--?
SCHIFF!
AAH!
THAT WASN'T "TAKING MY TEMPERATURE"!
NO, YOU'RE RIGHT-- I LIED.
THAT WAS A TRANSLATOR IMPLANT. CONGRATULATIONS, YOU NOW UNDERSTAND KOREAN.
YOU LIED?!
I'M A SUPER-SPY, I LIE ALL THE TIME.
TRY AND KEEP UP.
I DON'T THINK I LIKE MY NEW PARTNER.
THE JOB. TELL ME ABOUT THE JOB.
I LEAD TIGER DIVISION, THE N.I.S. SUPERHUMAN RESPONSE TEAM.
DO YOU KNOW OF TAEGUKGI, ONE OF OUR HEROES?
SURE. THE KOREAN HYPERION, RIGHT? HEAVY HITTER.
WE PREFER TO CALL HYPERION THE AMERICAN TAEGUKGI.
REGARDLESS, HE IS STRONG, INVULNERABLE, CAN FLY, ETC.
PATRIOT, HERO, AND THE HEART OF OUR TEAM.
HE'S ALSO BEEN COMPROMISED.

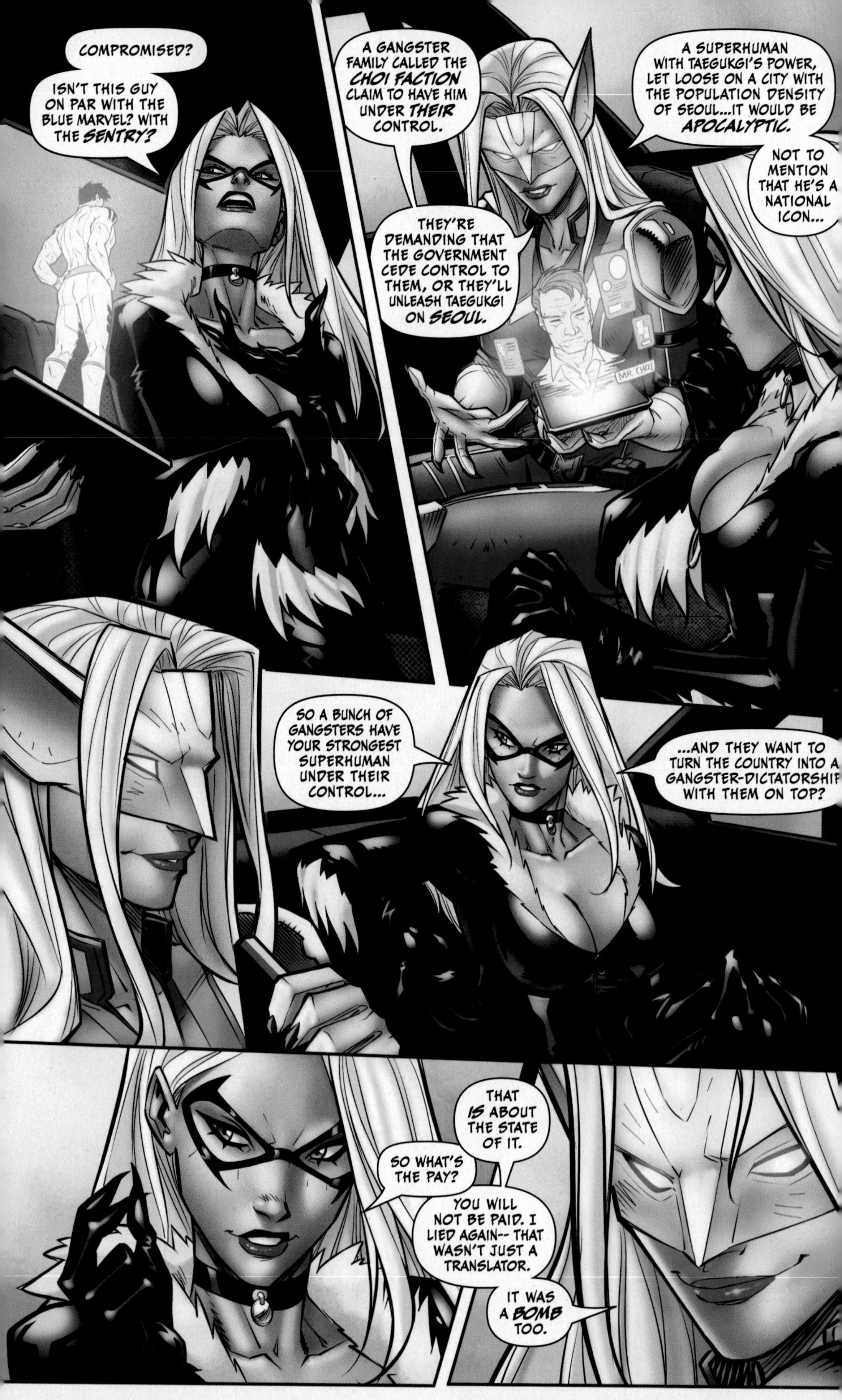

COMPROMISED?
ISN'T THIS GUY ON PAR WITH THE BLUE MARVEL? WITH THE SENTRY?
A GANGSTER FAMILY CALLED THE CHOI FACTION CLAIM TO HAVE HIM UNDER THEIR CONTROL.
THEY'RE DEMANDING THAT THE GOVERNMENT CEDE CONTROL TO THEM, OR THEY'LL UNLEASH TAEGUKGI ON SEOUL.
MR CHOI
A SUPERHUMAN WITH TAEGUKGI'S POWER, LET LOOSE ON A CITY WITH THE POPULATION DENSITY OF SEOUL...IT WOULD BE APOCALYPTIC.
NOT TO MENTION THAT HE'S A NATIONAL ICON...
SO A BUNCH OF GANGSTERS HAVE YOUR STRONGEST SUPERHUMAN UNDER THEIR CONTROL...
...AND THEY WANT TO TURN THE COUNTRY INTO A GANGSTER-DICTATORSHIP WITH THEM ON TOP?
THAT IS ABOUT THE STATE OF IT.
SO WHAT'S THE PAY?
YOU WILL NOT BE PAID. I LIED AGAIN-- THAT WASN'T JUST A TRANSLATOR.
IT WAS A BOMB TOO.

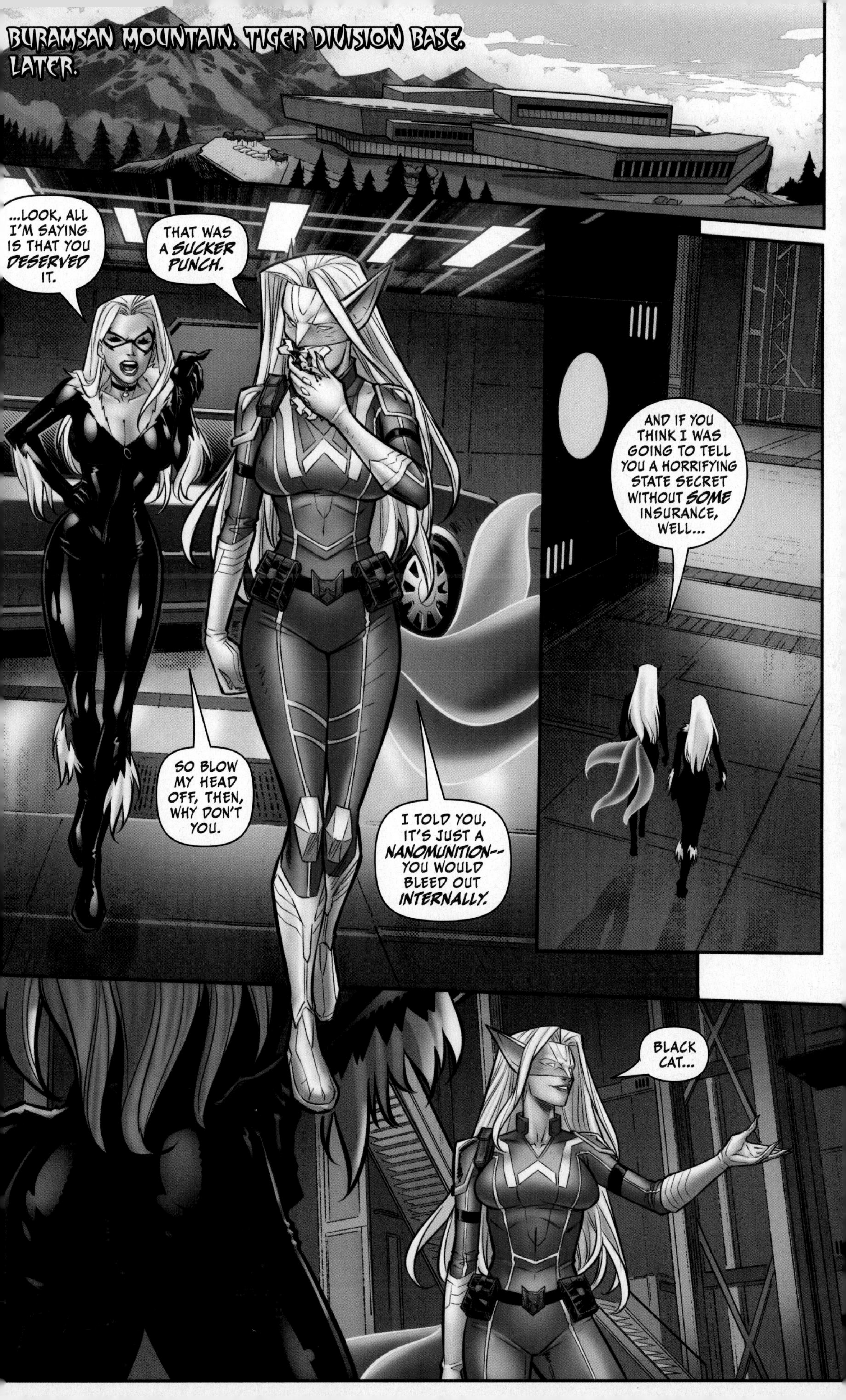

BURAMSAN MOUNTAIN. TIGER DIVISION BASE. LATER.
...LOOK, ALL I'M SAYING IS THAT YOU DESERVED IT.
THAT WAS A SUCKER PUNCH.
SO BLOW MY HEAD OFF, THEN, WHY DON'T YOU.
I TOLD YOU, IT'S JUST A NANOMUNITION-- YOU WOULD BLEED OUT INTERNALLY.
AND IF YOU THINK I WAS GOING TO TELL YOU A HORRIFYING STATE SECRET WITHOUT SOME INSURANCE, WELL...
BLACK CAT...

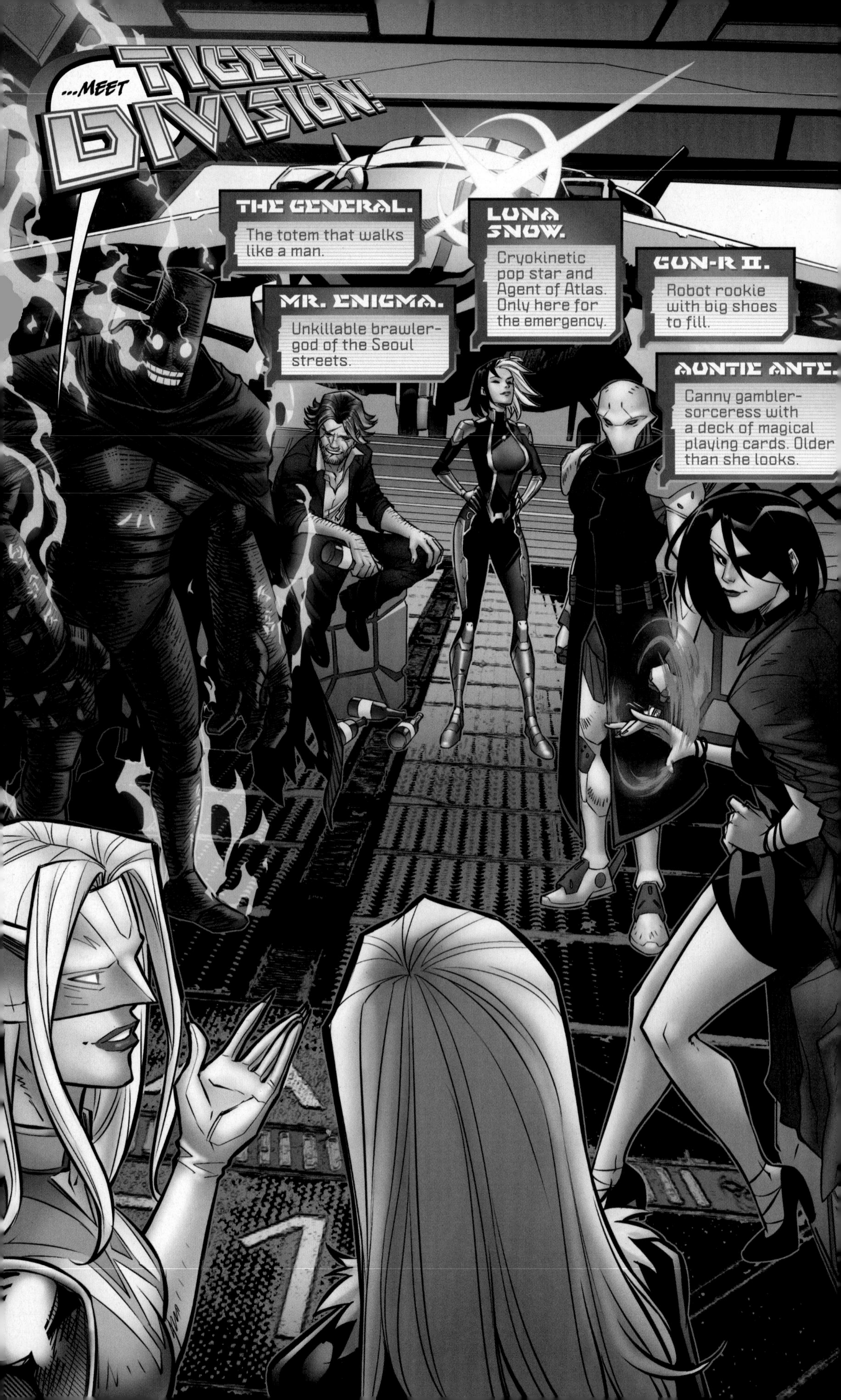
...MEET TIGER DIVISION!
THE GENERAL.
The totem that walks like a man.
MR. ENIGMA.
Unkillable brawler-god of the Seoul streets.
LUNA SNOW.
Cryokinetic pop star and Agent of Atlas. Only here for the emergency.
GUN-R II.
Robot rookie with big shoes to fill.
AUNTIE ANTE.
Canny gambler-sorceress with a deck of magical playing cards. Older than she looks.

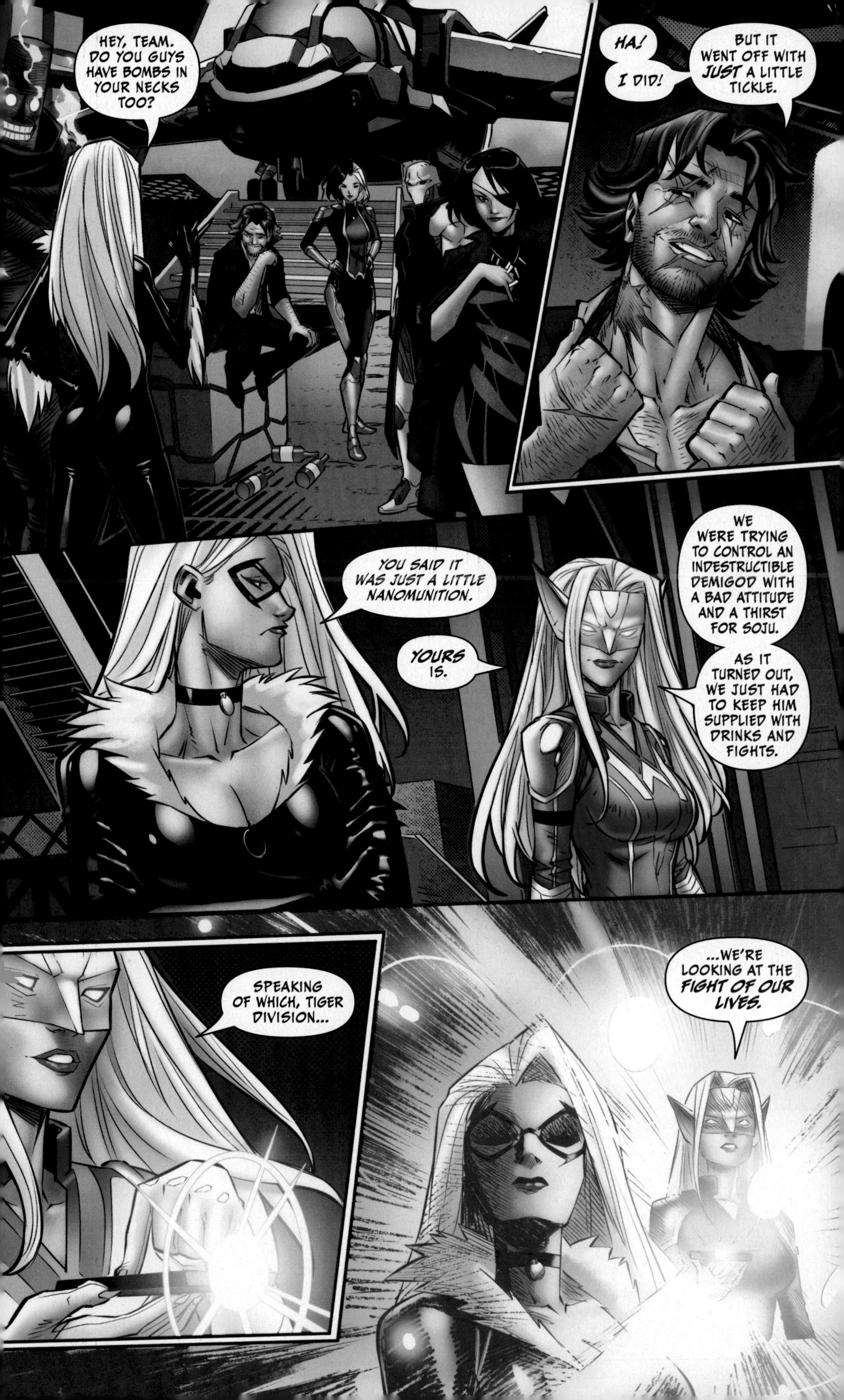
HEY, TEAM. DO YOU GUYS HAVE BOMBS IN YOUR NECKS TOO?
HA!
I DID!
BUT IT WENT OFF WITH JUST A LITTLE TICKLE.
YOU SAID IT WAS JUST A LITTLE NANOMUNITION.
YOURS IS.
WE WERE TRYING TO CONTROL AN INDESTRUCTIBLE DEMIGOD WITH A BAD ATTITUDE AND A THIRST FOR SOJU.
AS IT TURNED OUT, WE JUST HAD TO KEEP HIM SUPPLIED WITH DRINKS AND FIGHTS.
SPEAKING OF WHICH, TIGER DIVISION...
...WE'RE LOOKING AT THE FIGHT OF OUR LIVES.

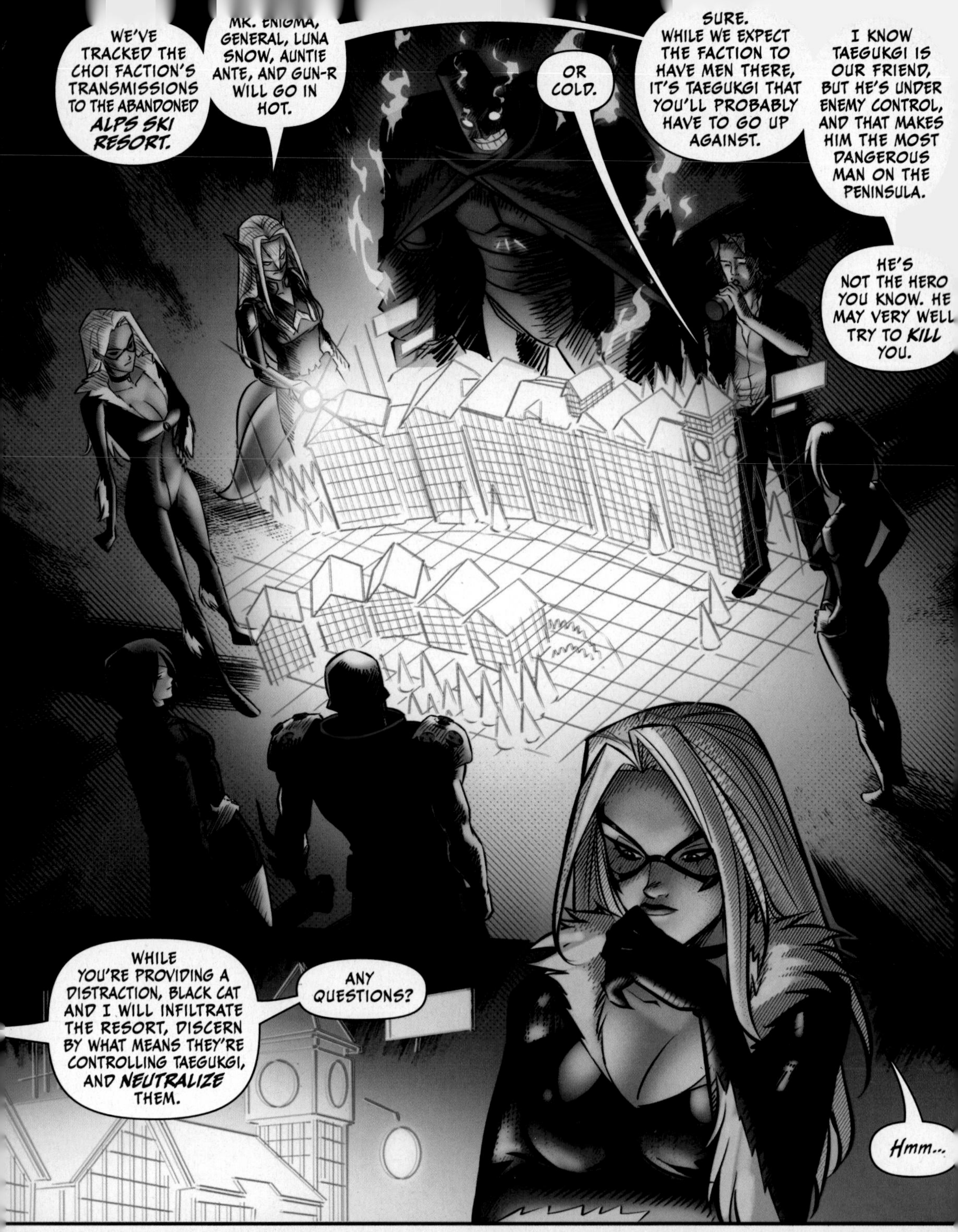
WE'VE TRACKED THE CHOI FACTION'S TRANSMISSIONS TO THE ABANDONED ALPS SKI RESORT.
MR. ENIGMA, GENERAL, LUNA SNOW, AUNTIE ANTE, AND GUN-R WILL GO IN HOT.
OR COLD.
SURE. WHILE WE EXPECT THE FACTION TO HAVE MEN THERE, IT'S TAEGUKGI THAT YOU'LL PROBABLY HAVE TO GO UP AGAINST.
I KNOW TAEGUKGI IS OUR FRIEND, BUT HE'S UNDER ENEMY CONTROL, AND THAT MAKES HIM THE MOST DANGEROUS MAN ON THE PENINSULA.
HE'S NOT THE HERO YOU KNOW. HE MAY VERY WELL TRY TO KILL YOU.
WHILE YOU'RE PROVIDING A DISTRACTION, BLACK CAT AND I WILL INFILTRATE THE RESORT, DISCERN BY WHAT MEANS THEY'RE CONTROLLING TAEGUKGI, AND NEUTRALIZE THEM.
ANY QUESTIONS?
Hmm...
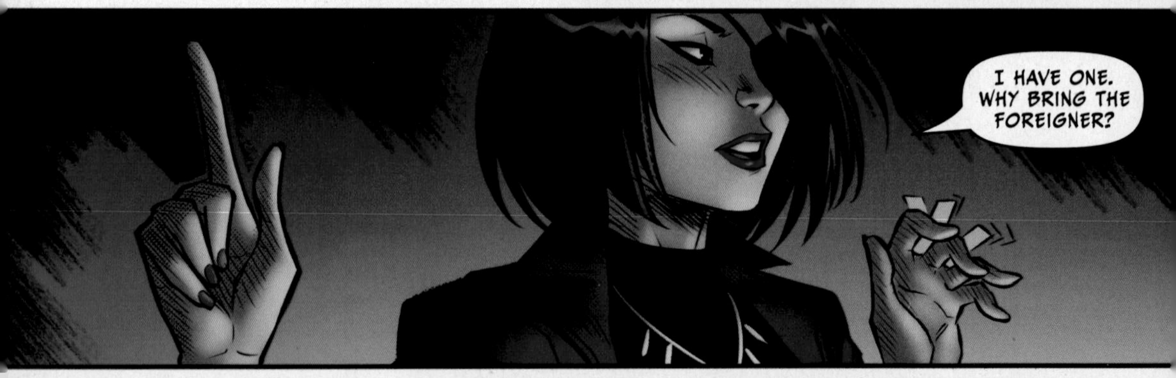
I HAVE ONE. WHY BRING THE FOREIGNER?

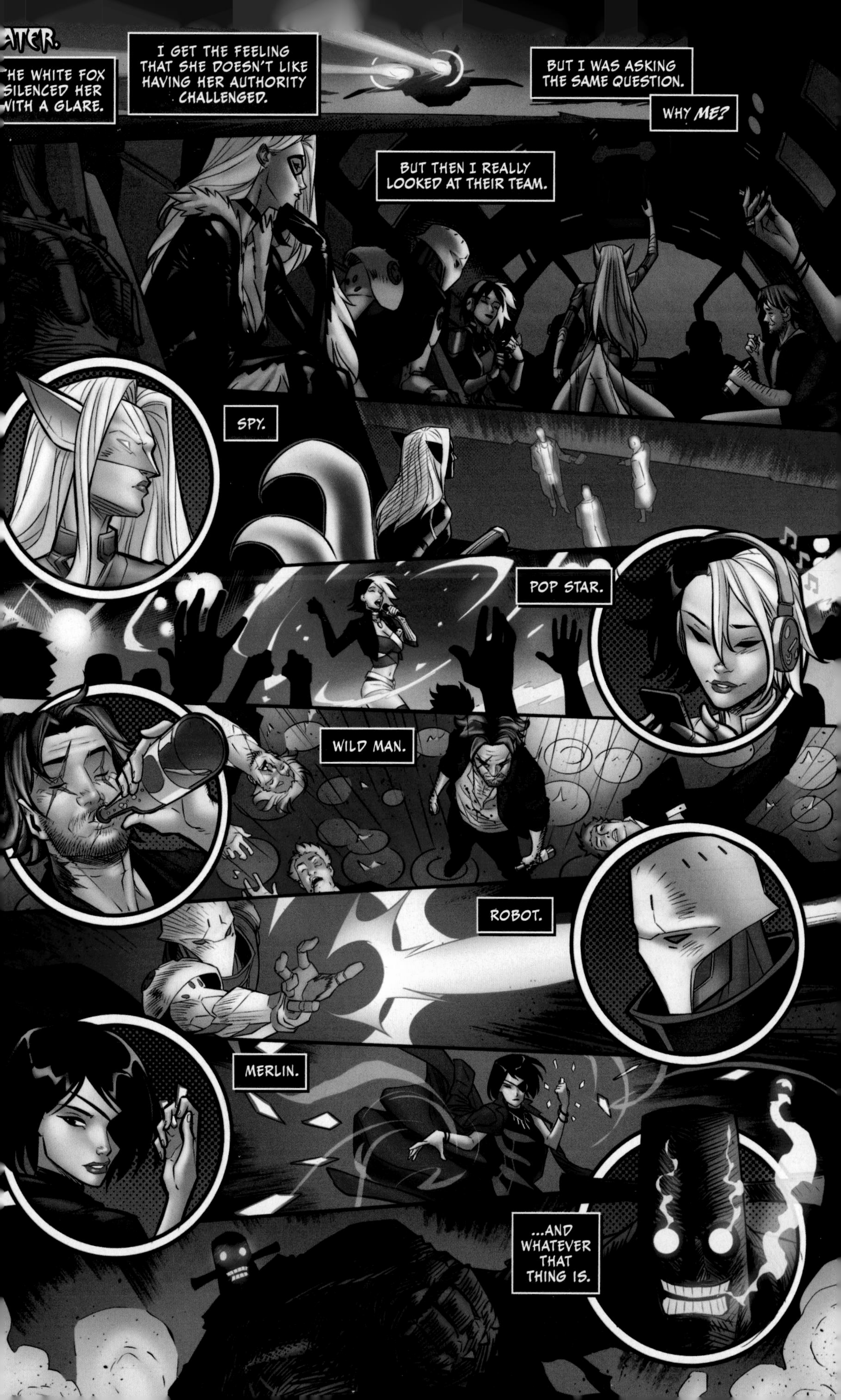

ATER.
HE WHITE FOX SILENCED HER WITH A GLARE.
I GET THE FEELING THAT SHE DOESN'T LIKE HAVING HER AUTHORITY CHALLENGED.
BUT I WAS ASKING THE SAME QUESTION.
WHY ME?
BUT THEN I REALLY LOOKED AT THEIR TEAM.
SPY.
POP STAR.
WILD MAN.
ROBOT.
MERLIN.
...AND WHATEVER THAT THING IS.

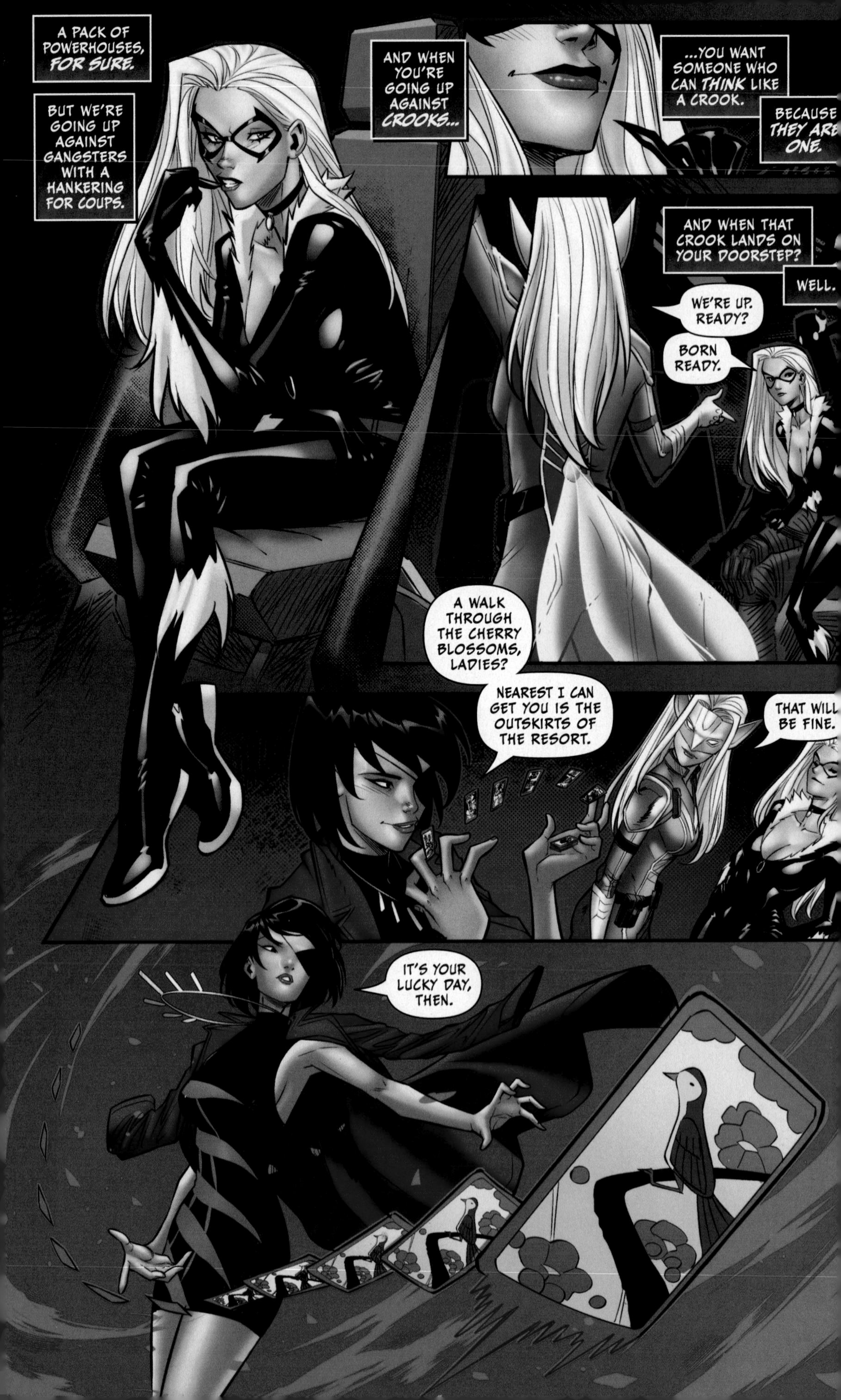
A PACK OF POWERHOUSES, FOR SURE.
BUT WE'RE GOING UP AGAINST GANGSTERS WITH A HANKERING FOR COUPS.
AND WHEN YOU'RE GOING UP AGAINST CROOKS...
...YOU WANT SOMEONE WHO CAN THINK LIKE A CROOK.
BECAUSE THEY ARE ONE.
AND WHEN THAT CROOK LANDS ON YOUR DOORSTEP?
WELL.
WE'RE UP. READY?
BORN READY.
A WALK THROUGH THE CHERRY BLOSSOMS, LADIES?
NEAREST I CAN GET YOU IS THE OUTSKIRTS OF THE RESORT.
THAT WILL BE FINE.
IT'S YOUR LUCKY DAY, THEN.

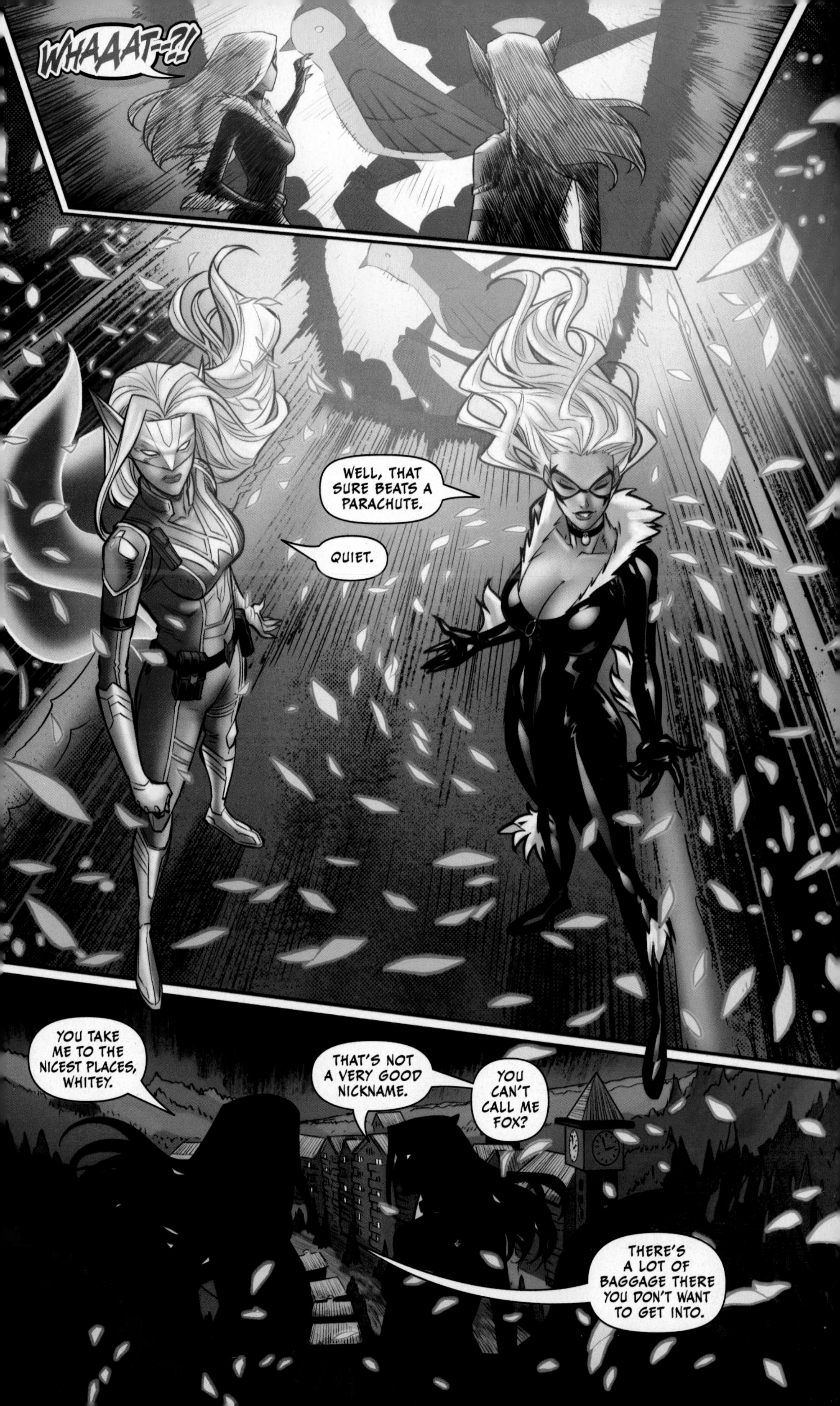
WHAAAT--?!
WELL, THAT SURE BEATS A PARACHUTE.
QUIET.
YOU TAKE ME TO THE NICEST PLACES, WHITEY.
THAT'S NOT A VERY GOOD NICKNAME.
YOU CAN'T CALL ME FOX?
THERE'S A LOT OF BAGGAGE THERE YOU DON'T WANT TO GET INTO.

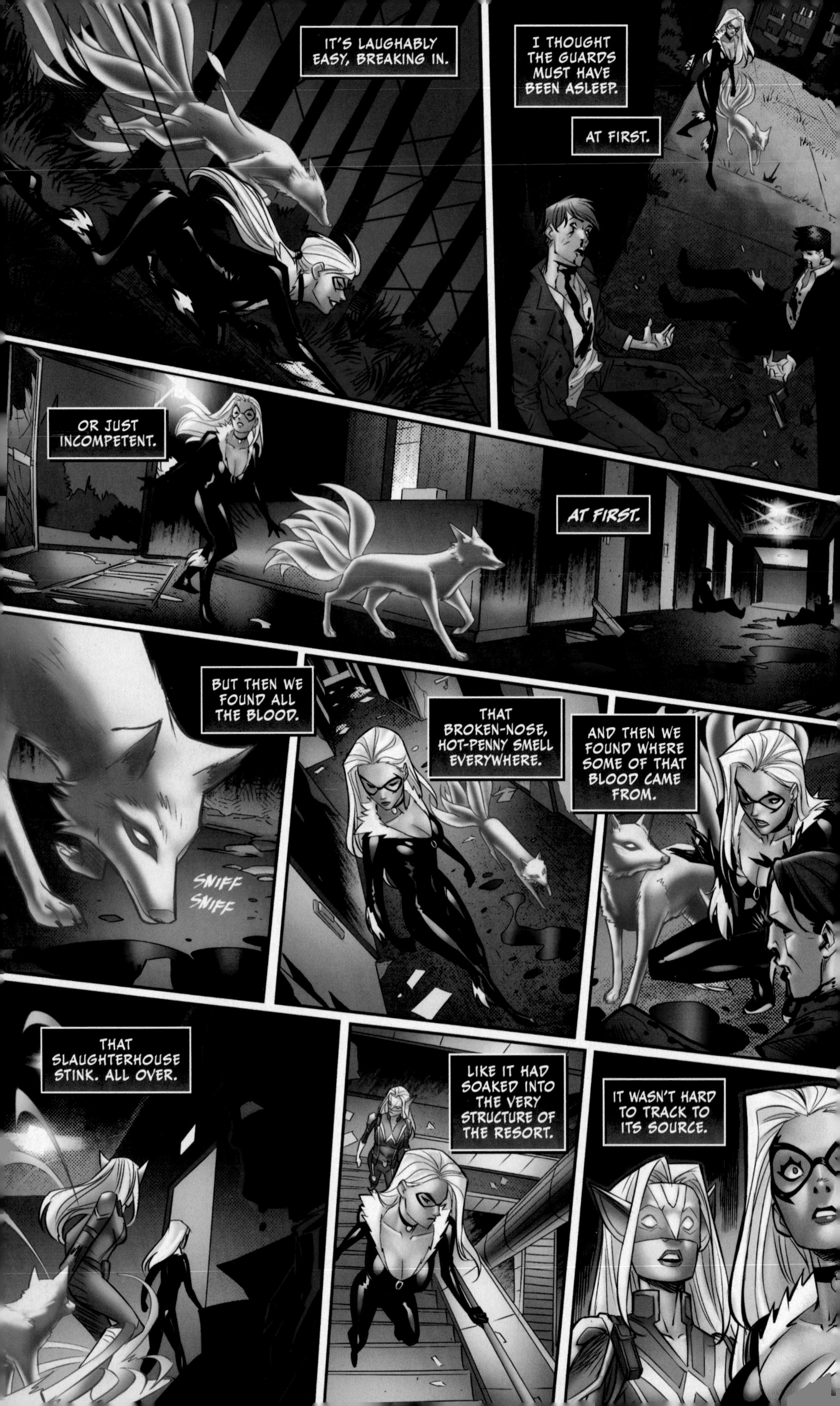
IT'S LAUGHABLY EASY, BREAKING IN.
I THOUGHT THE GUARDS MUST HAVE BEEN ASLEEP.
AT FIRST.
OR JUST INCOMPETENT.
AT FIRST.
BUT THEN WE FOUND ALL THE BLOOD.
SNIFF SNIFF
THAT BROKEN-NOSE, HOT-PENNY SMELL EVERYWHERE.
AND THEN WE FOUND WHERE SOME OF THAT BLOOD CAME FROM.
THAT SLAUGHTERHOUSE STINK. ALL OVER.
LIKE IT HAD SOAKED INTO THE VERY STRUCTURE OF THE RESORT.
IT WASN'T HARD TO TRACK TO ITS SOURCE.

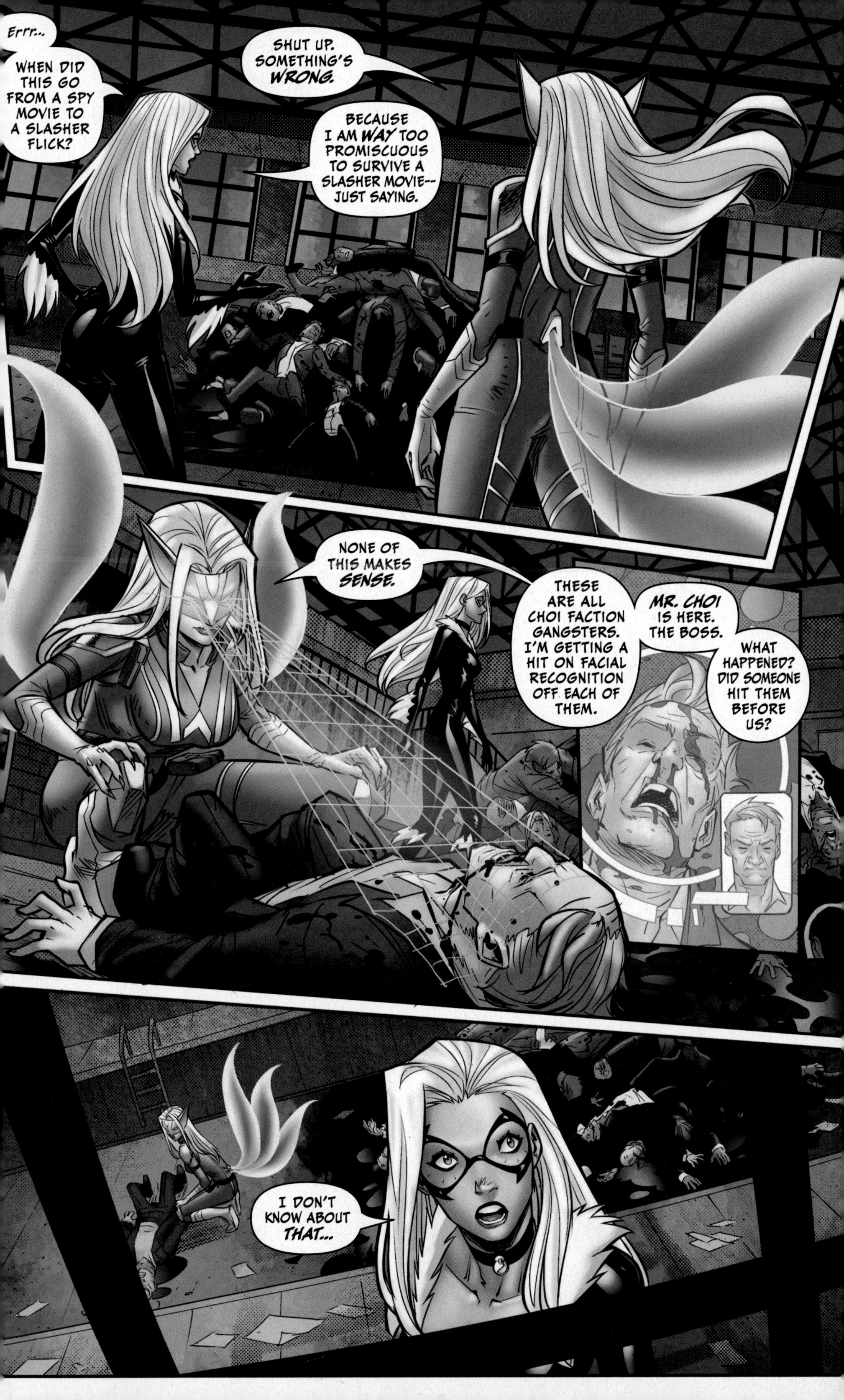

Errr...
WHEN DID THIS GO FROM A SPY MOVIE TO A SLASHER FLICK?
SHUT UP. SOMETHING'S WRONG.
BECAUSE I AM WAY TOO PROMISCUOUS TO SURVIVE A SLASHER MOVIE-- JUST SAYING.
NONE OF THIS MAKES SENSE.
THESE ARE ALL CHOI FACTION GANGSTERS. I'M GETTING A HIT ON FACIAL RECOGNITION OFF EACH OF THEM.
MR. CHOI IS HERE. THE BOSS.
WHAT HAPPENED? DID SOMEONE HIT THEM BEFORE US?
I DON'T KNOW ABOUT THAT...

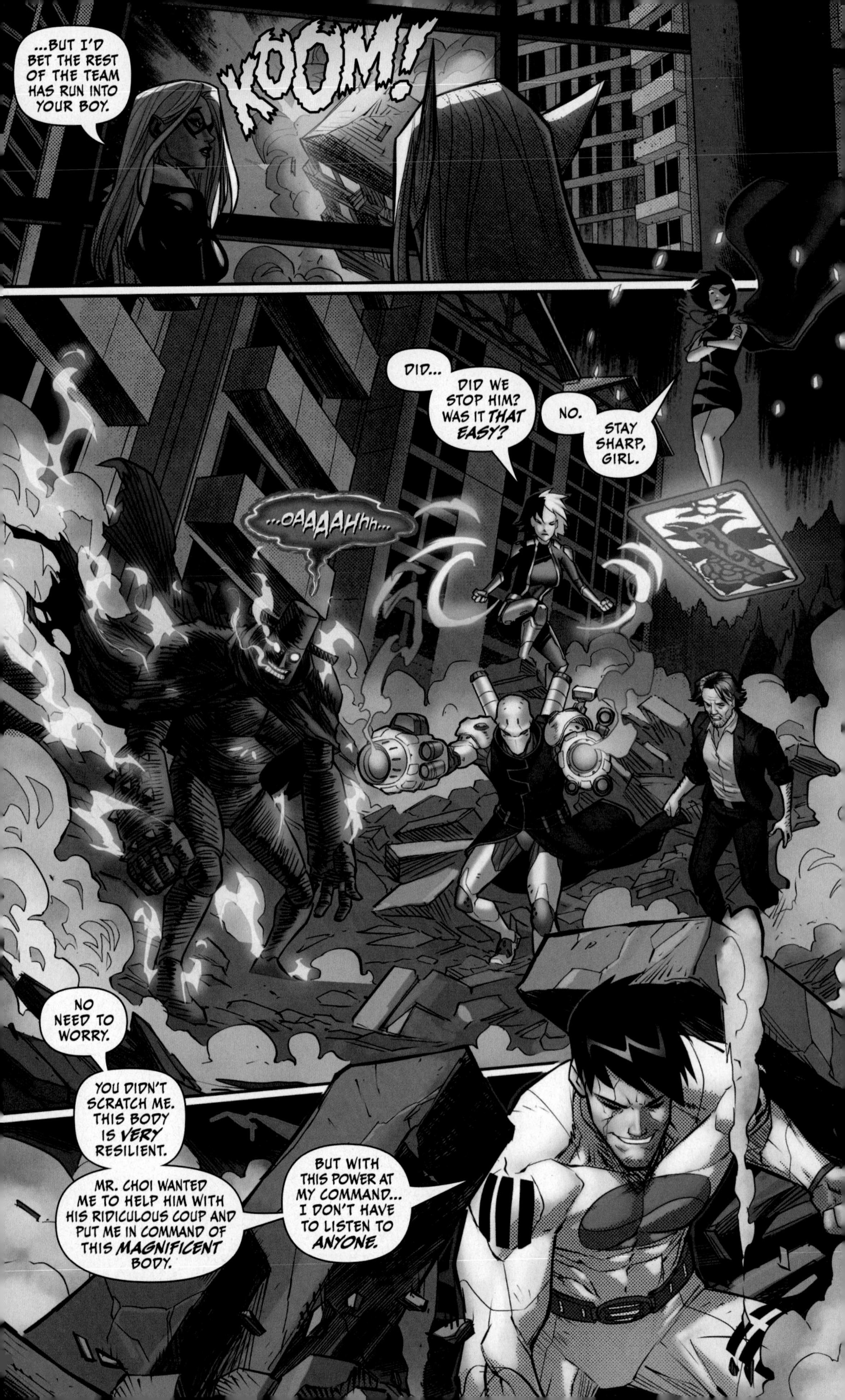
...BUT I'D BET THE REST OF THE TEAM HAS RUN INTO YOUR BOY.
KOOM!
DID... DID WE STOP HIM? WAS IT THAT EASY?
NO.
STAY SHARP, GIRL.
...OAAAAHhh...
NO NEED TO WORRY.
YOU DIDN'T SCRATCH ME. THIS BODY IS VERY RESILIENT.
MR. CHOI WANTED ME TO HELP HIM WITH HIS RIDICULOUS COUP AND PUT ME IN COMMAND OF THIS MAGNIFICENT BODY.
BUT WITH THIS POWER AT MY COMMAND... I DON'T HAVE TO LISTEN TO ANYONE.

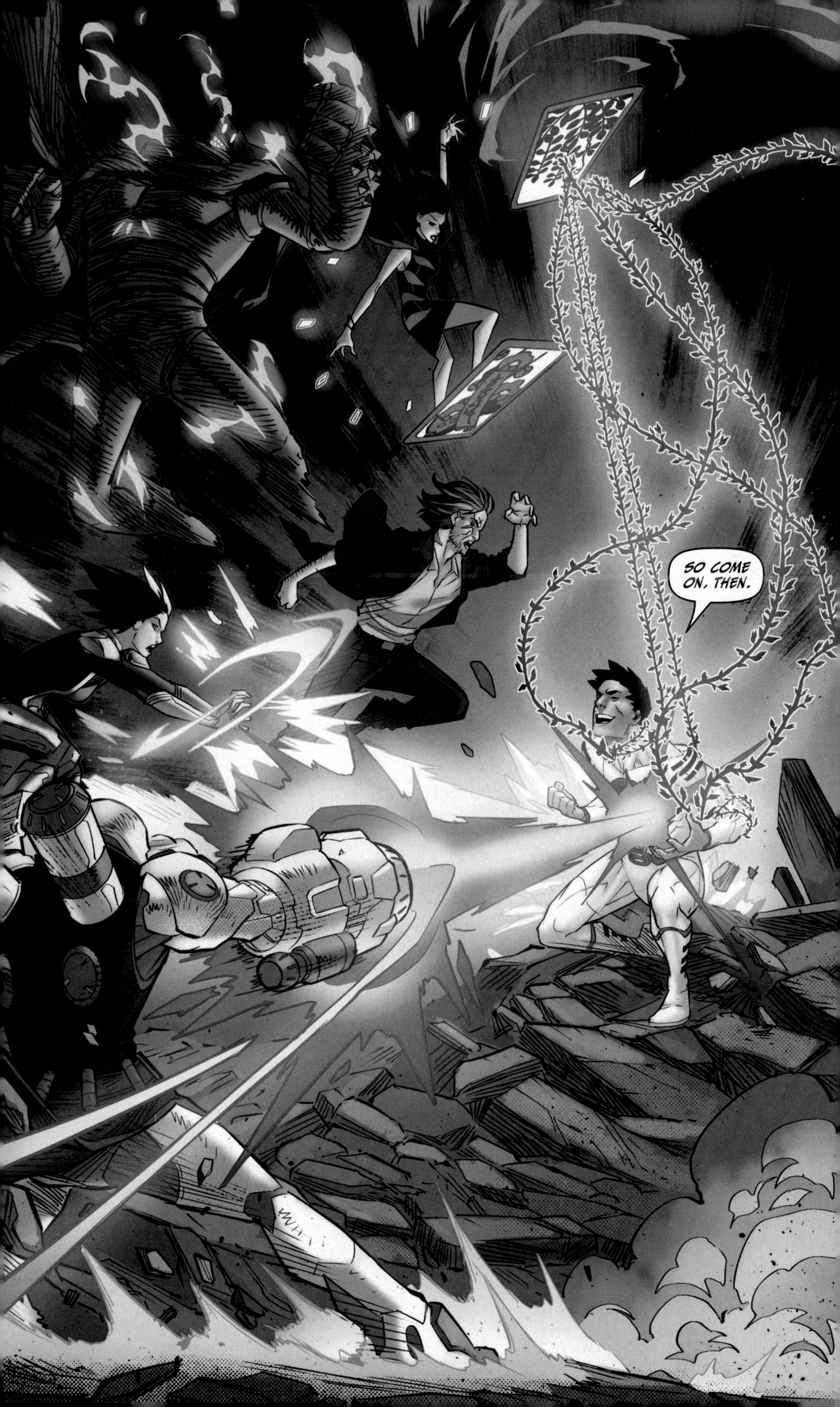
SO COME ON, THEN.

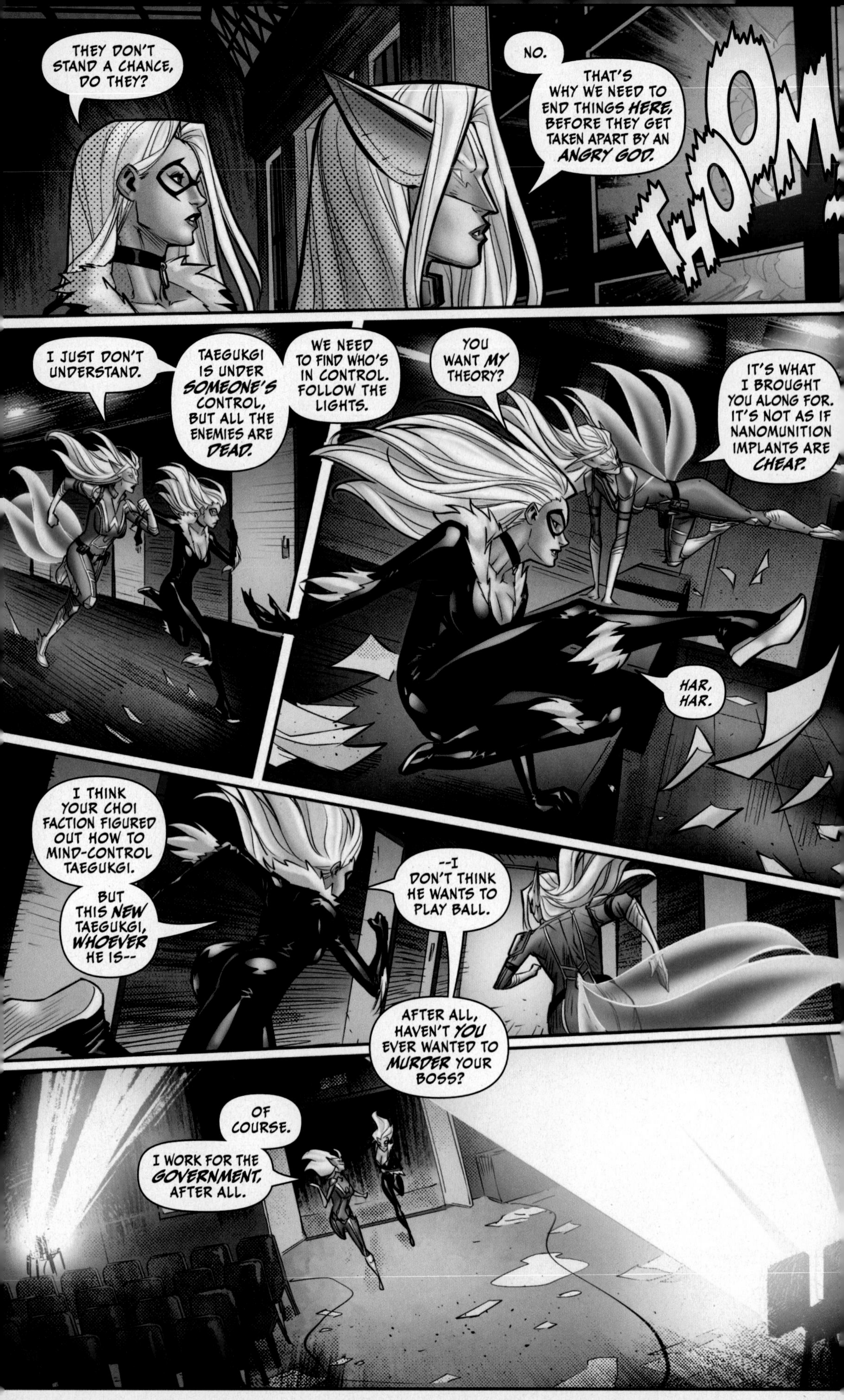

THEY DON'T STAND A CHANCE, DO THEY?
NO.
THAT'S WHY WE NEED TO END THINGS HERE, BEFORE THEY GET TAKEN APART BY AN ANGRY GOD.
THOOM
I JUST DON'T UNDERSTAND.
TAEGUKGI IS UNDER SOMEONE'S CONTROL, BUT ALL THE ENEMIES ARE DEAD.
WE NEED TO FIND WHO'S IN CONTROL. FOLLOW THE LIGHTS.
YOU WANT MY THEORY?
IT'S WHAT I BROUGHT YOU ALONG FOR. IT'S NOT AS IF NANOMUNITION IMPLANTS ARE CHEAP.
HAR, HAR.
I THINK YOUR CHOI FACTION FIGURED OUT HOW TO MIND-CONTROL TAEGUKGI.
BUT THIS NEW TAEGUKGI, WHOEVER HE IS--
--I DON'T THINK HE WANTS TO PLAY BALL.
AFTER ALL, HAVEN'T YOU EVER WANTED TO MURDER YOUR BOSS?
OF COURSE.
I WORK FOR THE GOVERNMENT, AFTER ALL.

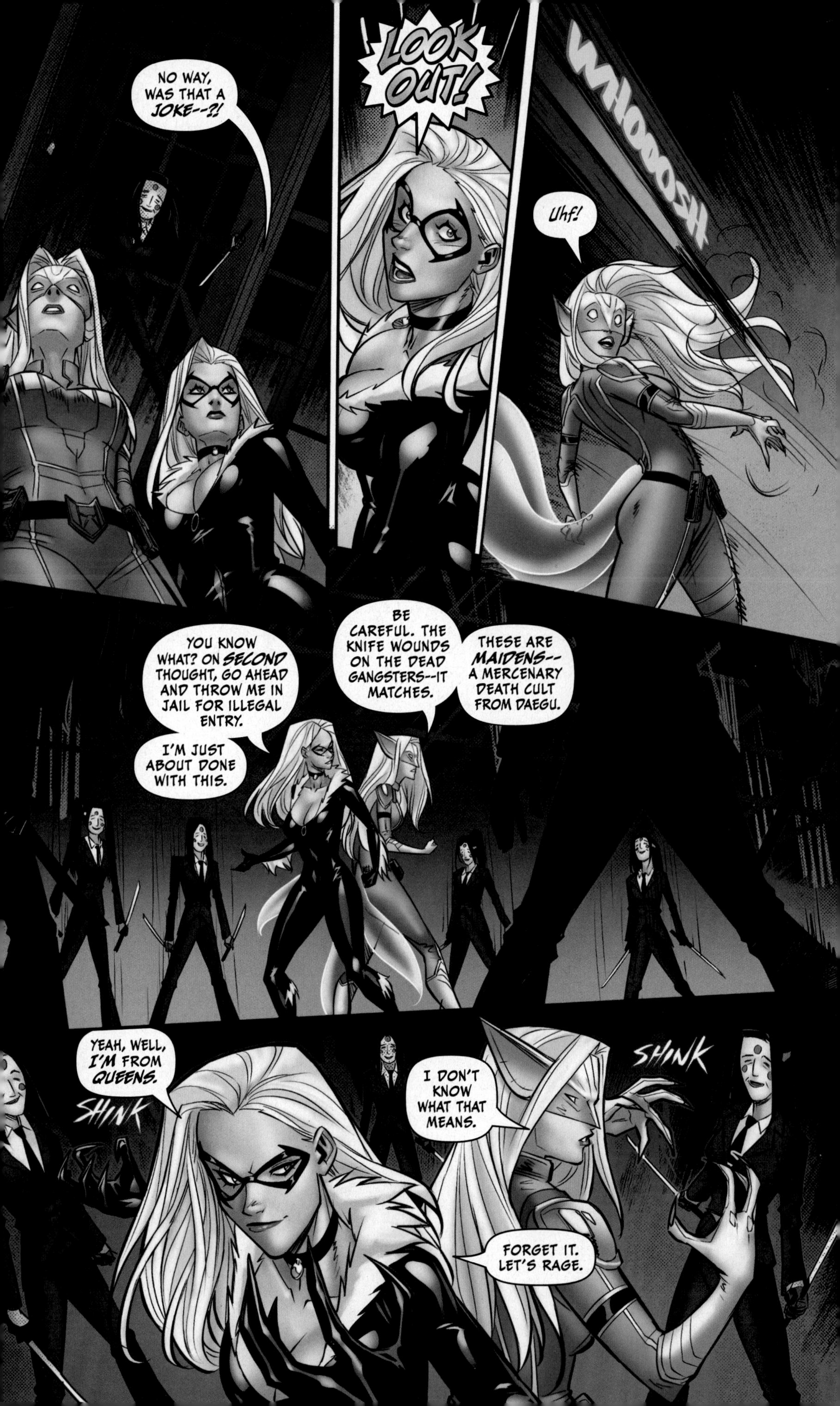

NO WAY, WAS THAT A JOKE--?!
LOOK OUT!
Uhf!
YOU KNOW WHAT? ON SECOND THOUGHT, GO AHEAD AND THROW ME IN JAIL FOR ILLEGAL ENTRY.
I'M JUST ABOUT DONE WITH THIS.
BE CAREFUL. THE KNIFE WOUNDS ON THE DEAD GANGSTERS--IT MATCHES.
THESE ARE MAIDENS--A MERCENARY DEATH CULT FROM DAEGU.
YEAH, WELL, I'M FROM QUEENS.
SHINK
I DON'T KNOW WHAT THAT MEANS.
SHINK
FORGET IT. LET'S RAGE.

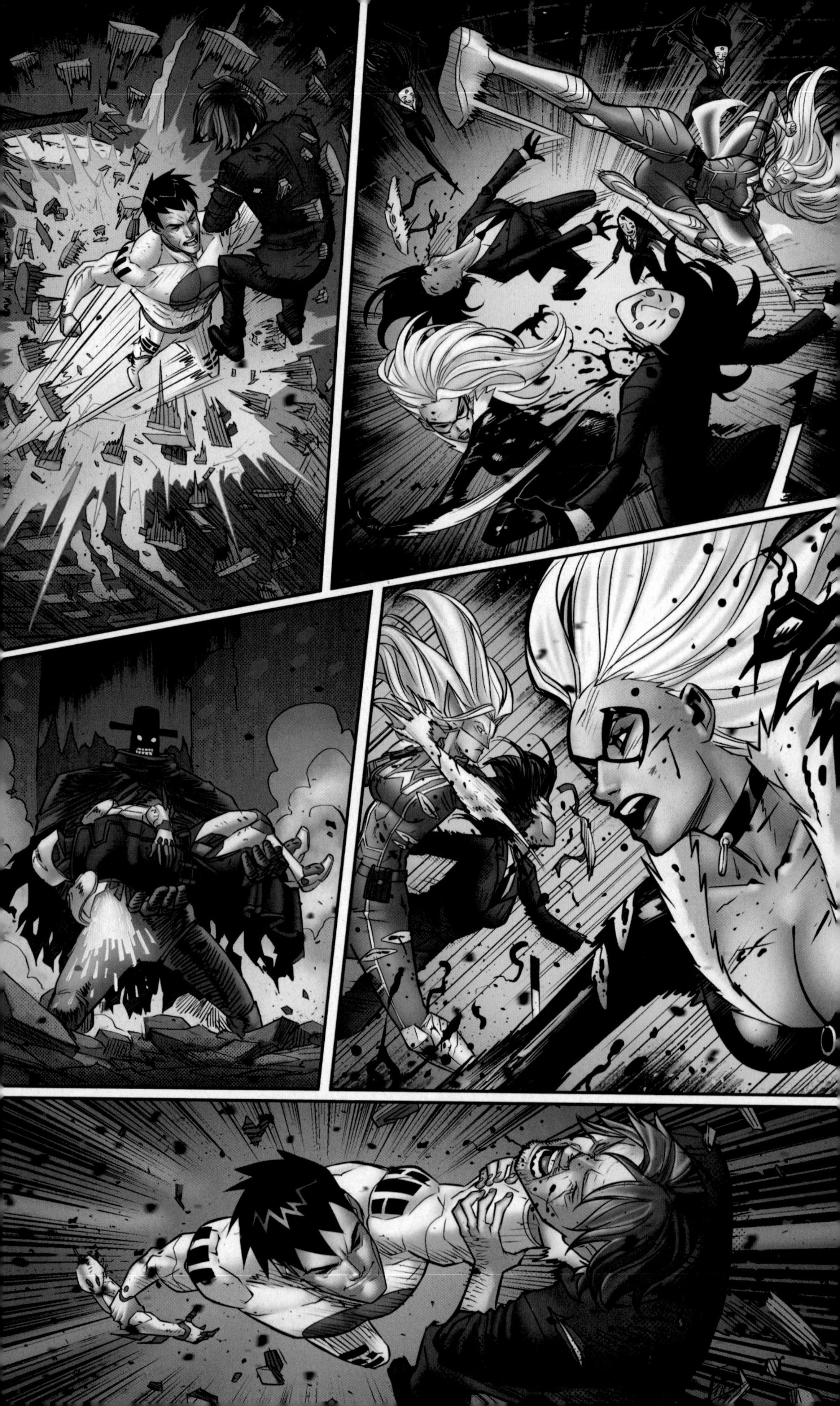

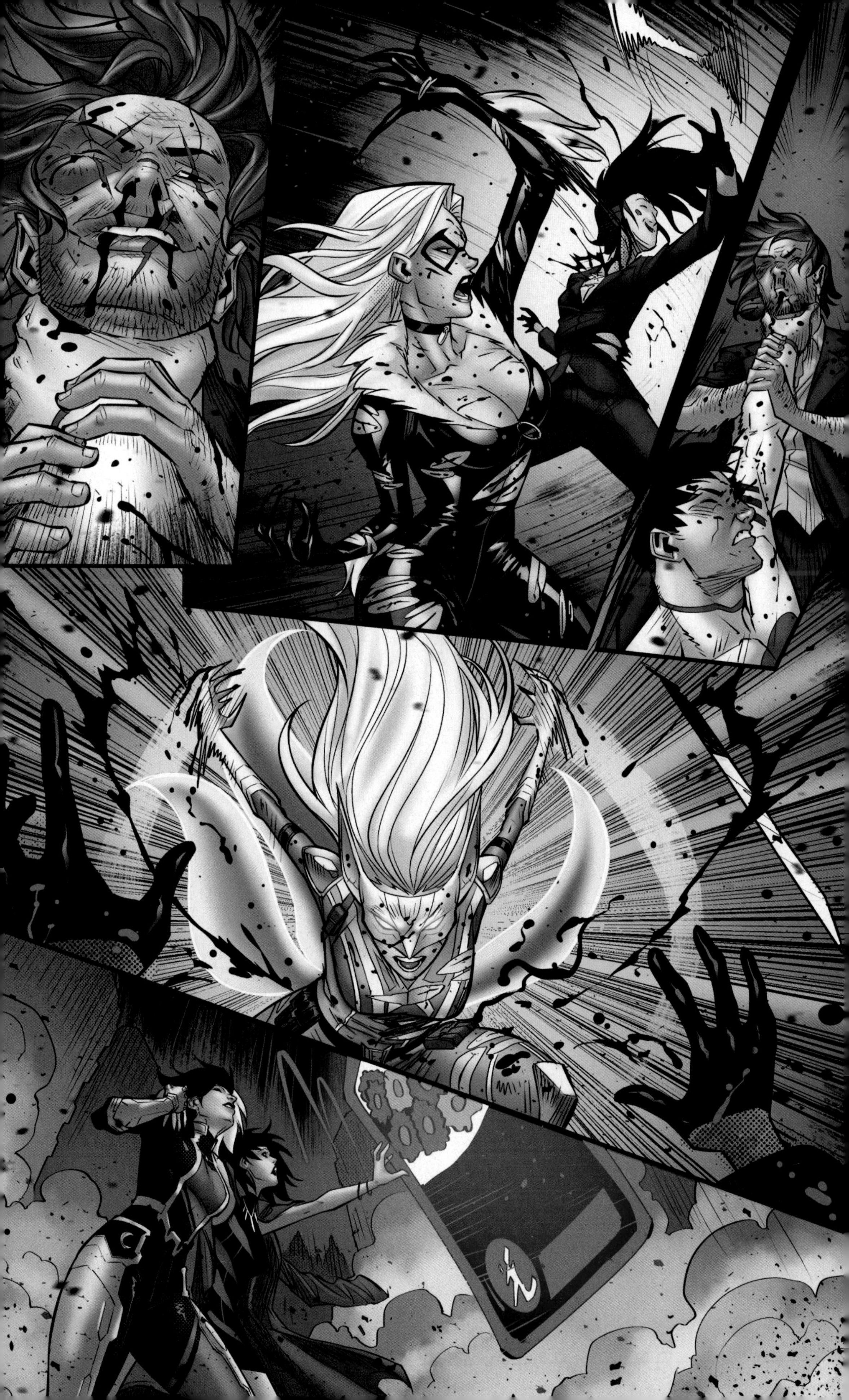

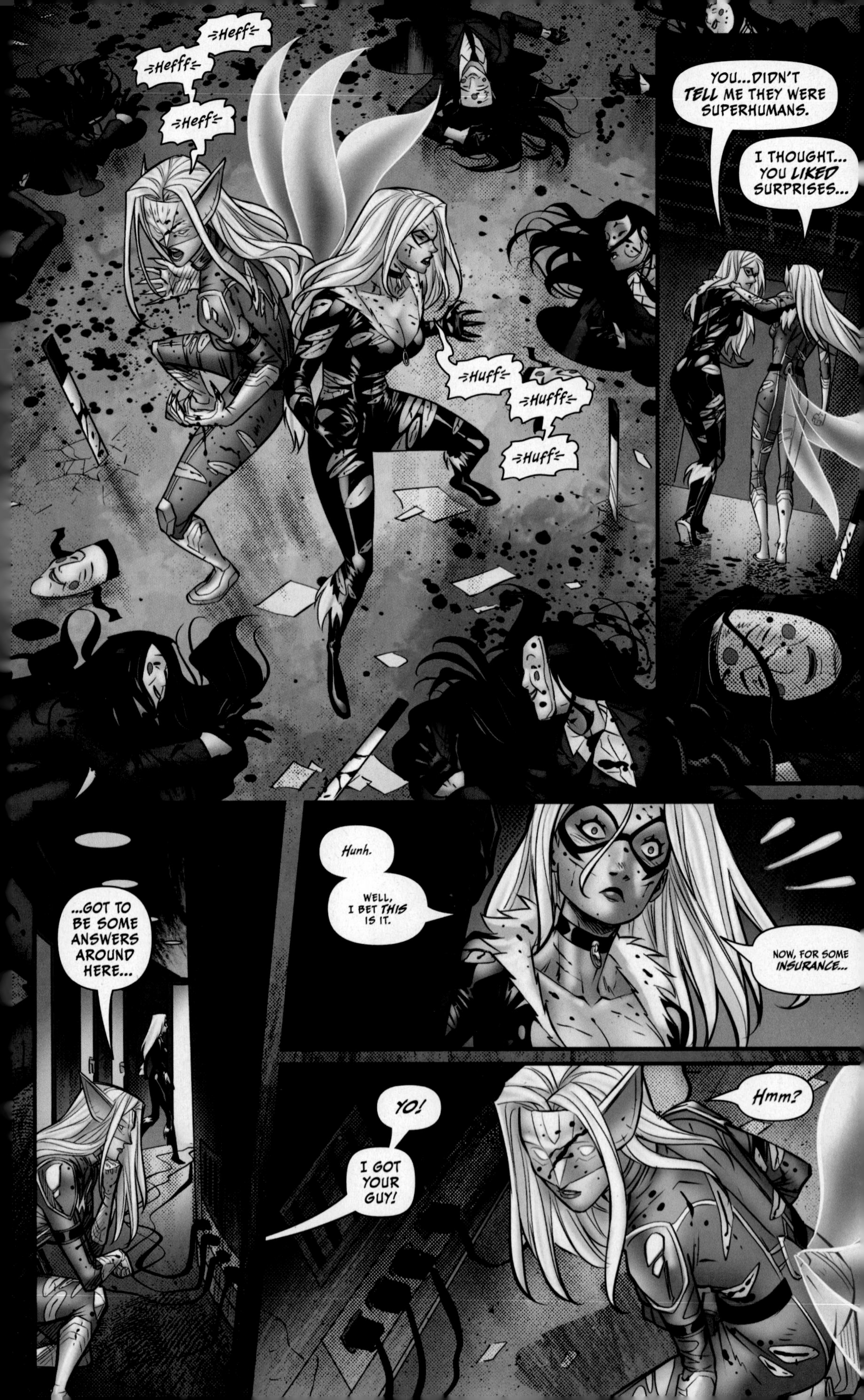

-Heff-
-Hefff-
-Heff-
-Huff-
-Hufff-
-Huff-
YOU...DIDN'T TELL ME THEY WERE SUPERHUMANS.
I THOUGHT... YOU LIKED SURPRISES...
...GOT TO BE SOME ANSWERS AROUND HERE...
Hunh.
WELL, I BET THIS IS IT.
NOW, FOR SOME INSURANCE...
YO!
I GOT YOUR GUY!
Hmm?

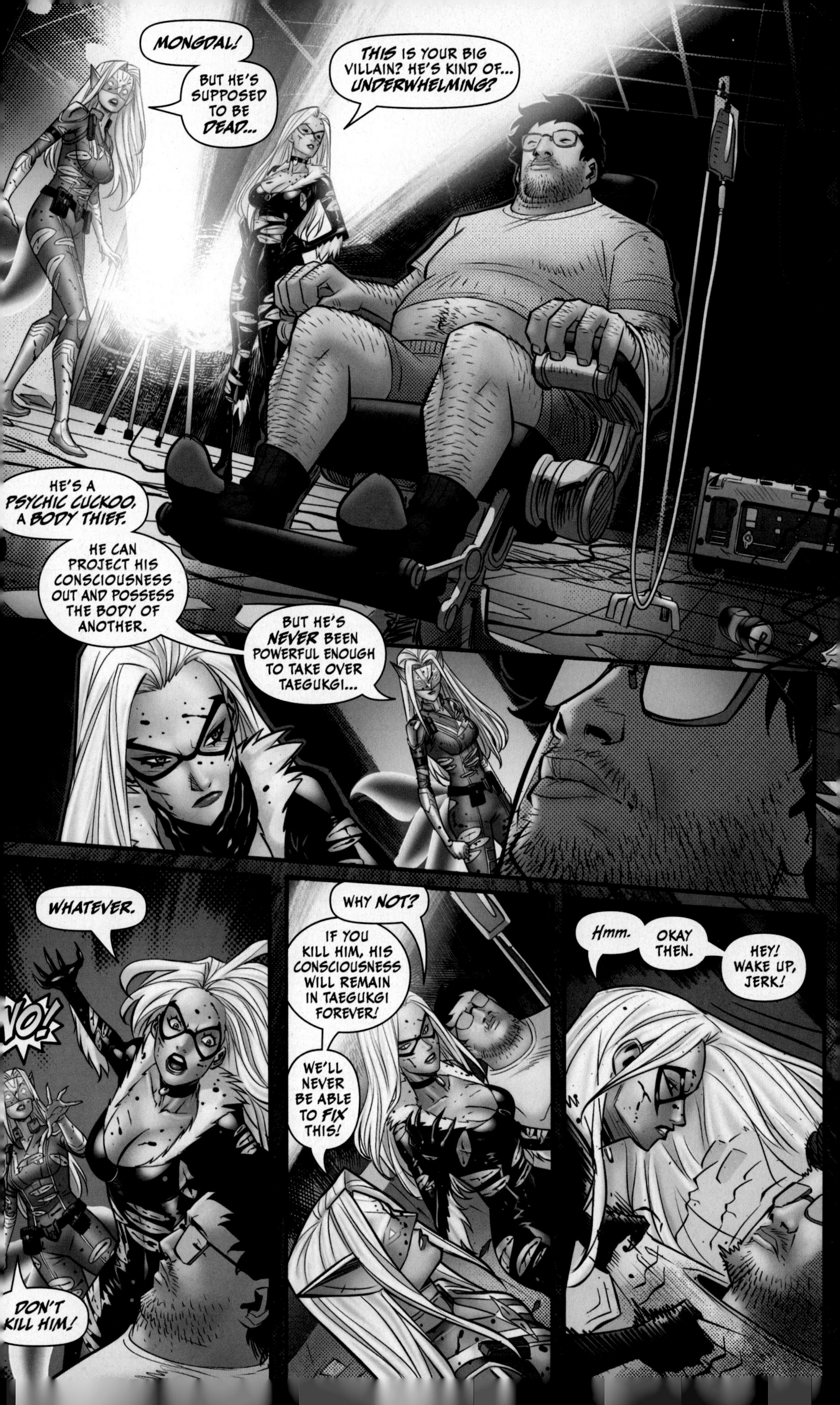

MONGDAL!
BUT HE'S SUPPOSED TO BE DEAD...
THIS IS YOUR BIG VILLAIN? HE'S KIND OF... UNDERWHELMING?
HE'S A PSYCHIC CUCKOO, A BODY THIEF.
HE CAN PROJECT HIS CONSCIOUSNESS OUT AND POSSESS THE BODY OF ANOTHER.
BUT HE'S NEVER BEEN POWERFUL ENOUGH TO TAKE OVER TAEGUKGI...
WHATEVER.
NO!
DON'T KILL HIM!
WHY NOT?
IF YOU KILL HIM, HIS CONSCIOUSNESS WILL REMAIN IN TAEGUKGI FOREVER!
WE'LL NEVER BE ABLE TO FIX THIS!
Hmm.
OKAY THEN.
HEY! WAKE UP, JERK!

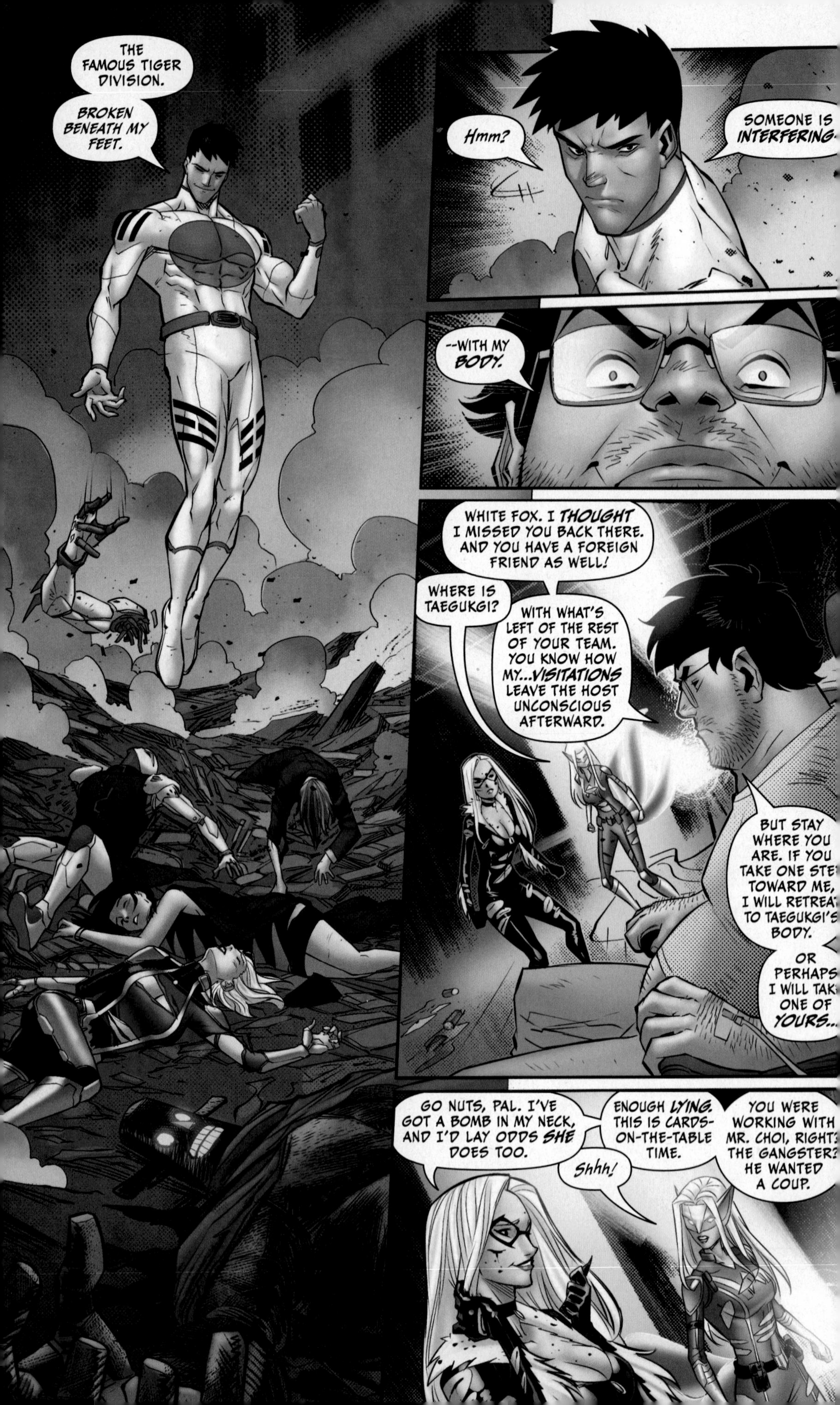
THE FAMOUS TIGER DIVISION.
BROKEN BENEATH MY FEET.
Hmm?
SOMEONE IS INTERFERING-
--WITH MY BODY.
WHITE FOX. I THOUGHT I MISSED YOU BACK THERE. AND YOU HAVE A FOREIGN FRIEND AS WELL!
WHERE IS TAEGUKGI?
WITH WHAT'S LEFT OF THE REST OF YOUR TEAM. YOU KNOW HOW MY...VISITATIONS LEAVE THE HOST UNCONSCIOUS AFTERWARD.
BUT STAY WHERE YOU ARE. IF YOU TAKE ONE STE TOWARD ME, I WILL RETREA TO TAEGUKGI'S BODY.
OR PERHAPS I WILL TAK ONE OF YOURS...
GO NUTS, PAL. I'VE GOT A BOMB IN MY NECK, AND I'D LAY ODDS SHE DOES TOO.
Shhh!
ENOUGH LYING. THIS IS CARDS-ON-THE-TABLE TIME.
YOU WERE WORKING WITH MR. CHOI, RIGHT? THE GANGSTER? HE WANTED A COUP.

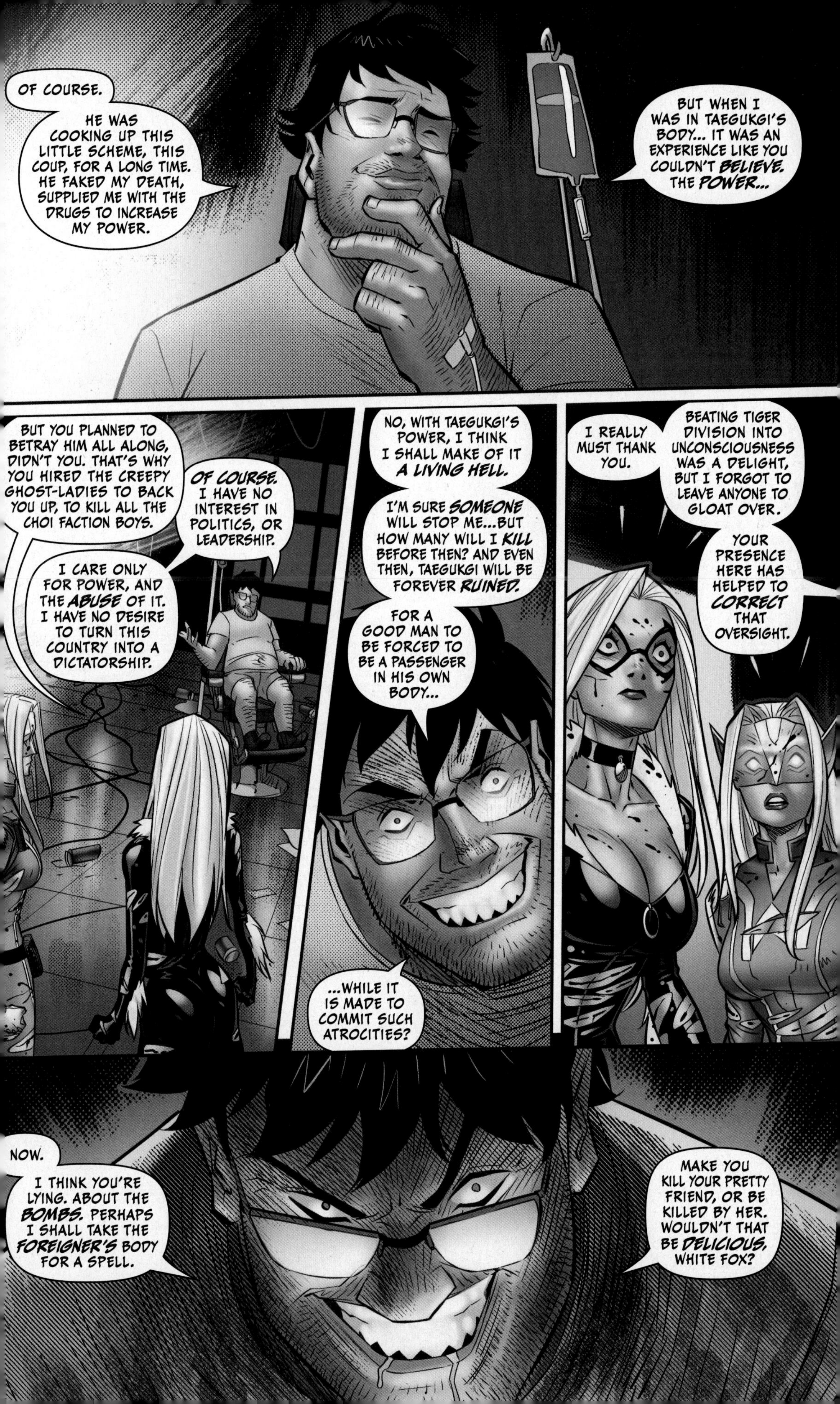
OF COURSE.
HE WAS COOKING UP THIS LITTLE SCHEME, THIS COUP, FOR A LONG TIME. HE FAKED MY DEATH, SUPPLIED ME WITH THE DRUGS TO INCREASE MY POWER.
BUT WHEN I WAS IN TAEGUKGI'S BODY... IT WAS AN EXPERIENCE LIKE YOU COULDN'T BELIEVE. THE POWER...
BUT YOU PLANNED TO BETRAY HIM ALL ALONG, DIDN'T YOU. THAT'S WHY YOU HIRED THE CREEPY GHOST-LADIES TO BACK YOU UP, TO KILL ALL THE CHOI FACTION BOYS.
OF COURSE. I HAVE NO INTEREST IN POLITICS, OR LEADERSHIP.
I CARE ONLY FOR POWER, AND THE ABUSE OF IT. I HAVE NO DESIRE TO TURN THIS COUNTRY INTO A DICTATORSHIP.
NO, WITH TAEGUKGI'S POWER, I THINK I SHALL MAKE OF IT A LIVING HELL.
I'M SURE SOMEONE WILL STOP ME...BUT HOW MANY WILL I KILL BEFORE THEN? AND EVEN THEN, TAEGUKGI WILL BE FOREVER RUINED.
FOR A GOOD MAN TO BE FORCED TO BE A PASSENGER IN HIS OWN BODY...
...WHILE IT IS MADE TO COMMIT SUCH ATROCITIES?
I REALLY MUST THANK YOU.
BEATING TIGER DIVISION INTO UNCONSCIOUSNESS WAS A DELIGHT, BUT I FORGOT TO LEAVE ANYONE TO GLOAT OVER.
YOUR PRESENCE HERE HAS HELPED TO CORRECT THAT OVERSIGHT.
NOW.
I THINK YOU'RE LYING. ABOUT THE BOMBS. PERHAPS I SHALL TAKE THE FOREIGNER'S BODY FOR A SPELL.
MAKE YOU KILL YOUR PRETTY FRIEND, OR BE KILLED BY HER. WOULDN'T THAT BE DELICIOUS, WHITE FOX?

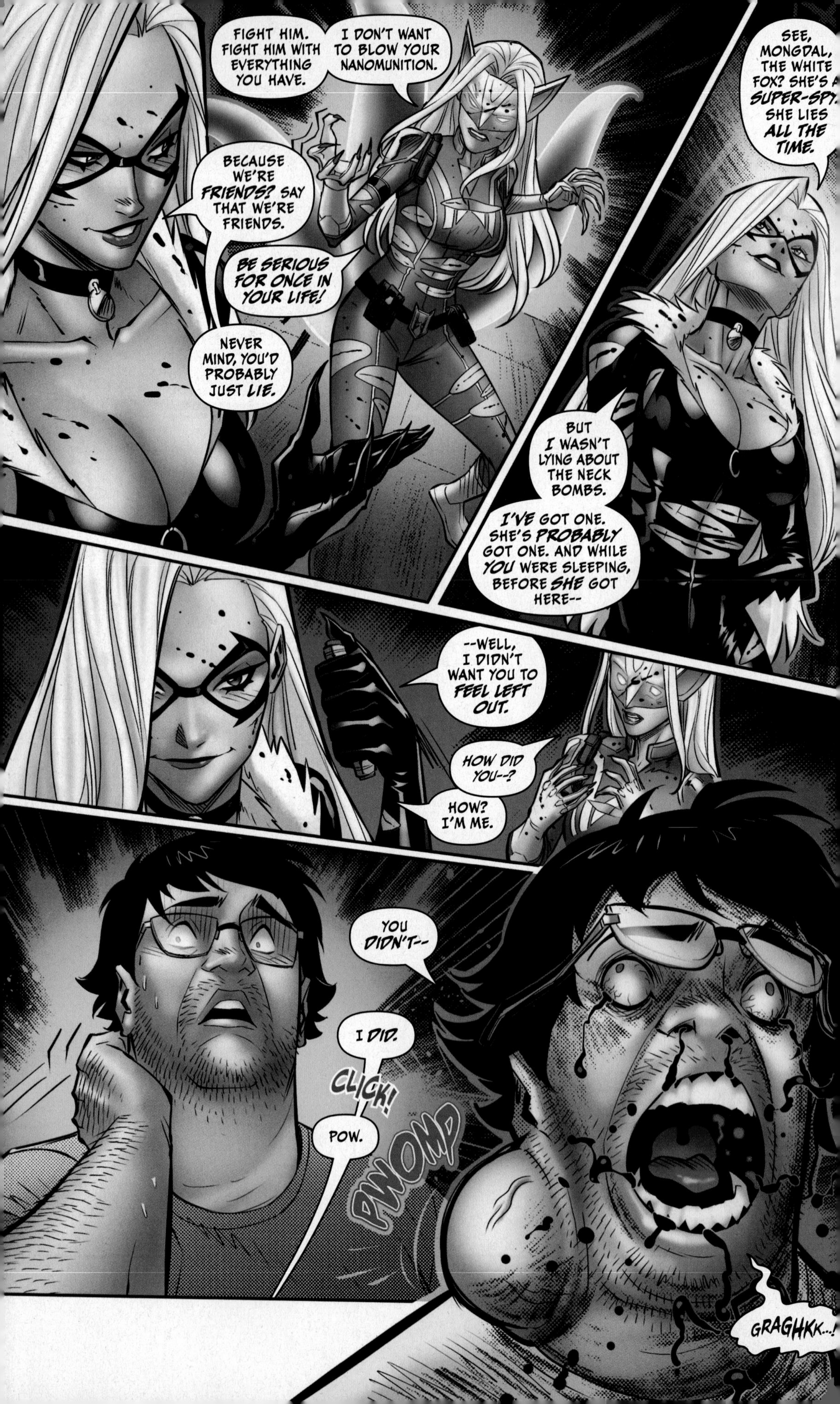
FIGHT HIM. FIGHT HIM WITH EVERYTHING YOU HAVE.
I DON'T WANT TO BLOW YOUR NANOMUNITION.
BECAUSE WE'RE FRIENDS? SAY THAT WE'RE FRIENDS.
BE SERIOUS FOR ONCE IN YOUR LIFE!
NEVER MIND, YOU'D PROBABLY JUST LIE.
SEE, MONGDAL, THE WHITE FOX? SHE'S A SUPER-SPY. SHE LIES ALL THE TIME.
BUT I WASN'T LYING ABOUT THE NECK BOMBS.
I'VE GOT ONE. SHE'S PROBABLY GOT ONE. AND WHILE YOU WERE SLEEPING, BEFORE SHE GOT HERE--
--WELL, I DIDN'T WANT YOU TO FEEL LEFT OUT.
HOW DID YOU--?
HOW? I'M ME.
YOU DIDN'T--
I DID.
CLICK!
POW.
PWOMP
GRAGHKK...!

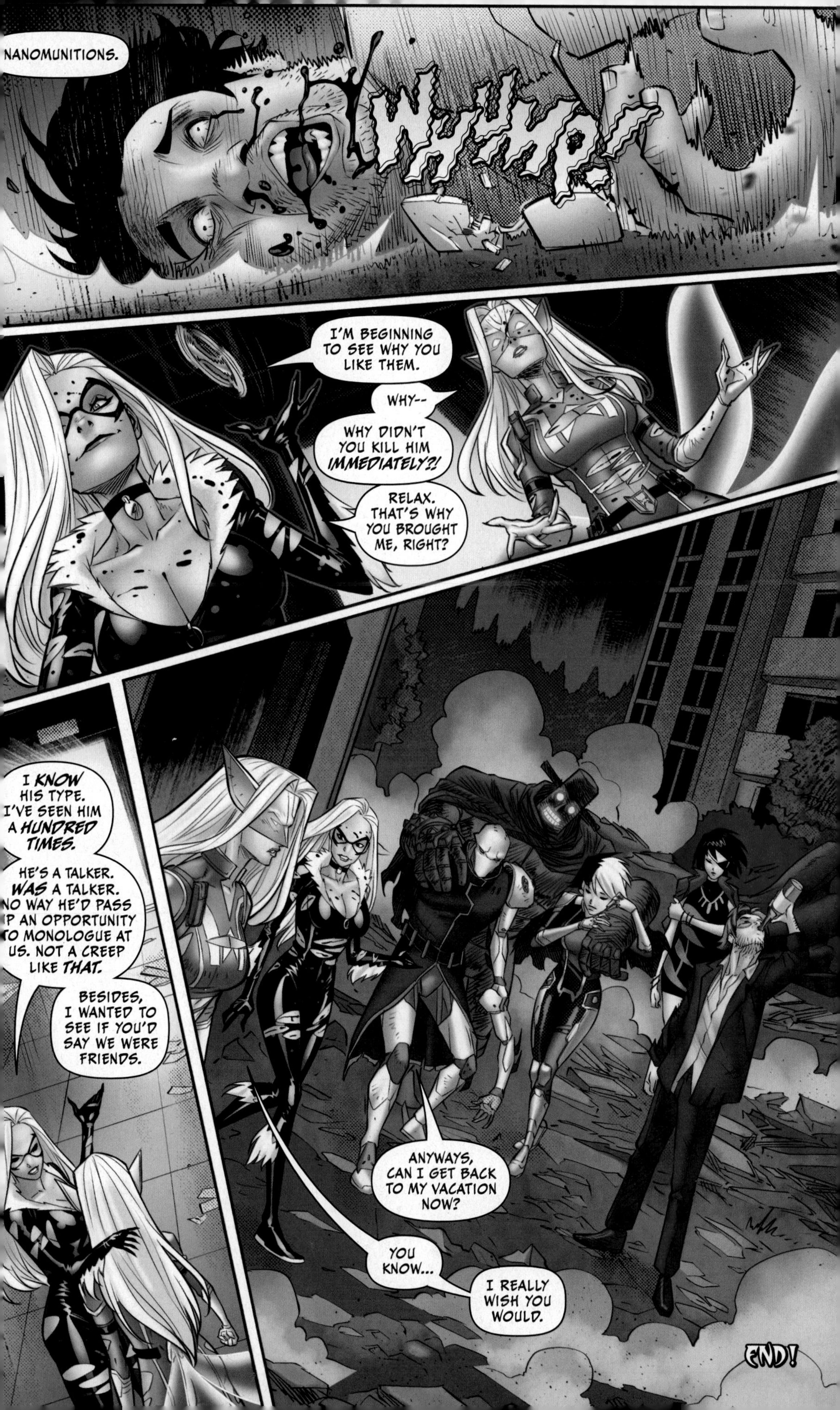

NANOMUNITIONS.
I'M BEGINNING TO SEE WHY YOU LIKE THEM.
WHY--
WHY DIDN'T YOU KILL HIM IMMEDIATELY?!
RELAX. THAT'S WHY YOU BROUGHT ME, RIGHT?
I KNOW HIS TYPE. I'VE SEEN HIM A HUNDRED TIMES.
HE'S A TALKER. WAS A TALKER. NO WAY HE'D PASS P AN OPPORTUNITY TO MONOLOGUE AT US. NOT A CREEP LIKE THAT.
BESIDES, I WANTED TO SEE IF YOU'D SAY WE WERE FRIENDS.
ANYWAYS, CAN I GET BACK TO MY VACATION NOW?
YOU KNOW...
I REALLY WISH YOU WOULD.
END!

You may recall this story from *Black Cat Vol. 1: Grand Theft Marvel*, but we wanted to include it here as well as it has a lot to do with the story you just read!

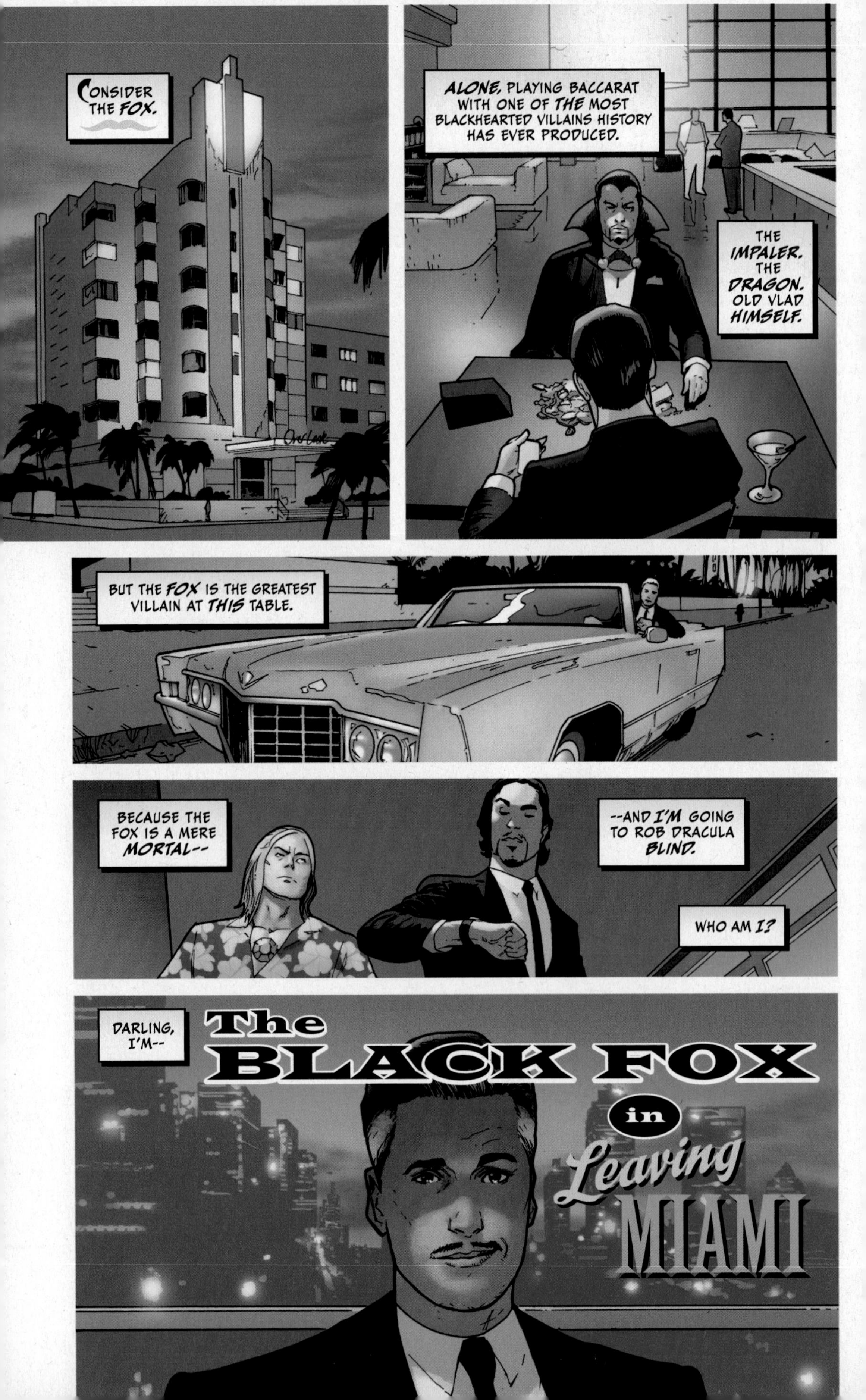

CONSIDER THE FOX.
ALONE, PLAYING BACCARAT WITH ONE OF THE MOST BLACKHEARTED VILLAINS HISTORY HAS EVER PRODUCED.
THE IMPALER. THE DRAGON. OLD VLAD HIMSELF.
BUT THE FOX IS THE GREATEST VILLAIN AT THIS TABLE.
BECAUSE THE FOX IS A MERE MORTAL--
--AND I'M GOING TO ROB DRACULA BLIND.
WHO AM I?
DARLING, I'M--
The BLACK FOX in Leaving MIAMI

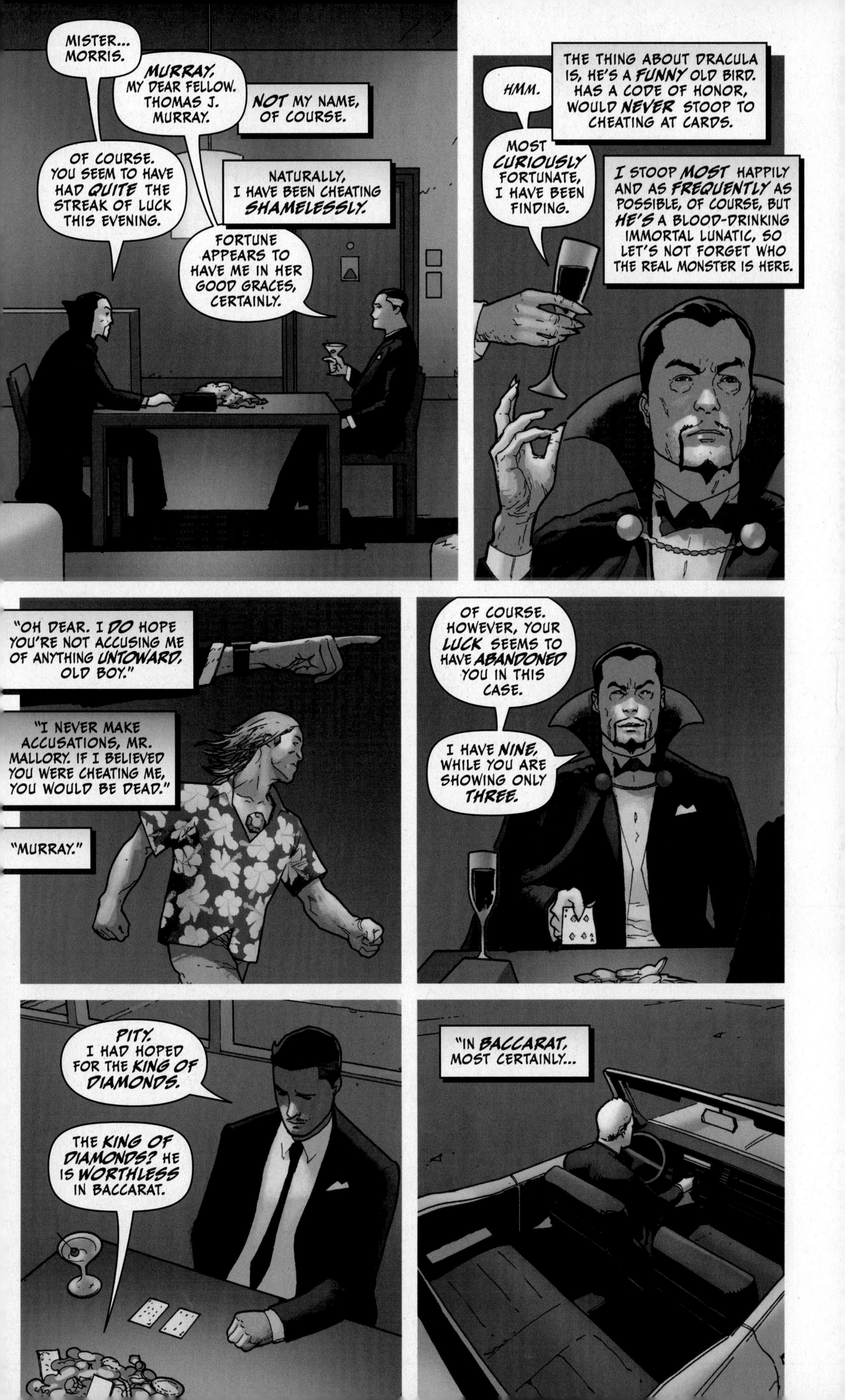
MISTER... MORRIS.
MURRAY, MY DEAR FELLOW. THOMAS J. MURRAY.
NOT MY NAME, OF COURSE.
OF COURSE. YOU SEEM TO HAVE HAD QUITE THE STREAK OF LUCK THIS EVENING.
NATURALLY, I HAVE BEEN CHEATING SHAMELESSLY.
FORTUNE APPEARS TO HAVE ME IN HER GOOD GRACES, CERTAINLY.
HMM.
THE THING ABOUT DRACULA IS, HE'S A FUNNY OLD BIRD. HAS A CODE OF HONOR, WOULD NEVER STOOP TO CHEATING AT CARDS.
MOST CURIOUSLY FORTUNATE, I HAVE BEEN FINDING.
I STOOP MOST HAPPILY AND AS FREQUENTLY AS POSSIBLE, OF COURSE, BUT HE'S A BLOOD-DRINKING IMMORTAL LUNATIC, SO LET'S NOT FORGET WHO THE REAL MONSTER IS HERE.
"OH DEAR. I DO HOPE YOU'RE NOT ACCUSING ME OF ANYTHING UNTOWARD, OLD BOY."
"I NEVER MAKE ACCUSATIONS, MR. MALLORY. IF I BELIEVED YOU WERE CHEATING ME, YOU WOULD BE DEAD."
"MURRAY."
OF COURSE. HOWEVER, YOUR LUCK SEEMS TO HAVE ABANDONED YOU IN THIS CASE.
I HAVE NINE, WHILE YOU ARE SHOWING ONLY THREE.
PITY. I HAD HOPED FOR THE KING OF DIAMONDS.
THE KING OF DIAMONDS? HE IS WORTHLESS IN BACCARAT.
"IN BACCARAT, MOST CERTAINLY...

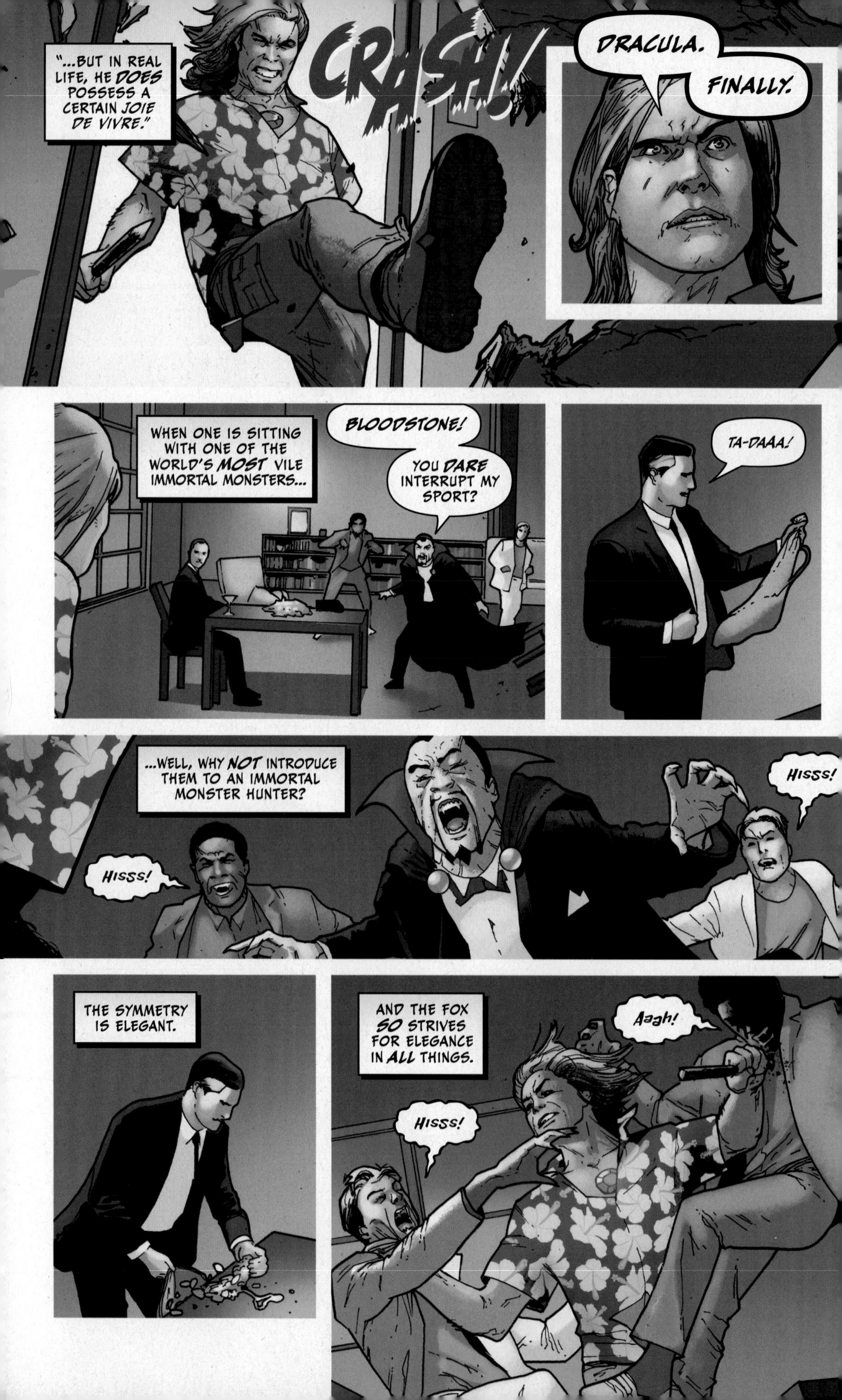

"...BUT IN REAL LIFE, HE DOES POSSESS A CERTAIN JOIE DE VIVRE."
CRASH!
DRACULA.
FINALLY.
WHEN ONE IS SITTING WITH ONE OF THE WORLD'S MOST VILE IMMORTAL MONSTERS...
BLOODSTONE!
YOU DARE INTERRUPT MY SPORT?
TA-DAAA!
...WELL, WHY NOT INTRODUCE THEM TO AN IMMORTAL MONSTER HUNTER?
HISSS!
HISSS!
THE SYMMETRY IS ELEGANT.
AND THE FOX SO STRIVES FOR ELEGANCE IN ALL THINGS.
Aaah!
HISSS!

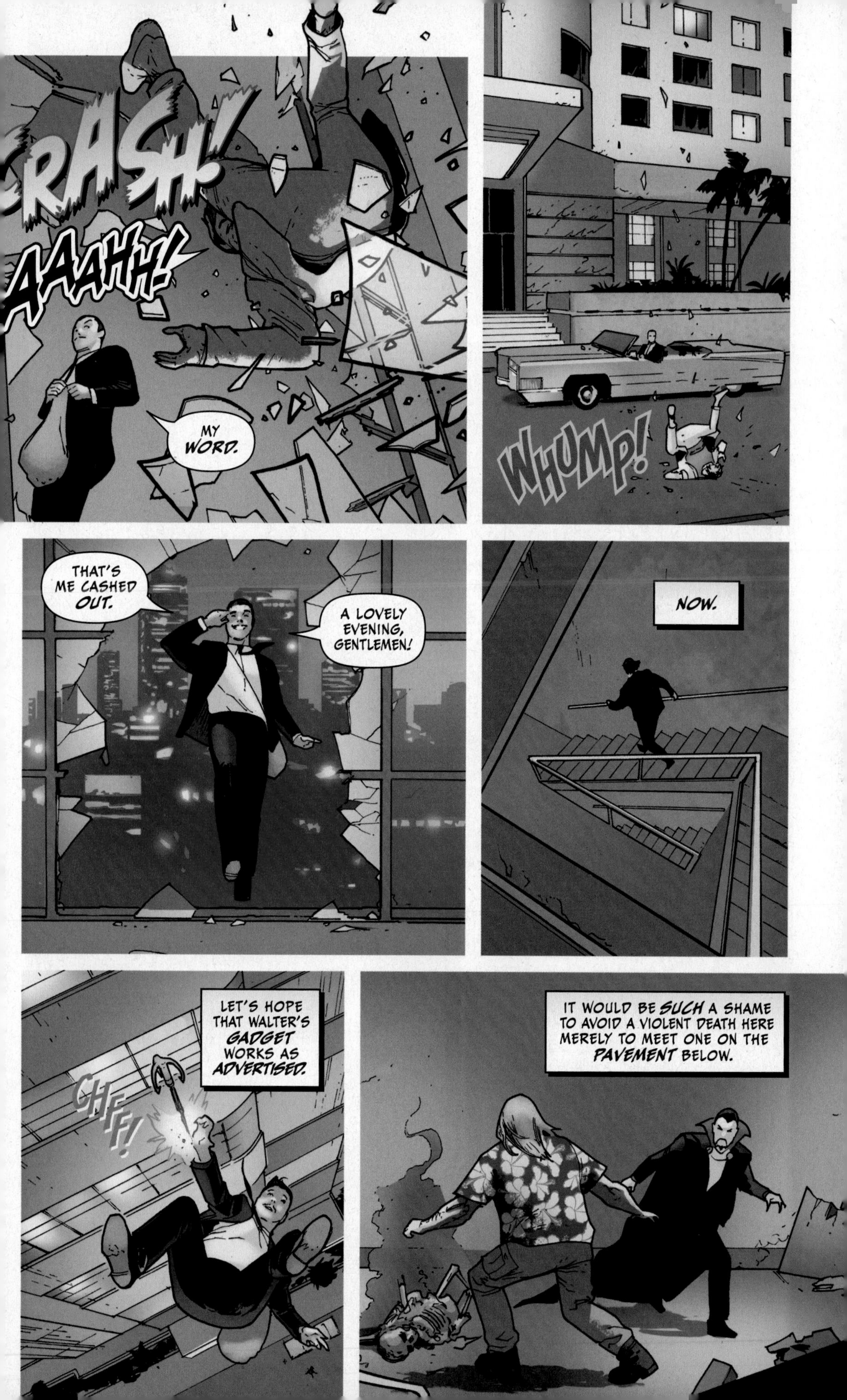
CRASH!
AAAHH!
MY WORD.
WHUMP!
THAT'S ME CASHED OUT.
A LOVELY EVENING, GENTLEMEN!
NOW.
LET'S HOPE THAT WALTER'S GADGET WORKS AS ADVERTISED.
CHFF!
IT WOULD BE SUCH A SHAME TO AVOID A VIOLENT DEATH HERE MERELY TO MEET ONE ON THE PAVEMENT BELOW.

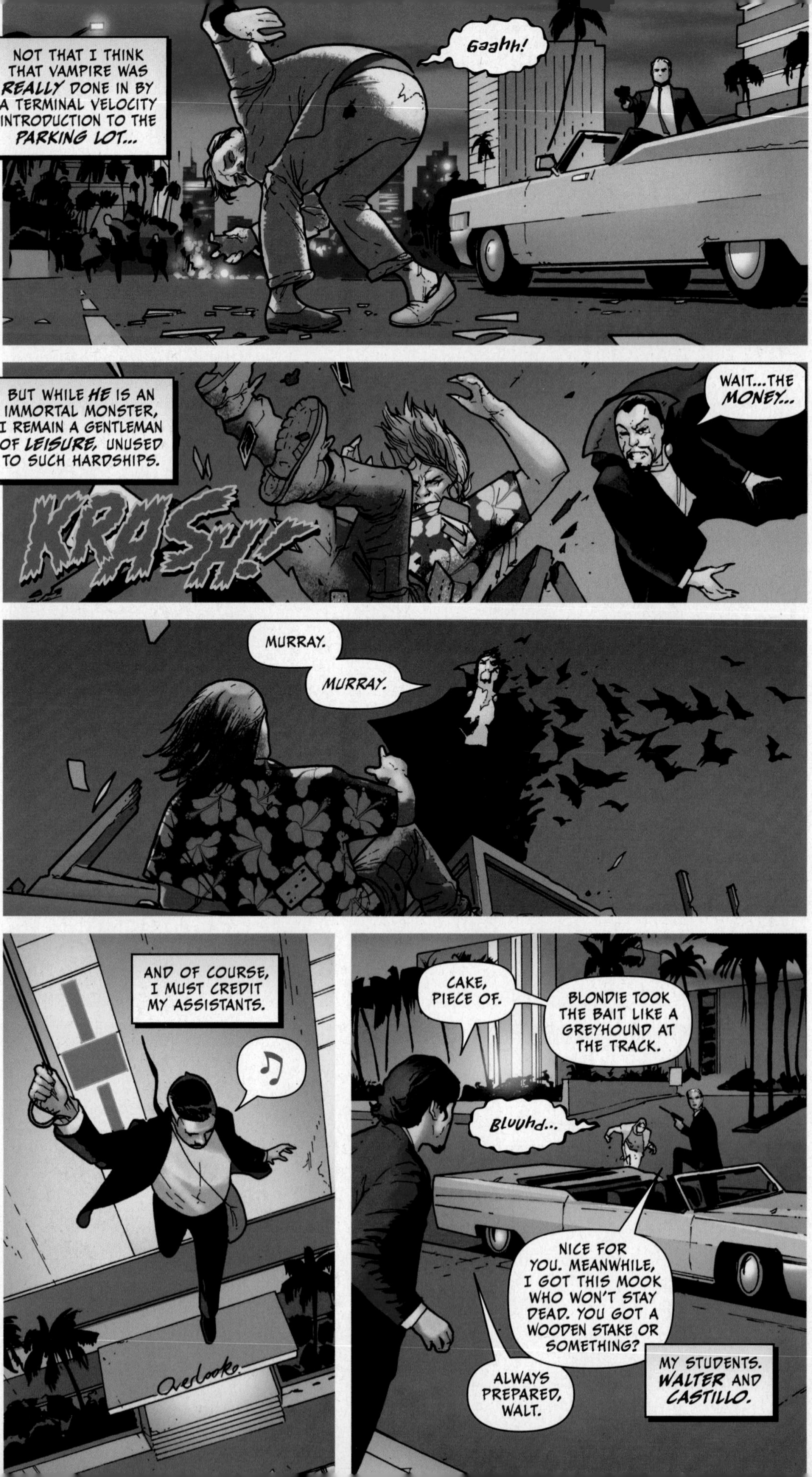

NOT THAT I THINK THAT VAMPIRE WAS REALLY DONE IN BY A TERMINAL VELOCITY INTRODUCTION TO THE PARKING LOT...
Gaahh!
BUT WHILE HE IS AN IMMORTAL MONSTER, I REMAIN A GENTLEMAN OF LEISURE, UNUSED TO SUCH HARDSHIPS.
KRASH!
WAIT...THE MONEY...
MURRAY.
MURRAY.
AND OF COURSE, I MUST CREDIT MY ASSISTANTS.
♫
CAKE, PIECE OF.
BLONDIE TOOK THE BAIT LIKE A GREYHOUND AT THE TRACK.
Bluuhd...
NICE FOR YOU. MEANWHILE, I GOT THIS MOOK WHO WON'T STAY DEAD. YOU GOT A WOODEN STAKE OR SOMETHING?
ALWAYS PREPARED, WALT.
MY STUDENTS. WALTER AND CASTILLO.
Overlook

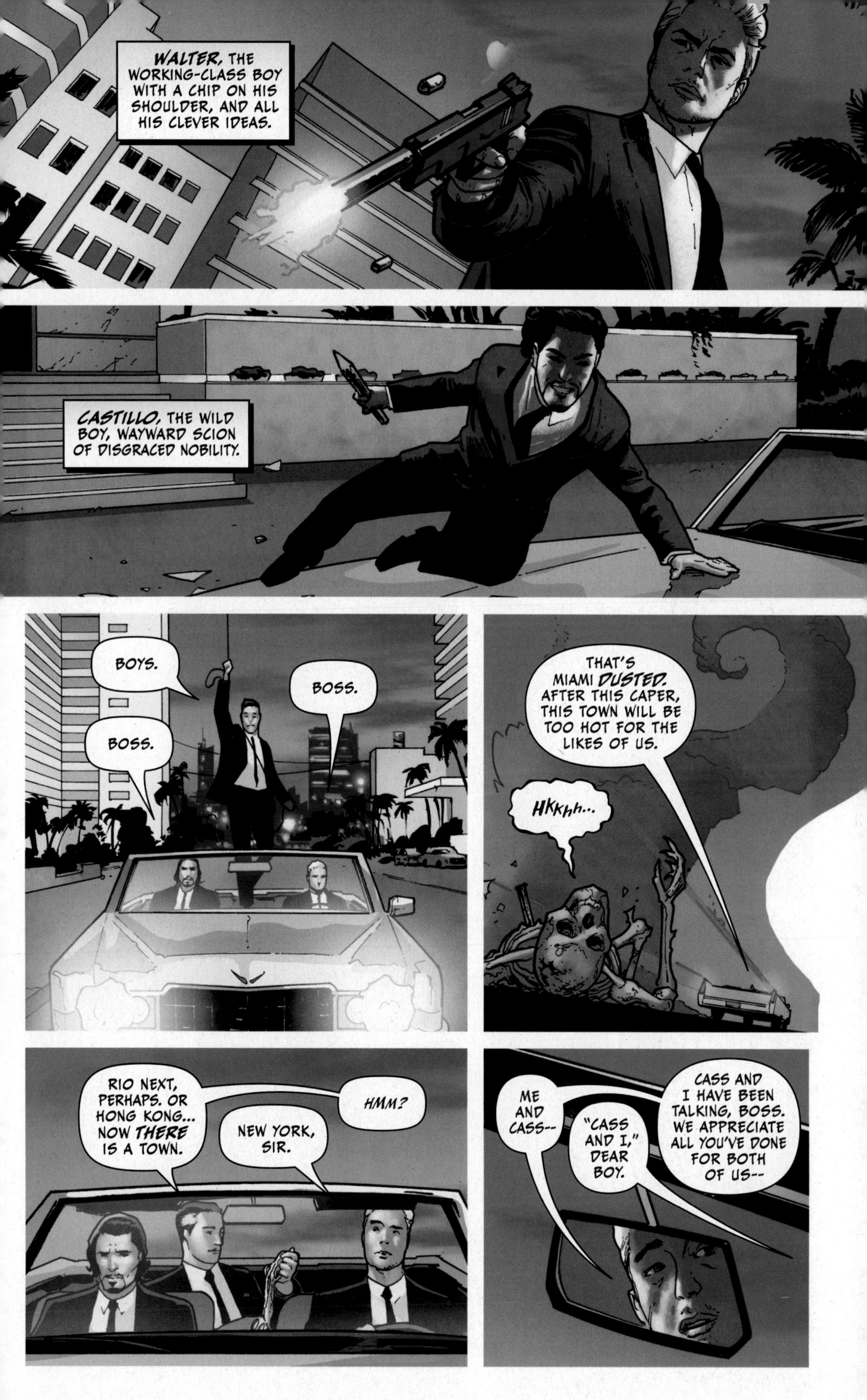
WALTER, THE WORKING-CLASS BOY WITH A CHIP ON HIS SHOULDER, AND ALL HIS CLEVER IDEAS.
CASTILLO, THE WILD BOY, WAYWARD SCION OF DISGRACED NOBILITY.
BOYS.
BOSS.
BOSS.
THAT'S MIAMI DUSTED. AFTER THIS CAPER, THIS TOWN WILL BE TOO HOT FOR THE LIKES OF US.
HKkhh...
RIO NEXT, PERHAPS. OR HONG KONG... NOW THERE IS A TOWN.
HMM?
NEW YORK, SIR.
ME AND CASS--
"CASS AND I," DEAR BOY.
CASS AND I HAVE BEEN TALKING, BOSS. WE APPRECIATE ALL YOU'VE DONE FOR BOTH OF US--

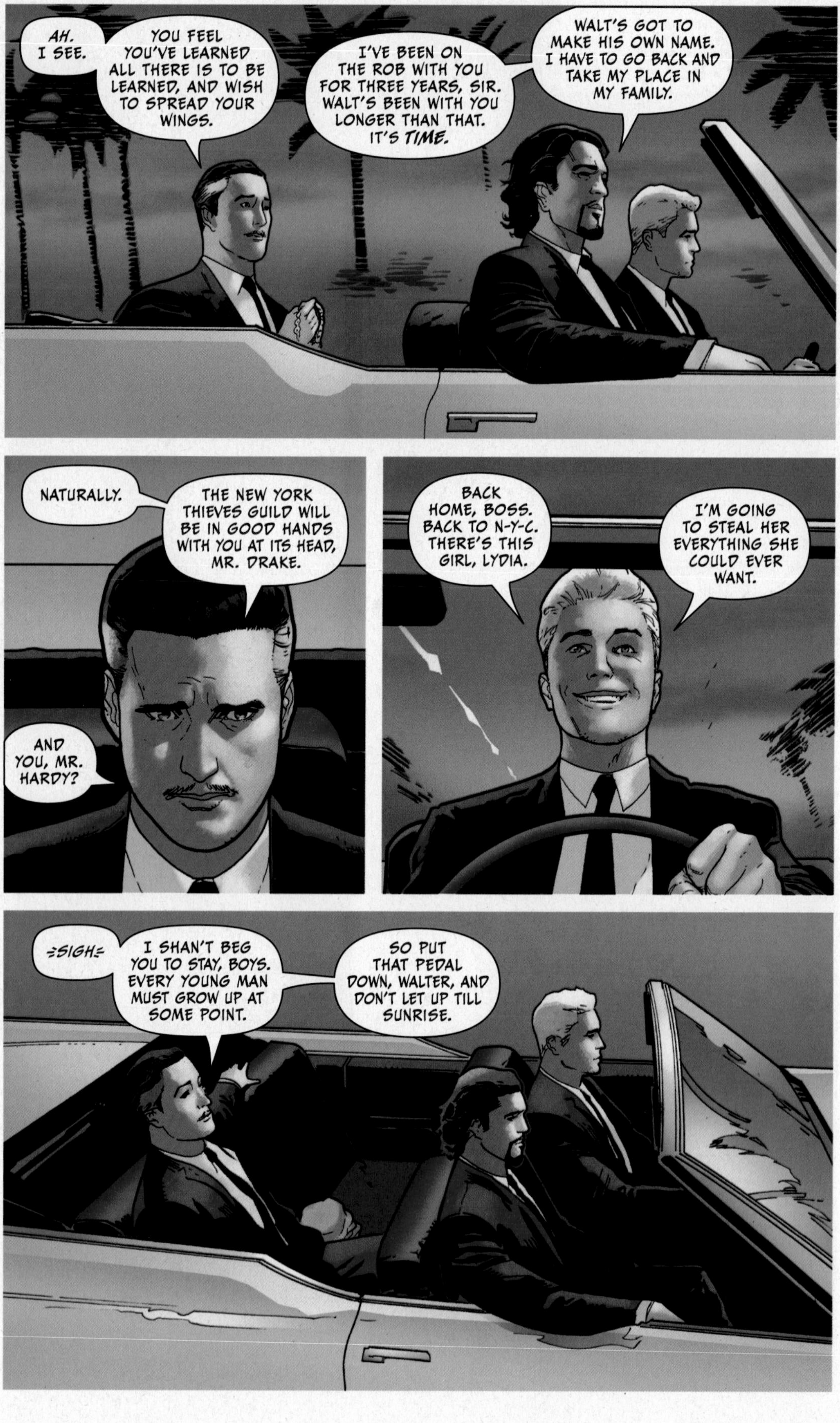
AH. I SEE.
YOU FEEL YOU'VE LEARNED ALL THERE IS TO BE LEARNED, AND WISH TO SPREAD YOUR WINGS.
I'VE BEEN ON THE ROB WITH YOU FOR THREE YEARS, SIR. WALT'S BEEN WITH YOU LONGER THAN THAT. IT'S TIME.
WALT'S GOT TO MAKE HIS OWN NAME. I HAVE TO GO BACK AND TAKE MY PLACE IN MY FAMILY.
NATURALLY.
THE NEW YORK THIEVES GUILD WILL BE IN GOOD HANDS WITH YOU AT ITS HEAD, MR. DRAKE.
AND YOU, MR. HARDY?
BACK HOME, BOSS. BACK TO N-Y-C. THERE'S THIS GIRL, LYDIA.
I'M GOING TO STEAL HER EVERYTHING SHE COULD EVER WANT.
=SIGH=
I SHAN'T BEG YOU TO STAY, BOYS. EVERY YOUNG MAN MUST GROW UP AT SOME POINT.
SO PUT THAT PEDAL DOWN, WALTER, AND DON'T LET UP TILL SUNRISE.

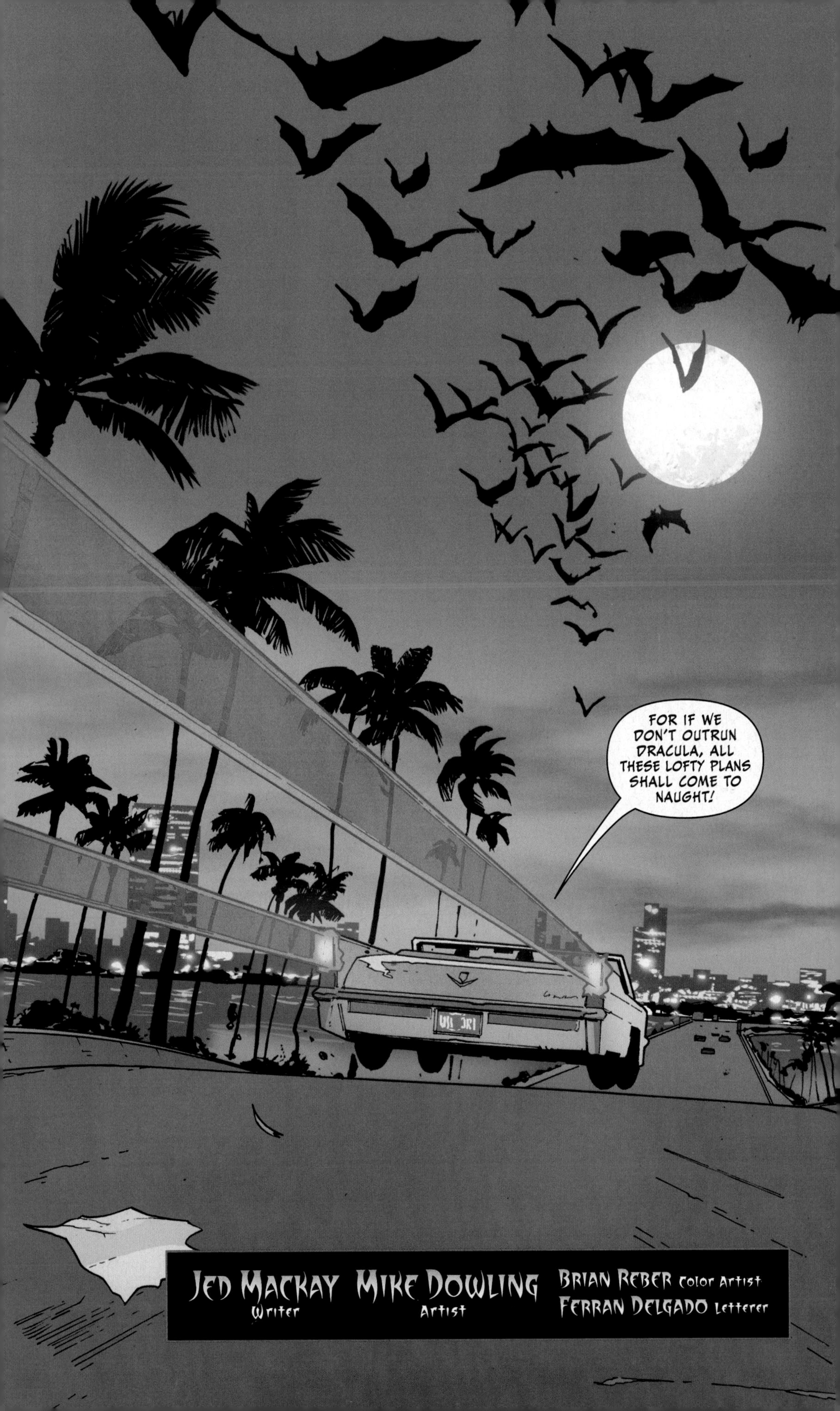
FOR IF WE DON'T OUTRUN DRACULA, ALL THESE LOFTY PLANS SHALL COME TO NAUGHT!
JED MACKAY Writer
MIKE DOWLING Artist
BRIAN REBER Color Artist
FERRAN DELGADO Letterer

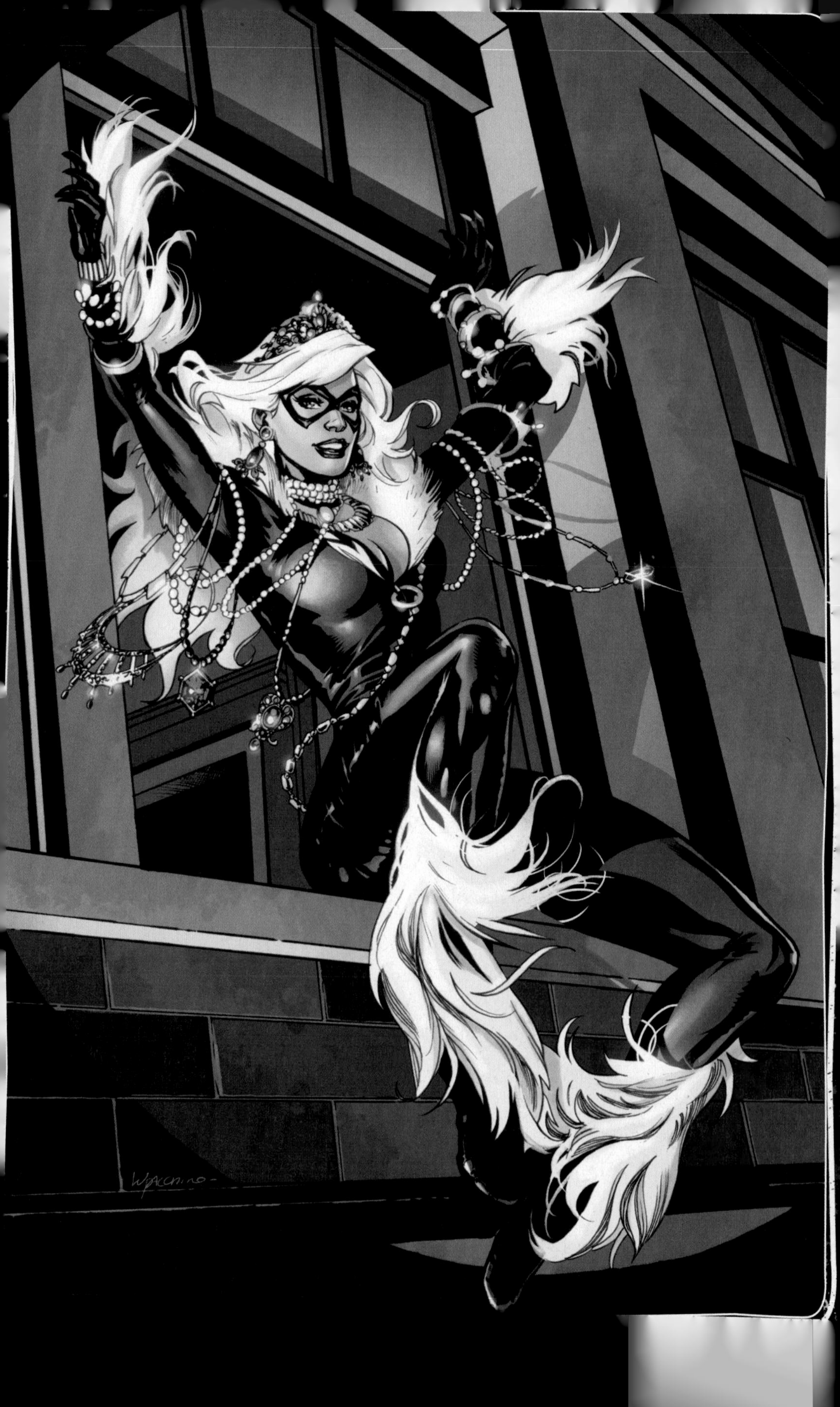

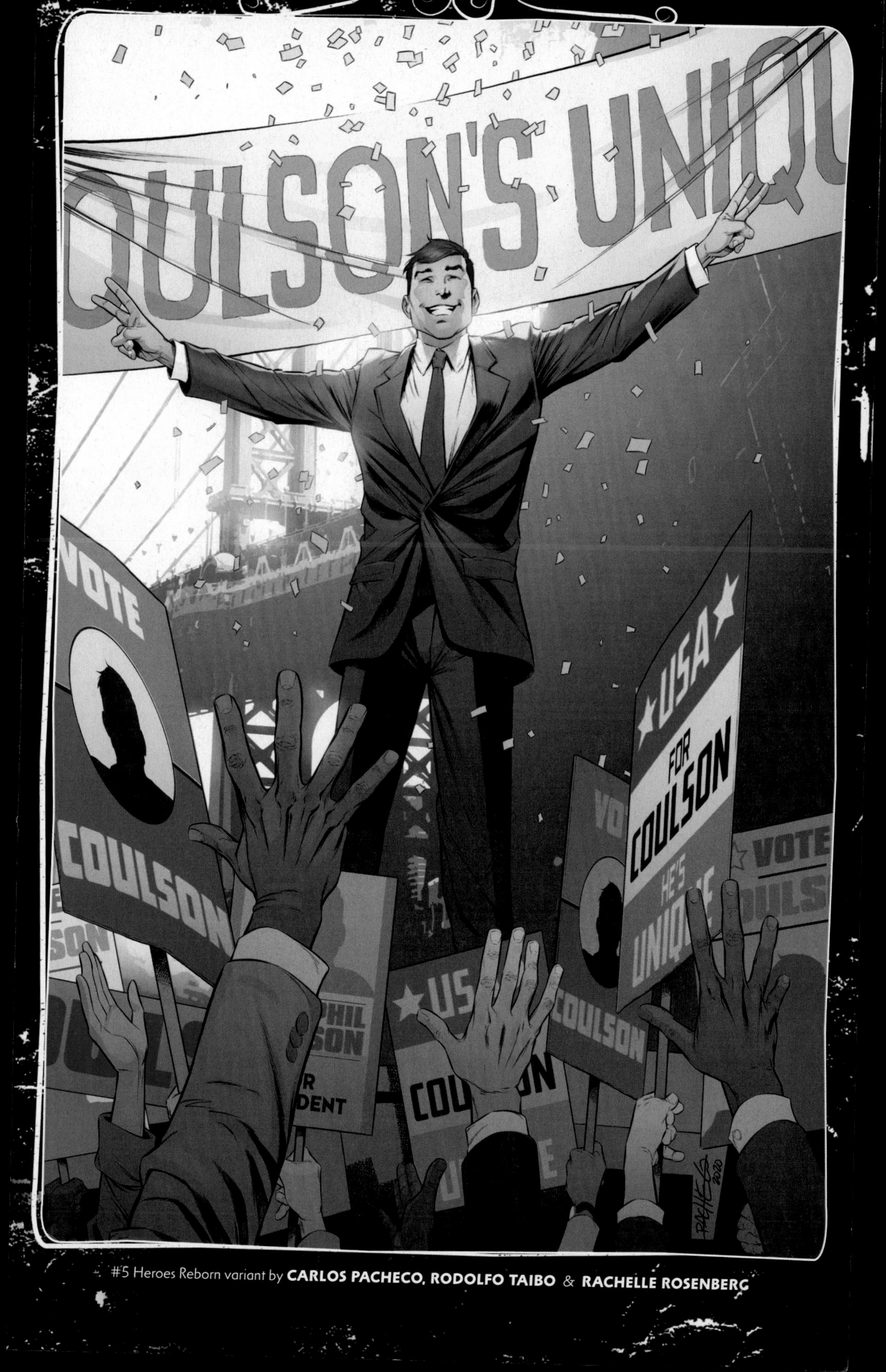
OULSON'S UNIQ
VOTE
COULSON
USA
FOR
COULSON
HE'S
UNIQUE
VOTE
COULSON

#5 Heroes Reborn variant by **CARLOS PACHECO, RODOLFO TAIBO** & **RACHELLE ROSENBERG**

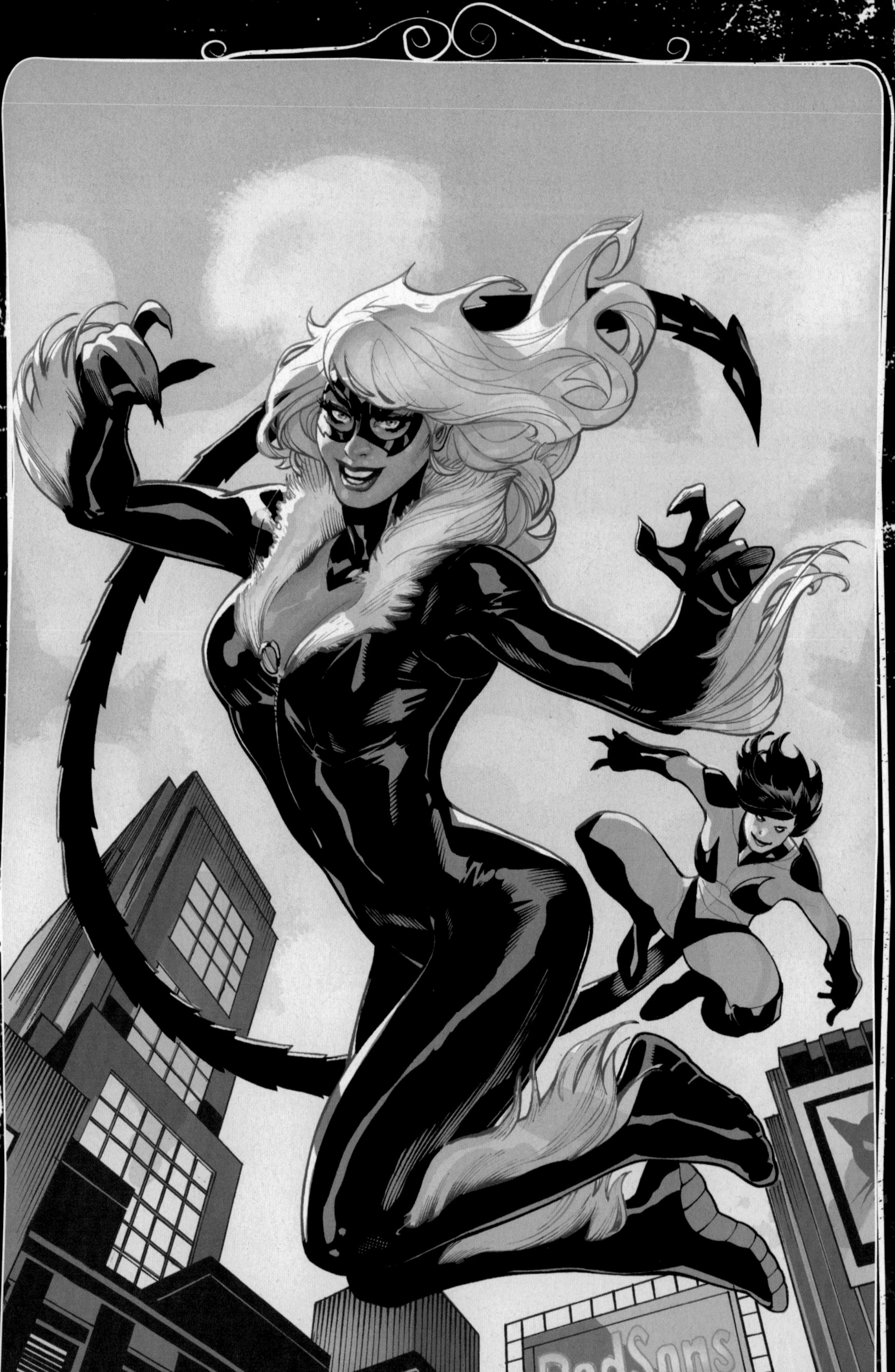
DodSons

#7 Spider-Man Villains variant by **TERRY DODSON** & **RACHEL DODSON**

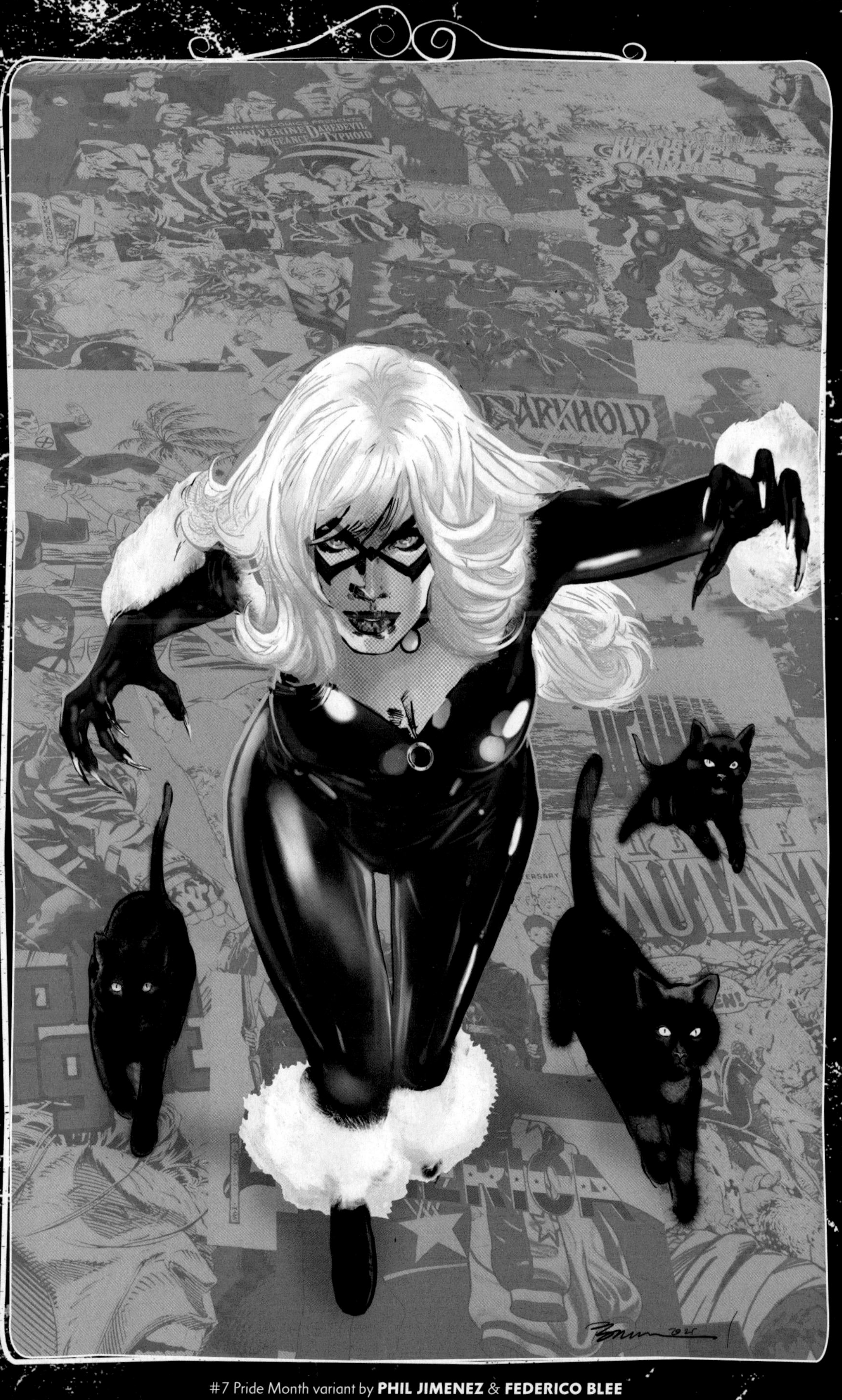

#7 Pride Month variant by **PHIL JIMENEZ** & **FEDERICO BLEE**

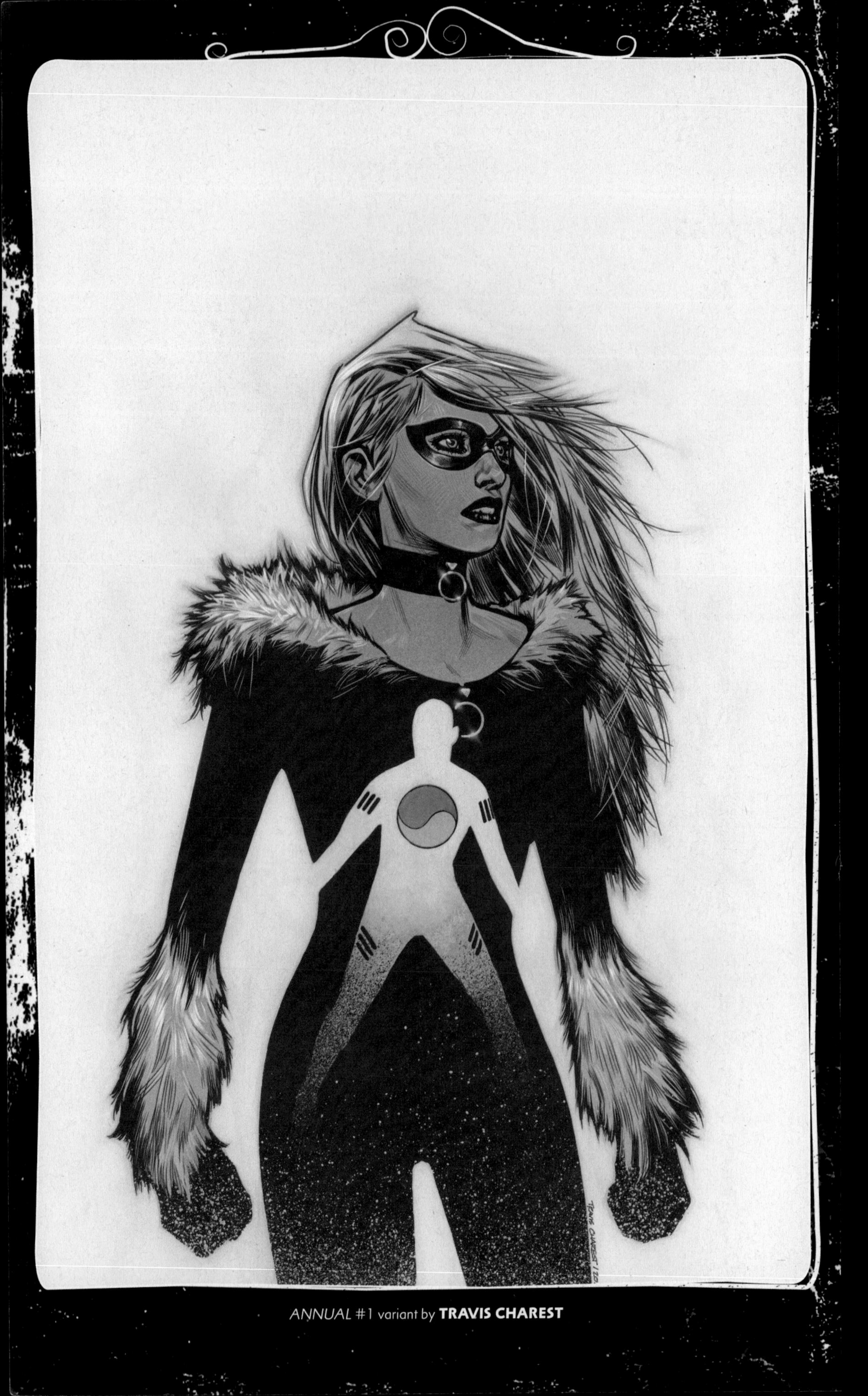

ANNUAL #1 variant by **TRAVIS CHAREST**

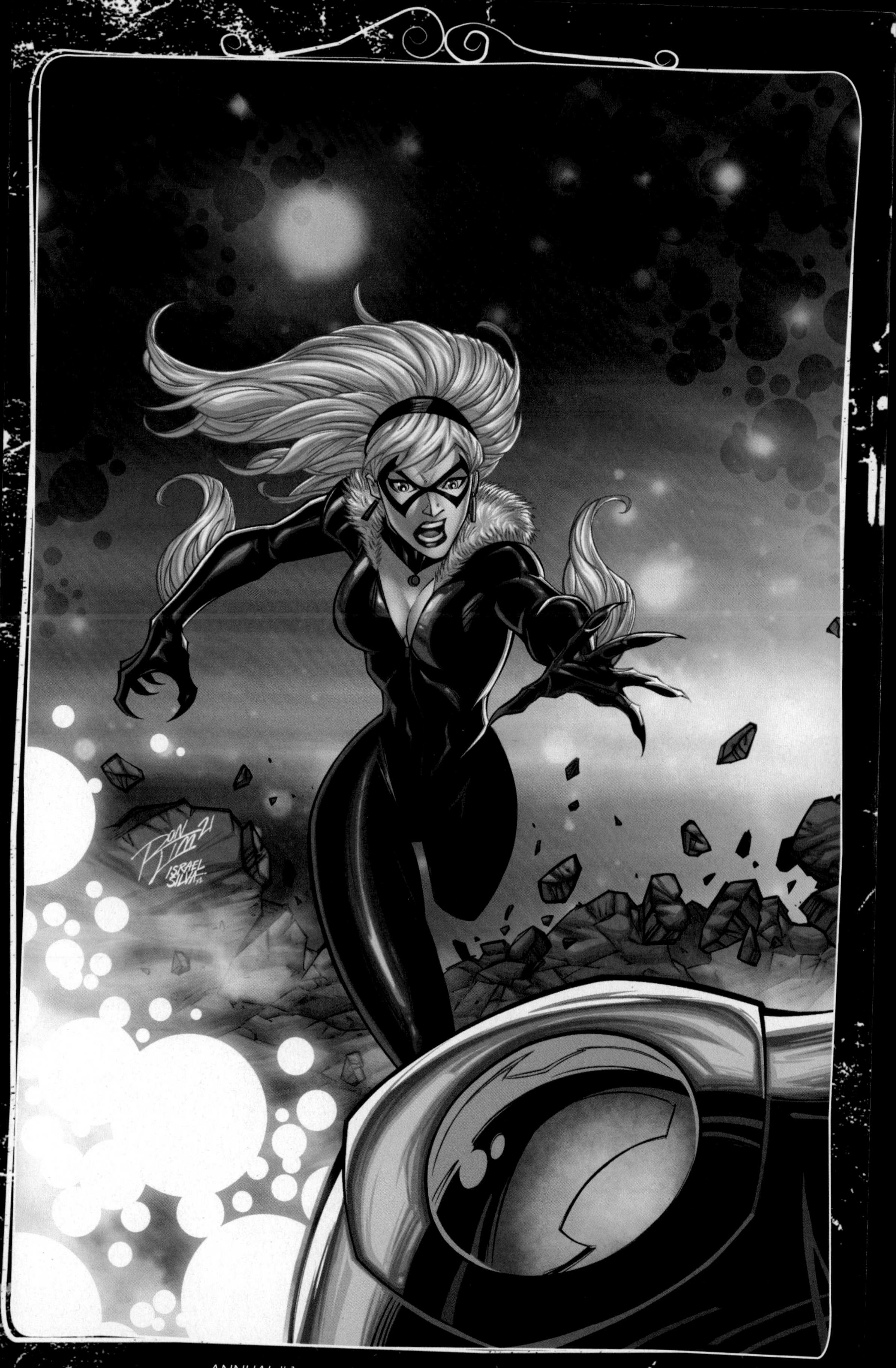

ANNUAL #1 connecting variant by **RON LIM** & **ISRAEL SILVA**

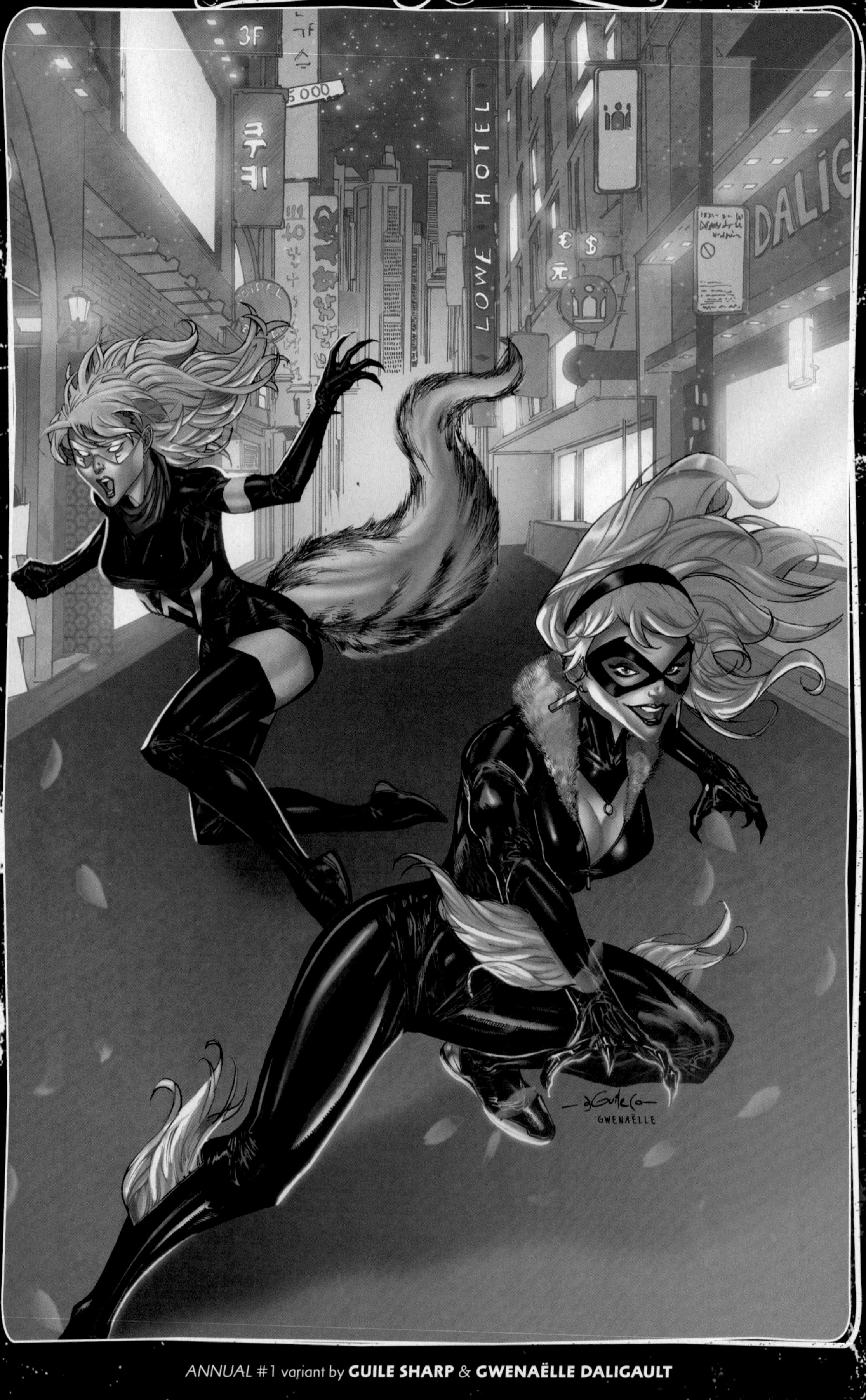
3F
5000
LOWE HOTEL
DALIG
GWENAËLLE

ANNUAL #1 variant by **GUILE SHARP** & **GWENAËLLE DALIGAULT**

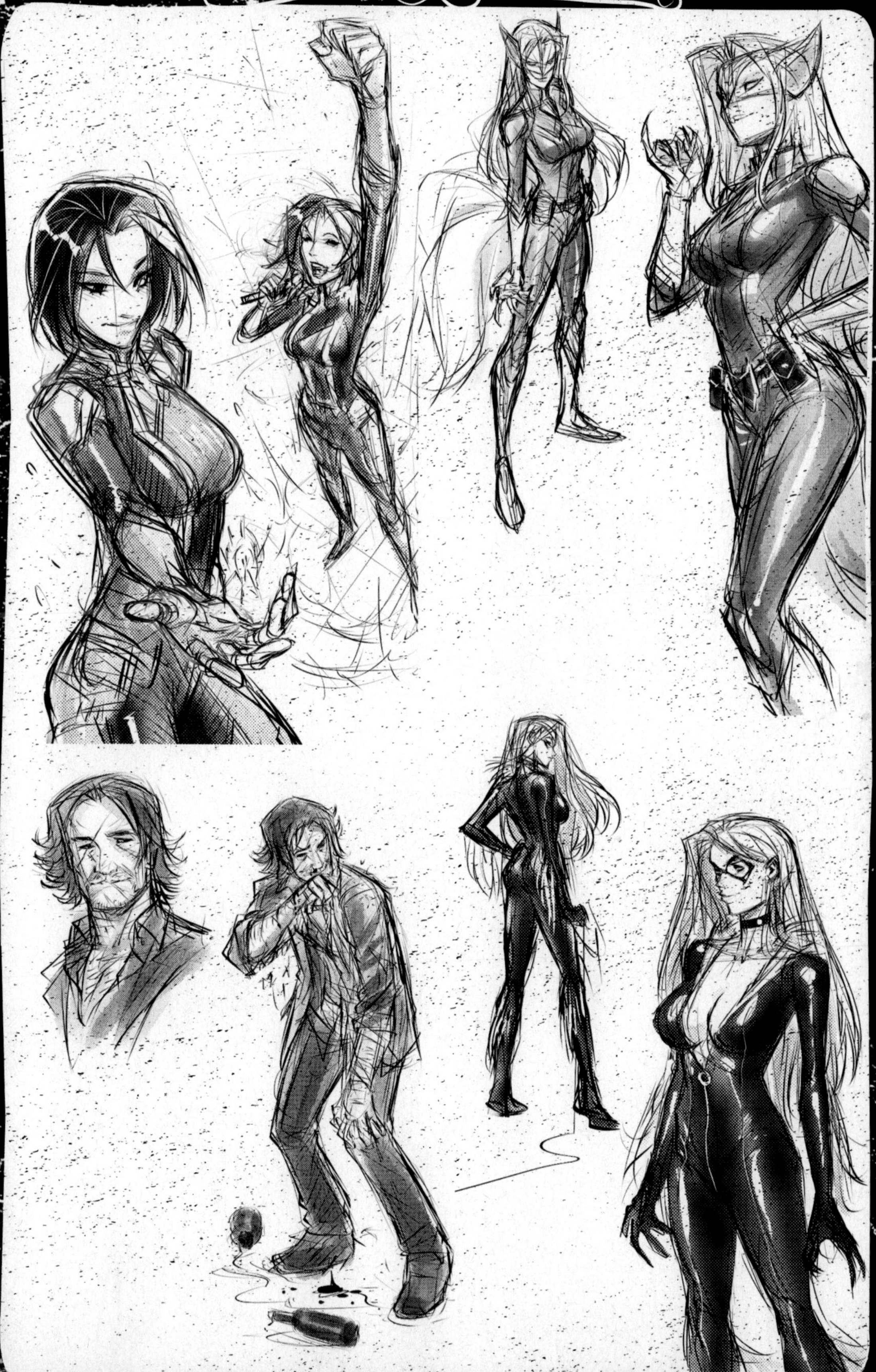

Character sketches by **JOEY VAZQUEZ**

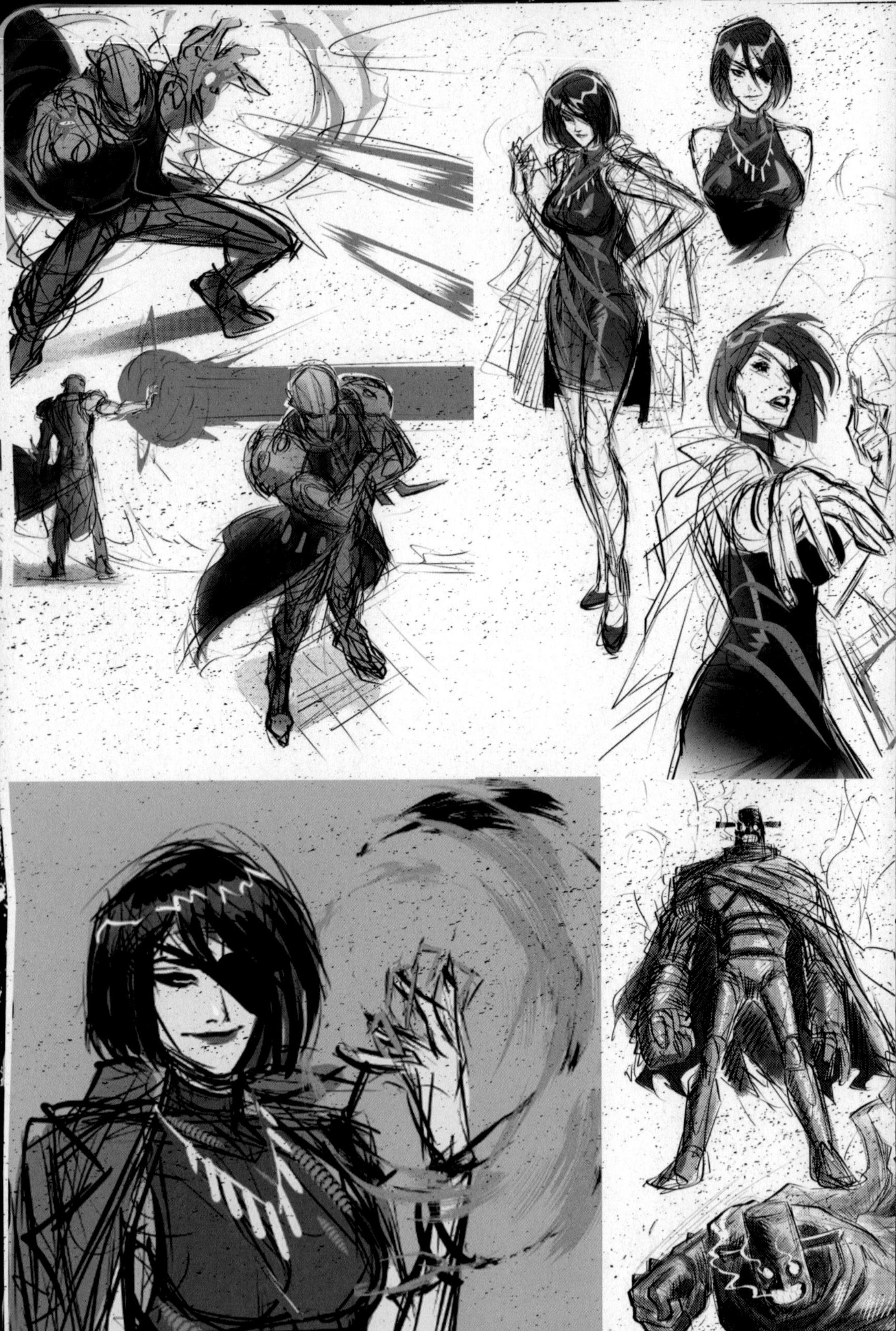

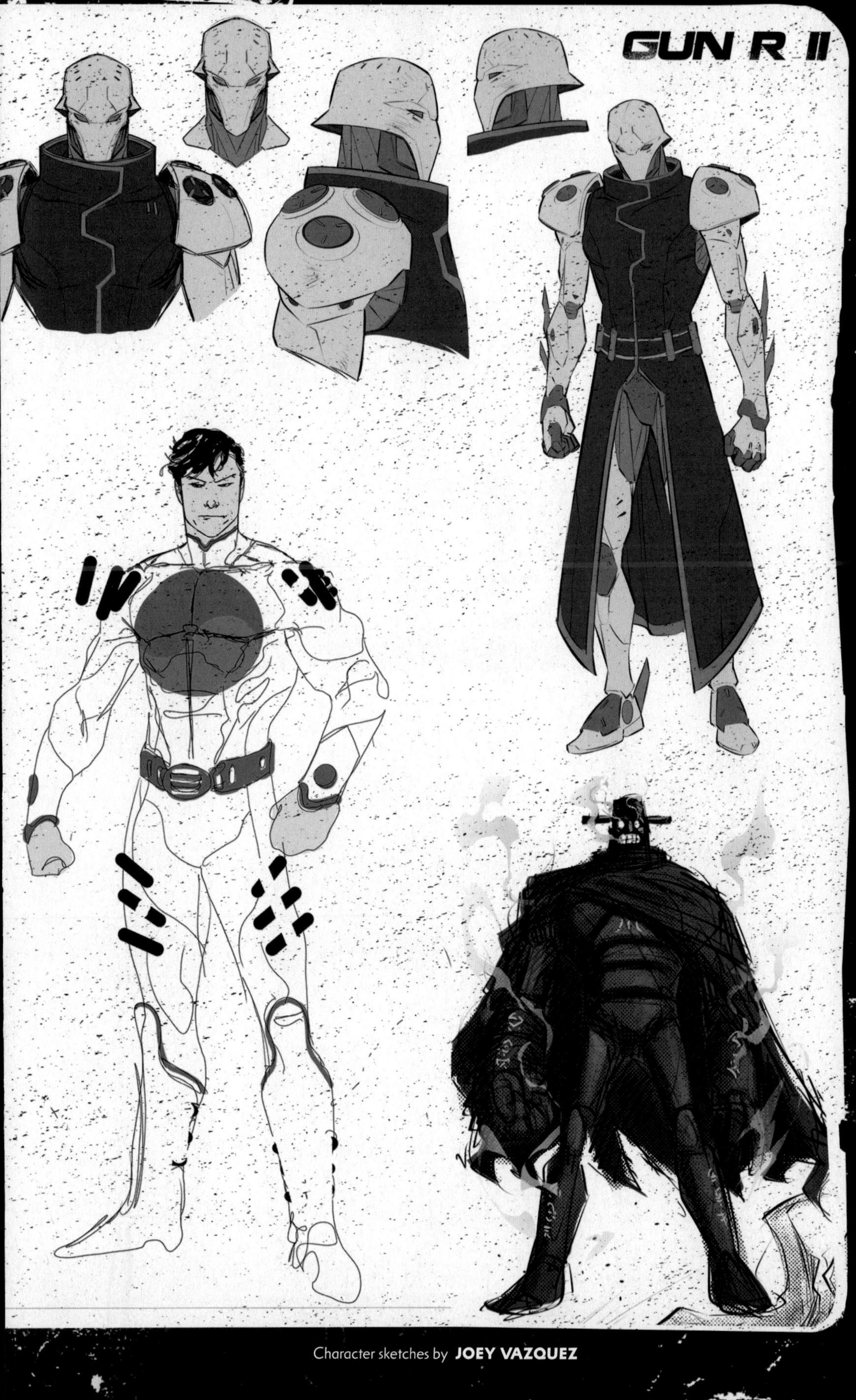
GUN R II

Character sketches by **JOEY VAZQUEZ**

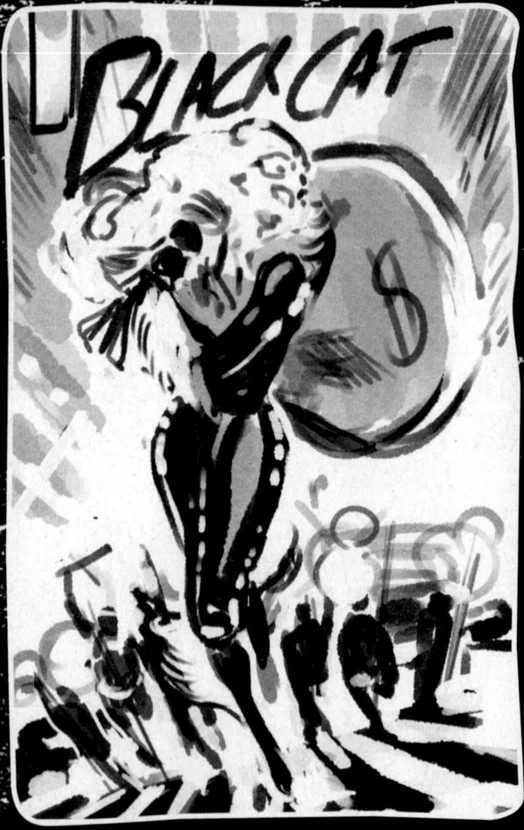
BLACK CAT

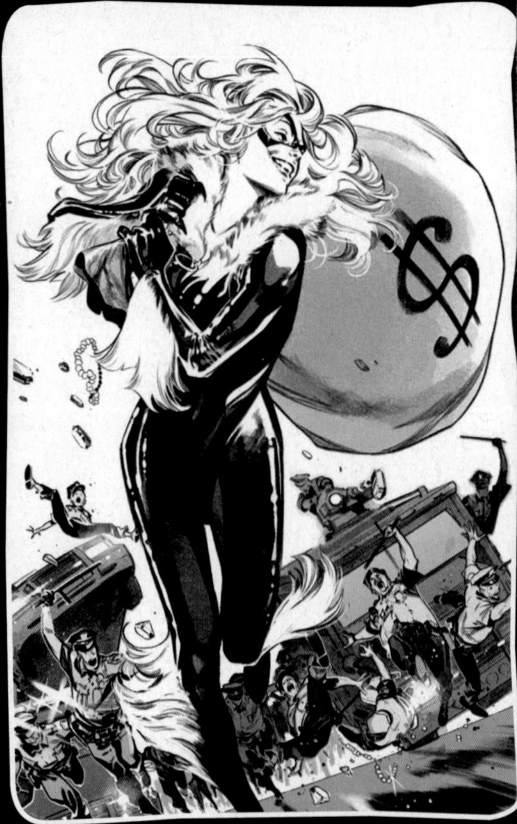

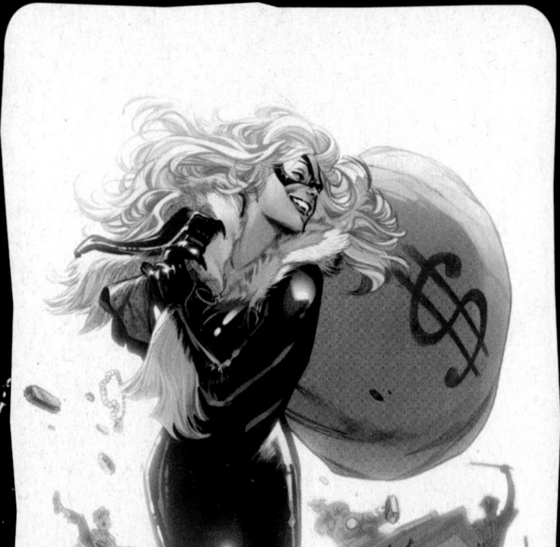

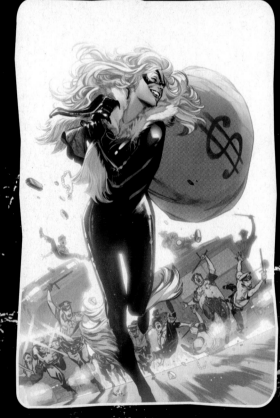

#7 cover process by **C.F. VILLA**